D e l i a   K h a n o

with best wishes

Delia Khano

By Eastern Windows

And not by eastern windows only,
When daylight comes, comes in the light.
ARTHUR HUGH CLOUGH

First published 1985 by Delia Khano
Oxford, England

Revised edition 1993 by Delia Khano
Ramallah, West Bank

Second revised edition 1995 by Delia Khano
Ramallah, West Bank

ISBN 0 9510795 0 6

Delia Khano, Guiding Star Ltd., P.O.Box 19421, Jerusalem 91193

Designed and Typeset by TD Turbo Design
Ramallah, West Bank, Tel. 02-9951262

Cover picture: Gabriel in St. Catherine's cloister, Bethlehem

To
my family
and the Palestinian people
who have been my friends
for many years

About the book

The writer is an Englishwoman who in 1960 met and
married Gabriel Khano, a Palestinian Christian. While
telling the story of an excursion to Petra, their wedding in
Bethlehem, and early married life in Jerusalem, she fills in
the details of Gabriel's eventful childhood and youth. She
mentions the forced migration from Turkey that his
parents endured as children, and records episodes that
impinged on the family from the explosive Arab-Jewish
situation before 1948. The creation of Israel in that year
made them refugees - his parents for the second time in
their lives - and they had a hard struggle to survive in the
early days of Jordan.

The highway of Gabriel's life proved to be the tourist
business, and it was as a guide that he first met Delia. She
briefly describes her family background in Britain before
shifting the scene back to Jerusalem where they started a
tourist agency called the Guiding Star. This was built on
snowballing recommendation and Gabriel's personality was
dominant: flamboyant, captivating, generous to a fault, a
Christian but despising humbug, he was mainly responsible
for the success that Guiding Star rapidly achieved.

The Arab-Israeli conflict is never absent - the 1967 war
found Gabriel outside the country and almost unable to
get in again - and politics take their place with the history,
religion and culture of the Holy Land, the true story of the
finding of the Dead Sea Scrolls, and tales of Gabriel's
little-known community, the Assyrians, to make a colourful
patchwork of information and biography.

Contents

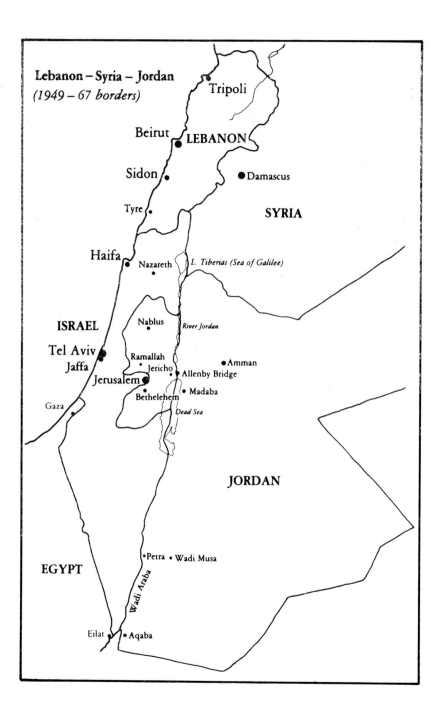

Lebanon – Syria – Jordan
(1949 – 67 borders)

Tripoli

Beirut **LEBANON**

Sidon

Damascus

Tyre

SYRIA

Haifa

Nazareth

L. Tiberias (Sea of Galilee)

Nablus

River Jordan

ISRAEL

Tel Aviv

Jaffa

Ramallah

Jericho

Amman

Jerusalem

Allenby Bridge

Bethelehem

Madaba

Gaza

Dead Sea

JORDAN

Petra • Wadi Musa

EGYPT

Wadi Araba

Eilat • Aqaba

Part I

The Birthplace

CHAPTER ONE

The Voice of the Archangel

'You've left something behind,' said Gabriel.

'What? Where?' I asked.

'There. Your footprint,' he said.

W E were on our first day of sightseeing in Jordan. I was the courier for the party of thirty-four English tourists and the only one who had been in the Middle East before. Gabriel was our guide.

The company organising the tour was called Wings, and when I went to the office in London to be briefed about my job, Mr. Welsman the General Manager had said, 'You will be perfectly all right in Jordan. Just leave everything to Gabriel.' He told me little else about this part of the tour except that Gabriel Khano was a Christian Arab who worked for the American Colony Hotel where we would be staying on the Jordanian side of Jerusalem.

With a few stops on the way out and the way back, the itinerary took in the Arab countries of Lebanon, Syria and the Hashemite Kingdom of Jordan, which at that time - the spring of 1960 - consisted not only of Transjordan but also of part of Palestine, and contained most of the main New Testament sites except Galilee and Nazareth.

3

The Lebanese capital Beirut was the gateway to the Middle East, and the sight of it as we flew in from the Mediterranean was breathtaking: its tall, light buildings seemed to be floating in the soft air between the blue of the sea and the deeper blue of the mountains behind. We covered most of Lebanon in our six days there: driving south along the coast road to Tyre and Sidon with the delicious scent of orange-blossom wafting through the car windows; from there inland to Beit-eddine to see a nineteenth century Arab palace of some splendour; eastward from Beirut through the ranges of the Lebanon and the Anti-Lebanon to see the magnificent Roman temples of Baalbeck; north from Beirut past the sweep of Jounieh Bay and the Dog River, site of many battles, with its graceful Roman bridge, to Byblos with remains going back to Phoenician times; and thence inland by winding mountain roads through little villages to the Cedars, where some of the famous trees still stood from past centuries.

Our guide was an elderly Lebanese Jew known as Alexander the Great, whose description of every site we visited was the same: 'This is Byblos. It is vairy, vairy old. See these stones. They are t'ousands of years old. Now slowly, slowly, ladies. Let Alexander the Great help you. Slowly, slowly, ladies, *please*,' as he handed the older ladies from ruin to ruin. It was the same with Tyre, Sidon, Baalbeck and the Cedars: all were 'vairy, vairy old.' But the obvious effort he put into guiding, or perhaps I should say escorting us, and the reverence he instilled in us for every stone did leave a certain impression on our minds which a more erudite explanation would not have done.

In the tenth century B.C. the Phoenician King Hiram supplied cedar-wood to Solomon for his Temple in Jerusalem, but no such peaceful commerce took place between Lebanon and modern Israel: there were Jews living in Lebanon and Arabs living in Israel, but the only contact between the two countries at that time was in acts of war and espionage, and in live broadcast messages on special radio programmes. The border between them was open only to United Nations officials, and so although it is only four hours' drive from Beirut to Jerusalem, ordinary people had to make a long detour by Damascus and Amman.

We stayed one night in Damascus, where the tour group was less interested in the historical sites than in the exotic bazaars with their brocades, inlaid wood, brass and copperware. The guides were only too happy to take them from shop to shop, because they got commission from whatever they purchased. I left them at one point with a particularly flamboyant shopkeeper who was stirring the visitors to frenzies of bargaining and buying with the rhythmic beat of a Bedouin coffee-pounder, and slipped away to the welcome silence of the Museum. I wandered round looking at the relics of past civilizations: Sumerian, Assyrian, Phoenician, Israelite, Hellenistic, Roman, Palmyrene, Byzantine. There was a relief of Zenobia, the powerful queen of the desert city of Palmyra, with an eagle holding an oak twig on her right and a dove holding an olive branch on her left, apparently an early proponent of cold warfare. And there were many Roman artefacts showing a high degree of sophistication: elaborate jewellery, cosmetics, dentistry tools, pottery, glass, weapons: even an ornate helmet for a woman, found beside a bronze breast-plate shaped like a brassière. But I spent the longest time looking at the delightful statues excavated from the ancient Sumerian city of Mari in Mesopotamia. The bearded King Itur-Shamagan stood four feet high, and the next in size was his buxom singer and dancer, Ur-Nina; the other members of the court, smaller because less important, included a little figure with covered head, who might have been the queen. The striking thing about them all was their expression: every one of them was smiling, and their eyes had a surprised look, for the irises, coloured with lapis-lazuli, were completely round and even had some of the white visible above them. It seemed as if the whole court shared some happy secret and was living in a state of cheerful and slightly mindless harmony: malice was obviously unknown in their fortunate circle. The alabaster figures were found in the temple of Ishtar, the goddess of the reproductive forces of nature, adopted by the Phoenicians as Astarte, and later probably merging into Aphrodite, the Greek goddess of love who rose from the foam off Cyprus.

In many ways ancient Mesopotamia was the cradle of our civilization: there the potter's wheel and the plough were first used: city dwelling first came into existence; cuneiform writing was invented; the earliest extant code of laws was written; astronomy and mathematics were studied. In Mesopotamia, too, the skull of Neanderthal man was found; and there are very early folk-tales telling of an earthly paradise and a great flood. From there the Semitic nomad Abraham set out to Canaan on the journey so fateful for his progeny and the history of the world; for his progeny were both the Hebrews by his wife Sarah and the Arabs by an earlier union with Sarah's slave-girl Hagar. He was the father of the three great monotheistic religions. Abandoning the gods of his homeland, Abraham directed his steps according to the instructions of the One God, and that God was pleased to reward him with another people's country. Genesis tells us that God entered into a covenant and promised to 'Abraham and his seed for ever' 'the land wherein he was a stranger,' the land of Canaan - or in another passage, the land from the Nile to the Euphrates. The Canaanites had no quarrel with Abraham's peaceful pastoral arrival; and it was only when his descendants returned to Canaan after their exile in Egypt that they became ambitious to overthrow the prosperous Canaanite cities and adopt their superior culture.

On Abraham's first visit to Jerusalem - or Salem as it was called in this passage of Genesis - he met the interesting figure of Melchizedek, Canaanite king and priest of the Most High God, who brought him not a sacrificial lamb but bread and wine.

We drove from Damascus to the Jordan side of the divided city of Jerusalem and arrived at the American Colony Hotel. It was there, after allotting the people their rooms, that I turned from the reception desk to find a tall, dark and strikingly handsome man regarding me keenly.

He came forward: 'I am Gabriel. Perhaps Mr. Welsman told you about me. I guided him on the last tour; it was the first one for the company, and he was very happy with my services. He is a very fine man. We like the British very much. I was with them in the NAAFI till they left in 1948. All our troubles started then. Can I get you a drink?'

The high forehead gave him a look of intelligence and distinction;

his nose was Semitic, his moustache typically Arab, his mouth well-drawn and sensitive; but it was his eyes that held me: they were large, black and compelling, and when he was animated, as he was now, the white showed above the iris. They were the eyes of the King and courtiers of Mari.

I collected myself. 'Thank you very much. Mr. Welsman certainly did tell me about you, and I'm glad to meet you. I think I'll have a orange juice.'

I went into the courtyard wile he fetched my drink, and looked round at the climbing plants, now in full bloom, and the fountain playing in the middle. The building had once been a private house belonging to one of the rich, long-established Arab families, and it had been bought and turned into a hotel by an American family called Vester. Mrs. Vester was now a beautiful old lady in her eighties, the doyenne of the large foreign community and renowned for her memories of General Gordon, T. E. Lawrence, General Allenby, Glubb Pasha and others who changed the course of Middle East history. Her parents, the Spaffords, had originally lived in the Old City and had founded the Colony as a sort of religious community. When the Vesters started the hotel, they turned the house in the Old City into a children's hospital. It was said of the family - and the present members laughed about it themselves - that they came to the Holy Land to do good and stayed to do well; but their hospital must have saved thousands of children's lives. When Gabriel came back with my orange juice, I said, 'Aren't you going to have something?'

'No, thank you. I don't feel like it now.'

I learnt afterwards that Mrs. Vester, who was called 'my lady' by the Arabs who worked for her, did not permit the guides to drink or dine in the hotel even when customers invited them. A guide was a guide, although from Mr. Welsman's testimonial and Gabriel's presentable appearance I would have called him a tour director or some other name without the slightly servile connotation of 'guide.' But he and his family had become refugees when Israel was treated in May 1948, and it was a very needy young man who had come to work at the Colony in 1953, struggling against great odds to make a decent

living for his parents and younger brothers and sisters. Mrs. Vester
was on visiting terms with the richer Arab families, but her policy with
the poorer ones was to keep them in what she considered their place,
not to encourage them to improve themselves. A natural attitude,
perhaps, for one of her generation, but it had led to an embarrassing situation when Gabriel guided Mr. and Mrs. Daggett Harvey of
Harvey Restaurants, a most enlightened couple from Chicago, who
thought very highly of him. The Vesters gave a party for them at
the Colony, and the Harveys were horrified that Gabriel was not to
be invited. Diplomatically but firmly they made it clear that Gabriel
was the person who had meant most to them during their stay, and
Mrs. Vester was forced to let him attend. But she was not pleased,
and he found it politic to leave the Colony shortly afterwards. They
asked him to come back again when they found their former clients
were recommending him to their friends. One of them was Aldous
Huxley who sent Gabriel his doctor to guide.

   I had not been talking to Gabriel very long when we were joined by
Anton Nahhas, the tour manager, and after he had made me a graceful speech of welcome, Gabriel and he had an animated conversation
in Arabic. I had been in the Mediterranean countries long enough
to know that a heated discussion was not necessarily an angry one:
it could mean passionate agreement in denunciation of a third party,
adamant refusal to accept a gift or favour - as when two friends com-
peted to pay each other's twopenny bus-fare - or just friendly banter.
But now it seemed something rather important was at stake, and Anton was begging Gabriel to do something he was refusing to do.

   'What's the matter?' I asked. 'Is it anything to do with our tour?'

   'Yes, ma'am,' said Anton apologetically. 'You see Gabriel told us
this morning he did not want to work for us any more.'

   My heart sank. 'Oh! but he must,' I said. 'Mr. Welsman told me
nothing about the arrangements here. He told me to leave everything
to Gabriel.'

   'I'm very sorry,' said Gabriel, 'but I shall not be able to help you.
I just came to ask you to give my regards to Mr. Welsman and to tell
you I am not working for the Colony any more.'

'Oh! but please,' I said.

'I'm sorry.' It was evident that he would have liked to oblige me, but some deep wound had been inflicted on his pride by the management which he could not overlook.

Anton joined my pleading: 'Now Gabriel, for Miss Boyd's sake.'

He shook his head, speechless now but still negative.

'No, not for my sake,' I said, 'but for Wings' sake, for Mr. Welsman's sake.'

The shaft went home. He could no longer in honour refuse. 'All right, for Mr. Welsman then, but not for the Colony.'

Thus began a week in which thirty-five people were entirely dominated by Gabriel's dynamic and unusual personality, and we gradually came to know when he was teasing us and when he was deadly serious. The tour members called him 'the Archangel Gabriel.' He was rather like Alexander the Great of Beirut in his exuberant way of carrying all before him and brooking no inattention or disbelief, but unlike him he had a superb command of his subject. He was a devout Christian and brought great intensity to his guiding in the holy places. His fervour was surprising and rather stimulating after the cold-blooded and chauvinistic Anglicanism we had known in England: he was too handsome and volatile for it to be embarrassing. He opened new vistas in linking not only the Old to the New Testament, but relating both to everyday life in Palestine in a way that made them seem suddenly relevant and important. He also brought out the symbolism of the events of the New Testament.

I remember particularly what he said at Gethesmane on the first morning. We saw the very old olive trees in the garden and then went into the adjoining Church of All Nations. The Church was built in 1926 and its focal point was a piece of flat rock in front of the altar. This was Gabriel's explanation: 'The word "Gethsemane" means in Aramaic "oil-press", and as you know Aramaic was the spoken language of Christ's time. Jesus and his disciples often came to rest in the peace and quiet of this olive grove, and we may imagine that the land-owner was a friend and sympathiser. Here you see the remains of the oil-press of that time. The olive and its oil were the most essential product in the East in those days, and for the humbler people they are still. Bread and olives are the basic diet of the poor; and the oil is used not only for food, but for light, for heat, for ritual anointing, for cleansing and for medicinal purposes. Even the stone is not wasted by the thrifty villager: it is used as fuel and the ashes are used as a fertilizer. The olive-branch was the sign of peace; the leaf, being evergreen, was the sign of eternal love; and olive-oil was the sign of joy, and the Jews of old would anoint their faces with it for festivals.

'To this day we can see oil-presses like this one operated as in biblical times: the massive round stone is turned by a mule, horse or camel, whose eyes are covered so that it should not become dizzy. As the stone turns, it presses the olives and the oil runs. There is significance in Jesus' connection with this place: here he was crushed by an agony of doubt and sorrow, and a sweat of blood ran from his body. Here olives were crushed and the oil ran to make the landowner rich and to give the people food, remedy, warmth, light and sacrament.'

On the Mount of Olives a little chapel had been built by the Crusaders on a high point of the rock to mark the site of the Ascension. There was a depression in the rock, revered since early times as the footprint left by Christ when he ascended to heaven.

Gabriel told us there had been an unbroken tradition of worship at this spot, but even if there had not been, the approximate place would have been known because it was 'a sabbath day's journey' from the Temple, that is the distance that the Ark was from the Israelites on their journey to the Promised Land, namely two thousand cubits or about a thousand yards.

'When I was a child,' he said, 'we lived near the Mea Shearim Quarter where the Hassidim, the ultra-Orthodox Jews, live. On Saturdays the rabbis would put on their fur hats and their ceremonial robes and walk to a certain point that was the distance permitted for the Sabbath from their synagogue. I and my friends would tug at the dangling side-pieces of their robes to make them take a step further, but they would cry "*Shabbat! shabbat!*" ("Sabbath! sabbath!") and push us away.'

We next visited the Pater Noster Church and entered a little cave nearby, which was one of the three caves over which Constantine built churches: the others being the cave of the Nativity and the cave of Christ's death and resurrection, that is the Sepulchre. This one on the Mount of Olives was the spot where according to the oral tradition of Constantine's time Christ told his disciples about his second coming, a central point in his teaching. It could have been from here that he disappeared from their sight.

We drove down to one of the eight gates of the Old City, and left the cars to make our way on foot through the narrow lanes to the Church of the Holy Sepulchre. Shopkeepers, pedlars and hangers-on crowded round us calling 'Jabra, Jabra' - which I discovered was 'Gabriel' in Arabic - asking him to recommend their wares. But he was not primarily interested in commissions like the Damascus guides: he was determined we were to see everything even if it nearly killed us. 'Keep close behind me,' he said. 'We are coming to the most dangerous shops;' and we threaded our way between a sort of Scylla and Charybdis of souvenir stalls.

When we entered the church, which at that time, before its restoration, was very dark, a crowd of little choir-boys in crimson and white surplices, dimly-seen in a cloud of incense, were coming up the steps from Queen Helena's Chapel in the tenebral depths below; some of them were carrying candles, and the flames picked out the indentations of thousands of little crosses cut in the walls by bygone pilgrims. The church was divided between the Roman Catholic (or Latin), Greek Orthodox, Armenian, Coptic and Syrian Orthodox churches. In the Greek Orthodox section was a stone known as the Omphalos (or navel) which was said to mark the centre of the world.

When there was time for conversation, Gabriel told me he lived in Bethlehem: he had been born there, the eldest child of his parents, but the following year they had moved to Jerusalem. When they became refugees in 1948, they again came to live in Bethlehem. I asked him what church he belonged to.

'The Syrian Orthodox Church, whose language is Syriac or Ara-

maic. It is a very ancient church. You see we are Assyrians.* My
father came from the Upper Tigris in Turkey.'

'Assyrians! You mean there are still Assyrians alive today? Well,
no wonder you look like the people of Mari.' I told him about Itur-
Shamagan and his court in the Damascus Museum, and he said that
the village his father came from was mid-way between Mari and Mount
Ararat, not very far from the great inland sea of Lake Van.

He usually referred to himself as an Arab, but he was only that
inasmuch as Arabic was his first language and Jordanian his nation-
ality. There was no Arab blood in his veins. Many of those who bore
the name 'Arab' did not in fact have their origins in Arabia; they were
Canaanites, Moabites, Philistines, Phoenicians, Greeks, Jews, or members of other races who lived or came to live in the Middle East, and
either became Christians in very early days or accepted Islam when
the conquering Arabs came in the seventh century A.D., and in both
cases adopted the Arabic language at the Arab conquest. There were
also many descendants of the Crusaders among those called Arabs,
one Bethlehem family even bearing a name that means 'Crusader.'
Some 'Arabs' are blue-eyed, some are fair, some even red-haired. Only
some of the Bedouin are really dark-skinned, and those inhabitants of
Jericho who originated from Africa.

Most people know of the great Turkish persecution of the Armenians that caused the preacher at St Paul's Cathedral one Sunday early
in the First World War to start his sermon 'God damn the Sultan!'
but not so many known that another community of Christians living
in eastern Turkey was also involved, namely the Assyrians. Gabriel's
father was Assyrian and his mother half Assyrian and half Armenian,
and they were among those who were driven out of Turkey and came
to Palestine. A dispersed people like their fellow-Semites the Jews, the
Assyrians had no Zionism to give them political unity and a country
of return; but they were fervent Christians, and the Holy Land drew
them when they had to leave their homes. There were now Assyr-

---

*The Syrian Orthodox people usually call themselves 'Syriani' but I call them
'Assyrians' because of their Mesopotamian origins & to distingish them from the
people of Syria.

ian communities in Jerusalem and Bethlehem, and about one in four
adults, including Gabriel, spoke Aramaic; its literary equivalent, Syriac, being the language of their liturgy. Aramaic is a Semitic language
like Canaanite, Hebrew and Arabic, and it was the *lingua franca* of
the whole Fertile Crescent from the time of the Assyrian conquests of
the eighth century B.C. to the Arab conquest. The Arabs used to say,
'A man must know ten words of Aramaic before he can go to Heaven.'
There were pockets of Aramaic-speaking people in Maloula in Syria,
but they were more properly described as Aramaeans, and some of
them accepted Islam at the Arab conquest: only those who originated
from Mesopotamia, ancient Assyria, could be regarded as true Assyrians; there were still villages in Northern Iraq where the people spoke
Aramaic as their first language and belonged to Gabriel's church or
the Chaldean or Nestorian churches.

Gabriel's parents became refugees for the second time - and Gabriel
and his brothers and sisters for the first time - when Israel was created
in 1948, and apart from the minimal rations provided by UNRWA, the
United Nations relief agency, the family depended on what Gabriel was
able to bring home from various abysmally-paid jobs. In 1953 when the
first tourists started to come after the fighting, he decided to put to use
his knowledge of the Bible and the holy places by picking up guiding
work. One of the interesting visitors who stayed at the Colony in 1954
and had Gabriel as his guide was Aldous Huxley. He described their
young Christian refugee guide in an essay called '*Usually Destroyed*',
using his situation to illustrate the sufferings endured through the
centuries by the innocent people of the Holy Land amid the waves of
conquest and reconquest, destruction, rebuilding and destruction. 'He
was a sad, embittered young man,' he wrote. 'The surprising thing
was not his bitterness, but the melancholy resignation with which it
was tempered.'

Paradox was the keynote of Gabriel's personality as it is of the
whole Middle East; and while one side was all darkness and plunging
intensity, the obverse glittered with soaring high spirits. He was, as
a schoolmaster of his used to say, 'half angel and half devil.' On one
occasion, finding the other people in the car were congenial, he told us

about some of the American Fundamentalists he had guided (that is, Protestants who believe in every word of the Bible as literally true):

'Once I was guiding a group of thirty Baptist ministers from the southern states of America, which is the most fanatical sort of Baptist there is. I was told by the agent I was working for that I shouldn't smoke or drink so as not to offend their beliefs. I was bringing some of them overland from Damascus to Amman, and round about the Plains of Jabbok I felt a great desire for a cigarette and a sip of whisky. I stopped the cars, got the ministers out into the fields and said:

' "Now we are in the Plains of Jabbok where Jacob wrestled with God, and God blessed him and changed his name to Israel, 'the Wrestler.' But my brothers, I see you standing and doing nothing. Who are you that you should stand idle where our father Jacob had his struggle with God? Can you not kneel down, struggle and pray that you too may be blessed by the Lord?"

'And soon they were all kneeling on the ground, their eyes closed, praying as if their lives depended on it; and I was able to go behind the taxis, light my cigarette and smoke it between swigs from my flask of whisky. Then I said, "All right, you can take pictures now, and then back to the cars, please." And we went on our way to Amman.'

When we went to Bethlehem, we stopped at Rachel's Tomb on the outskirts of the town, and Gabriel reminded us of the story of Jacob, Leah and Rachel.

'When Jacob was in the land of the people of the east, he saw Rachel at the well, and he fell in love with her. He worked seven years for her; but at the wedding ceremony, when he was already bound in marriage, he discovered that he had been given the elder sister Leah, for the bride was so heavily veiled that he could not tell who it was. He had to work another seven years before he could marry the younger sister.

'This custom still survives in some families in this country. I know a family in Bethlehem where there are several daughters, and because the eldest did not marry the others could not either.'

He also told us of something he saw at the tomb as a child:

'This tomb has for centuries been venerated by Jews, Christians and Moslems, especially women. My mother often came here to pray, and one day when I was quite small she brought me with her. A Jewish woman was there with a long rope in her hand, and she came up and asked me to hold one end on the tomb. Then she went seven times round the tomb with the rest of the rope, and finally lifted up her skirts and tied the end round her belly. I was much abashed, and turning away I asked my mother in a whisper what the matter was with her. My mother replied, "She is barren and she is longing for a child, and she envies others having children as Rachel envied her sister Leah. She does this that God may grant her wish and end her barrenness as He did to Rachel. For she gave birth to Joseph and Benjamin." '

He also told us about the Milk Grotto though he did not take us there, as it was not an authentic site. There was an old legend that Mary, Joseph and the infant Jesus hid in the grotto just before they fled to Egypt, and from the fear she was feeling Mary's milk dried up. She broke off a piece of the whitish-coloured rock of the cave and put it in a cup of water. When she drank the liquid, her milk was restored. Bethlehemite mothers who did not have enough milk used to do the same thing.

In Bethlehem Gabriel suddenly stopped the car and disappeared into a house beside the road. When he came out he was carrying a lovely embroidered, blue velvet cape. 'This is for you. My sister made it.'

This was not so: his sister had not made it, but the idea that she had at the same time increased the cape's value and enhanced his family's reputation. And there was a sort of higher truth about it: for some-one Gabriel wished to please his sister would have sat up at night working her fingers to the bone over the highly-skilled couching embroidery - if she had known how. The craft dated from Crusader times, and peasants in Georgia still wore capes and jackets like those made in Bethlehem. For a group of Crusaders settled there on their way back from the Holy Land, and legend had it that they brought the Holy Manger with them.

The manger was probably neither that one nor the one in Santa Maria Maggiore in Rome. It would have been simply a trough cut out of the rock. For the Nativity took place not in a building but in a natural cave that was used as a stable. There were still such stable-caves with stone mangers under houses in Bethlehem; and the traditional birth-place, revered from the earliest times, was in the huge cave over which the sixth-century Church of the Nativity stood. Here the holy child was swathed with white cloths as he was thirty-three years later at his death, and laid in a feeding-trough that was cut from the rock as his tomb was. The swaddling clothes and the trough, signs of his mortality, were to identify him to the shepherds as the Messiah.

In the cave, which was elaborately decorated with hangings and lamps in the eastern style, Gabriel preached us a sermon on the message of Christmas and led us in a rather quavering rendering of 'O Little Town of Bethlehem,' of which, needless to say, we did not know the words. However it meant much more than the tinsel-glitter of Oxford Street in December, and with serious thoughts we followed Gabriel's lean, purposeful figure through the cloisters of the neighbouring St. Catherine's Church. Gabriel met some children he knew coming out of the nearby school, and while he talked and joked with them, turning back to see if we were coming, there was a sudden lightening of the atmosphere as if the sun had come out after an English rainstorm.

CHAPTER TWO

'A Rose-Red City
Half as Old as Time'

'THIS will be my sixty-eighth trip to Petra.' At four o'clock in
the morning of our fourth day, Gabriel was wide-awake, full of a lithe
animal magnetism, and appropriately dressed for our journey into the
desert. There was a distinctly histrionic streak in him, particularly
evident when he was in high spirits, and with his white *keffieh* (Arab
headdress) he would have been perfectly cast as the Great Sheikh. He
had brought a white *keffieh* for me too - 'My sister embroidered it.
See how soft it feels against your face' - and it was the best protection
against the dust of the road, and against heat or cold.

The group was ready, and putting on my headdress I took the seat
beside Gabriel and the driver in our seven-seater taxi, and we started
on the long, lonely drive to the mysterious city of caves in the south
of Jordan. Lost for hundreds of years, Petra was now inhabited only
by a few very poor Bedouin and their goats, and the staff of the rough
and ready guest-house known as Nazzal's Camp. We were to spend
two nights there, and then we returned to England and I was to bring
out a second and final tour.

First we had to drive east down the winding road to the deep rift
valley of the Jordan. It became steadily hotter as we dropped lower

17

between the barren hills of the Judean wilderness, now sparsely coated with green after the winter rain, and came within sight of the Dead Sea, a muted blue in the heat haze.

We passed a sign saying 'Sea Level.'

'Shut your windows,' said Gabriel in an urgent voice.

One of the women next to a back window obeyed hurriedly. After some suffocating moments, 'Why do we have to shut the windows?' she asked timidly, seeing that no-one else had obeyed.

'We are below sea level now,' said Gabriel, 'and the water might come in.'

On the East Bank of the Jordan we turned south and took the biblical 'King's Highway' through the Mountains of Moab and Edom; for the Desert Road from Amman to Aqaba was not built at that time. It was remote, beautiful terrain where undulating grassland alternated with plunging gorges. Gabriel told us stories of his early guiding days before the road was tarmacked, when they had to enlist the help of passing Bedouin to push the cars through river-beds and up precipitous screes.

Our driver, who was called Ata, was about five foot high and completely rotund, and Gabriel loved teasing him. Gabriel told us that once he and some other drivers were in Syria with Ata, and they plotted with some friendly Syrian policemen to get Ata arrested. As they had dinner in a restaurant, the two policemen appeared and asked to see their passports. When they came to Ata's, they pounced on him saying, 'This is our man.'

'What's up?' asked Ata.

'It's no use protesting,' they said. 'We know all about you. You have come here to spy for King Hussein.'

'King Hussein! What have I got to do with King Hussein? I am just a simple taxi-driver. Ask anyone you like about me.'

'Where are the papers?' they demanded.

'What papers? I haven't got any papers,' said poor Ata desperately.

'Come along with us to the police-station,' they said, almost dragging him off his short legs, and they took him out to the street where they had a motor-cycle and side-car. They tried first to get him into the side-car, but this proved quite impossible. He was then placed on the back of the motor-bike overlapping on every side, and Gabriel and the others collapsed with laughter as he was driven off protesting still and wobbling perilously.

At the police-station the policemen kept up the pretence, even going to the lengths of beating poor Ata, until finally their commanding officer came in and asked them what they were doing. When Ata realised it was a trick, he flew out of the station as fast as his squat figure would allow and came breathlessly to Gabriel and his fellow-conspirators: they just laughed helplessly as, gasping for breath, he dredged up unrepeatable imprecations from the murky depths of the Arabic language.

There was another occasion when Ata was beaten by the police, this time in earnest. He was driving behind a lorry carrying some Bedouin when one of them fell off into the road and was killed. Ata picked up the dead man and took him to a police-station, but the police thought *he* had killed him and proceeded to beat him while he tried desperately to explain what had happened.

Another time when Gabriel was going to Petra with Ata, one of the wheels of the car came off and bounded along the rough road in front of them. 'Look, some-one's lost a wheel,' they said, looking round for the car. But there were no other cars, and it dawned on them with horror that this was *their* wheel. Panicking and both talking at once, they crashed the car into a wall of rock rather than plunge into the precipice on the other side.

In the winter Nazzal's Camp was closed and the only place for people to stay was in the police-post outside Petra, where conditions were pretty primitive. Gabriel and some drivers again made a plot against the unfortunate Ata. This time they caught a rat and put it in his sleeping-bag while he was outside. When he got into bed the rat started to bite him, and at first he moved around the bag unable to understand what was happening. When he realised, he shot out of bed, across the room and slap into the door which he thought was open.

I was feeling a good deal of sympathy for Ata by this time, and I asked him through Gabriel how many children he had. Delighted to show off his linguistic powers, he let go of the steering-wheel and cupped his hands over his chest saying 'This' - to intimate the female sex - and then held up four fingers. Then 'This', wiggling his middle finger up and down to intimate the male sex, and he held up three fingers. We realised he was telling us he had four girls and three boys, and laughed at his triumph over the language barrier, and I asked him by signs how many children Gabriel had. I understood by the sweeping outward and downward gesture of his upturned hand that he had none, and from further gesticulations that he was not married. Gabriel interpreted what Ata was saying: 'He says it is time I settled down and got married. What do you think?' 'I should think it probably is, but I don't know how old you are.' He said, 'I'm thirty-three.' 'Well, then, I think it is time you settled.'

We made the steep descent into the valley of the Brook Arnon, and by the dry river-bed we stopped in the shade of some fig-trees to have our picnic lunch. Gabriel, Ata and the drivers of the other taxis had their own supplies: small, juicy cucumbers, enormous tomatoes, raw onions, hot peppers, pickles, some of the delicious salads made with the paste of sesame meal, slices of white goat cheese and a very highly spiced sausage. They drank arak, called by the Bedouin 'tigress' milk', which was the aniseed drink like pernod that went cloudy when water was added. This seemed very much more appetizing than the austere sandwiches and lemonade provided by the hotel, and I accepted Gabriel's invitation to join them. Gabriel ate several of the fiery hot peppers: 'This is what I like,' he said, looking at me.

We were joined half way through the meal by a Bedouin who sat down with us and started talking. After an exchange of conversation, Gabriel told me: 'He says he and his tribe love and respect the English, and you and the others are welcome to drink coffee in his tent if you would like to.'

A moment's thought made me realise we could not really spare the time. 'I should simply love to, but I'm afraid it would make us late arriving in Petra, wouldn't it?'

'Yes. We should be there before sunset.' After further talk between them, the Bedouin left us and we went back to the taxis.

On the road once more Gabriel said, 'That Bedouin spoke the purest classical Arabic. His words could have come straight from the Bible.'

'It certainly confirms all one has heard about Arab hospitality, asking thirty complete strangers to coffee.'

'We love it,' said Gabriel. 'It is in our blood.'

I was interested in the Bedouin's declared liking for the English. 'After our government's double-dealing over the Palestine question', I said, 'I would not have thought the Arabs had much love and respect left for us'.

'Don't think that,' he said with more than his usual animation. 'We owe England so much. Look how much they did in the Gulf States before the discovery of the oil. Look at Palestine - apart from the political mix-up - look what they did in the field of education, law, civil government, roads, missions and so on. That was the British colonialism: now we have American colonialism, the colonialism of the dollar'.

'Is that what it is?' I asked.

He tapped my arm to emphasise what he was saying. 'Once I was the guide of the Admiral of the Sixth Fleet, and he asked "What do you people do with all these dollars you make from the tourists?"

"Sir," I said, "We work hard year after year collecting the dollars one by one, until at last after many years we make eight thousand. Then we put them in an envelope, address them to the United States and send them back so that we can buy a nice big shiny American car for the American tourists." He asked me no more. No, don't underestimate what the British did in the Arab world.'

'It's very interesting to hear this from you. I imagined before that everyone under the British yoke could not wait to be rid of it.' I thought back to a time when I had felt unusual political indignation.

'You must have hated us at the time of Suez,' I said.

'That was hard,' he said, looking away over the countryside which was changed to a sort of moonscape as we got nearer Petra. He evidently did not want to talk about it very much. 'There were no tourists for six months. It was like the years after 48 again.'

We left the cars at the police-post at El-Ji and prepared for the last stretch of the way to Petra which had to be on horseback. Mark Twain called the Arab horse he rode in Palestine 'Baalbeck' because it was a magnificent ruin; but the moth-eaten state of our mounts left little sign of their original beauty of contour. However their owners, the tribe of the village of Wadi Mousa, were little better-fed or groomed themselves. I was adopted by a wily-looking old man called Abu Ali, 'the father of Ali,' who was the leader of the assorted horse-men and boys who were crowding round us recommending their animals; and when one of the tourists wanted to take a photograph of the scene, Abu Ali seized my left arm to pose for her. The horses were chosen and the terms agreed, and we started on the dramatic ride into the heart of the ancient caravan stronghold.

Petra is surrounded by cliffs and the only way in from the east is by 'the Syk', a deep rock cleft a mile long and only a few yards wide. The Nabataeans of Petra, an Arab tribe descended from Esau, had from about 300 B.C. to 300 A.D. exacted tolls from the trading caravans on the north-south route, and their amazing cave-city became rich and famous. In 106 A.D. Trajan annexed it to the Roman Empire, and twenty-five years later that intrepid traveller Hadrian visited it. After 300 A.D. Petra declined and was in time completely deserted except for the very poor Bedouin who lived in some of the caves.

The city's fame lived on, but it was sealed off from foreign visitors by the Bedouin of the area. For Moses' brother Aaron was supposed to be buried on the second highest peak in Petra and no infidel was to go anywhere near. The city might have remained hidden from western eyes till this century had it not been for the Swiss traveller Burckhardt. In 1812 he journeyed through the desert disguised as a sheikh and told the people of Wadi Mousa he wanted to sacrifice a goat to Aaron. As he entered Petra by the Syk accompanied by a party of local Bedouin, Burckhardt hardly dared to look at the marvels that appeared before him in case they might penetrate his disguise; but he returned to Europe to tell his story, and others followed in his steps. Westerners always went with an armed escort until about 1930. By then the Wadi Mousa tribe was more interested in the money the visitors brought than in keeping the city undefiled.

Wadi Mousa means the Valley of Moses, and just outside the Syk is Ein Mousa, 'Moses' Spring,' which was said to be the spot where Moses struck the rock and water gushed forth. There was a deep trough of water where we saw the villagers filling their black goat-skins, and then we entered the Syk.

The Syk was formed millennia ago by water collecting from the higher ground by Wadi Mousa and carving a way through the soft sandstone of the encircling cliffs; and it could by very dangerous in wet weather. In 1964 a French group under the leadership of a priest went against the advice of the Bedouin and entered the Syk during a storm. Twenty-three of them, including the priest and a Bedouin guide, were washed away to their deaths by the accumulated force of the rainwater rushing down the Syk like a tidal wave. Only three survived: two women and a tourist policeman climbed up the side of the Syk and the policeman held on to them till the water subsided. Later the ancient channel of Nabataean times was reopened, which diverted the water from the Syk so that such a tragedy should not happen again.

The Syk's towering sides almost shut out the sky and the chill deepened as we went further in: it was the perfect place for an ambush. Where it became still darker and it seemed that the walls must meet round the next corner, suddenly a streak of pink light appeared ahead. It gradually grew wider until we emerged from the Syk to see the most beautiful of Petra's monuments in all the glory of the dying sun. Carved out of the wall of rock which was part of the cross-gorge to the Syk, the Treasury's columns, broken pediments, relief figures and crowning urn were a glowing pink even without a sunset.

'The Bedouin call it "the Treasury",' Gabriel told us, 'because they thought the urn you see on top contained gold. You may see the bullet holes from their shooting at it to release the treasure.

'The Treasury and the Deir, which we will see tomorrow, are the most striking monuments in Petra. They were built by the Nabataeans

at the peak of their power, but whether as temples to their gods or
tombs for their kings we do not know. They worshipped two gods, a
male and a female, Dushara and his consort Allat, the sun-god and
the moon-goddess, personifying light and darkness. Later we will see
where the Nabataeans hewed away a whole mountain-top to leave two
obelisks of stone facing each other, probably representing these insepa-
rable deities of Arabia. The highest peak of Petra was levelled to make
a high place of sacrifice, for like other primitive peoples they believed
that the higher you were the nearer you were to the Ultimate.'

We let the boys hold the horses while we went into the inner cham-
bers of the Treasury, and the photographers of the party returned to
the Syk to capture that first breathtaking glimpse. I sat on a rock between flowering oleander bushes, and looking up saw blue-black birds
darting with a high sweet cry from cliff to cliff, perching momentarily
on the stunted trees that sprouted high up the rock-face, and then
swooping down into the cross-gorge. They were Tristram's Grackles
which are only found in the rift valley area. A blue lizard crawled
across my rock. Time was utterly irrelevant, something belonging
to another planet, but with an effort I wrenched myself back to the
present.

When I glanced at my wrist, my watch was not there. I looked
round for Gabriel, and found he had been sitting beside me in a moment of rare relaxation. 'Gabriel. My watch. I think Abu Ali must
have taken it when he held my arm to be photographed.' I spoke
quietly because I did not want the others to hear.

His mood changed instantly. 'Don't say anything yet. Maybe it
fell off in the Syk. Can you take the people on to the Camp while I
ride back?'

'If I dropped it on the way, you'll never be able to find it.' But he
was already galloping back up the Syk, and I was glad he had picked
the best horse. His horse-boy started off in his wake.

We passed a Roman-type theatre roughly fashioned from the rock,
and hundreds of Nabataean cave-dwellings, as the cross-gorge gradually widened. It finally opened out into an area about a quarter of a
mile square bounded by cliffs on every side, and one could see how su-

perb the natural defences were: a handful of men in the Syk could hold a city against a great army. We clattered down a Roman road which English archaeologists had recently excavated, under a triumphal arch built for Hadrian, and arrived at the hostelry known as 'the Camp.' A plain stone building with twelve bedrooms, it was dwarfed by the only other masonry building in Petra which stood nearby, probably a temple from Roman days but known by the romantic name of 'the Castle of Pharaoh's Daughter.'

I tried to dismiss the horse-boys by saying in my very limited Arabic, 'Half-past five the day after tomorrow,' but they did not move till I said, '*Baksheesh* the day after tomorrow.' Then Abu Ali gave them the word, and they mounted and galloped off with whooping cries to encourage their steeds, leaving an echoing silence behind them.

Some of us had cubicles in the caves near the hotel; and after having a shower in the main building, I changed and emerged from my cave to find a dusty and exhausted Gabriel walking into the camp in the semi-darkness. His horse-boy had not wanted to return alone after sunset, and so he had walked most of the way back. He came up and looked at me intently as he held up the missing watch.

'You've got it!' I said, 'Where was it?'

'I rode right back to where we mounted the horses, looking for it all the way. And there it was in the sand where you got on your horse.'

'Poor Abu Ali,' I said. 'I was wrong about him. It's lucky I didn't accuse him.'

The strap was broken but it was still going: though time could be irrelevant here, it was not out of joint. The Assyrian of old was boring his way into my soul with his hypnotic eyes. 'You said I would never find it, but I did. You have no other invitations here; please have a drink with me after dinner this evening.' He had invited me out when we were in Jerusalem, but I had always been going to see some of the English community I had known on my previous visit.

When we came out on the terrace after dinner, the others talked to us for a short time, and then said 'Goodnight' and dispersed to their rooms and caves, leaving Gabriel and me alone. The moon had risen and a jackal was howling in the distance. It was strangely, eerily beautiful, and I could not help thinking of the Marabar Caves in '*Passage to India*', where the cry 'Mrs. Moore, Mrs. Moore' seemed to echo down the years. It was there Miss Quested thought she had been insulted.'

'I must go in', I said.

Gabriel said, 'I was fascinated when I first saw you. Couldn't you stay a bit longer?'

'No. I must go in'.

'Why?'

'I'm here for such a short time. There's no point.' But as I spoke I knew this was my chessboard.

'Could you come back after the tours?'

'Well, I might. Goodnight.'

'Then who knows what may be behind the curtain for us? You must come.'

The next morning Gabriel came up as soon as he saw me: 'I wanted to bring you an extra blanket last night. I was afraid you might be cold.' Petra has a desert climate: hot by day and cold by night; but I assured him I had not been cold, because I had been warmed by the sun in the afternoon.

All that day, in the intervals of explaining to the group the monuments, inscriptions and sacrificial sites, he hovered near me like an insect, fervid and persistent. On the way up to the Deir, we passed a shallow trough with the sculptured relief of a lion above it. Gabriel said, as he walked beside me with springing step, his eyes alight: 'Once when I was going up to the Deir, I had a terrible thirst. The trough was empty, but when I came back, it was full of water. It was a miracle.' I felt sure that if at that moment I could have seen the whole of his head under his *keffieh*, I would have seen the goat-ears of a satyr.

The Deir was another monument like the Treasury, but here the finely-grained sandstone was not of the same glowing pink; and the facade, though not so ornate, was in an almost perfect state of preservation. The Treasury had been carved out of a perpendicular rock-face, but for the Deir a section of the mountain had been cut back to get the same height. It was on a very sacred spot, for it faced Jebel

Harun, 'Aaron's Mountain', and perhaps an idol of Dushara formerly stood in one of the niches. The Deir was on a plateau, and a David Roberts print of 1839 showed the huge bases of columns in a line about fifty yards away - probably the relics of a Roman temple. The Byzantines were said to have used the Deir as a place of Christian worship - whence the name which means 'the Monastery' - but the only signs of this era were two large red crosses painted on the interior walls.

The far edge of the plateau dropped sheer away to the deep rift of the Wadi Arabah, a valley that, disregarding political frontiers, sliced majestically through Palestine-Transjordan or Israel-Jordan, only changing its name as it went northward: the Arabah, the Jordan Valley, the Beit Shean Valley, the Huleh Valley; and in its trough it held the lethal waters of the Dead Sea, the sweet waters of Galilee, and the Jordan meandering between.

I said to Gabriel, 'Do you remember we used to come this way when we were children?'

'Could I forget?' he said. He kept me behind the others when we started for the Camp, and we wandered back slowly through the tall oleanders that fringed the stream that flowed from the spring that bubbled up near the Monastery.

CHAPTER THREE

The Golden String

IT was not only because of my friendship with Gabriel but also because of the very special atmosphere of Arab Jerusalem that, when I returned with the second tour, I felt as if I were coming home. Foreigners enjoyed a privileged position there, and the local population treated them with respect and friendliness. Personal considerations, not material ones, were paramount, and memories were long. The Palestinians had known Turkish rule for four hundred years, and British rule from 1917 to 1948, and now, under King Hussein, they were enjoying the nearest thing to self-rule they had ever known. Though not nationalistic, they did have a great ethnic pride in showing themselves and their country in a good light to visitors, and their very deep-rooted tradition of hospitality found its perfect expression in the tourist industry.

As the whole subject of Jerusalem, Palestine, Israel, Jordan, Jews and Arabs is a complicated one on which the most way-out misconceptions exist, it is perhaps the moment to say a little more about the political background.

In the Baedeker edition of 1912 we see that in the province of the Turkish *mutesarrif* of Jerusalem at the time of the census of 1896, there were less than forty thousand Jews, and there were forty-four thousand Christians and more than two hundred and fifty thousand Moslems. And yet in 1917 Lord Balfour, taking a leaf out of God's

Book, made his famous 'declaration' to the effect that 'His Majesty's Government view with favour the establishment in Palestine of a National Home for the Jewish people, and will use their best endeavours to facilitate the achievement of this object,' though he did add the proviso, 'it being clearly understood that nothing shall be done which may prejudice the civil and religious rights of existing non-Jewish communities in Palestine.' Although this declaration was really just a letter without any binding legality, it was used in the coming years as justification for the Zionist ambition to regain the Promised Land; and God's Covenant with Abraham was also invoked. Then the Nazi persecution aroused such desperation in the Jews and such horrified pity in the western powers that the dream of a Jewish state became reality in May 1948, while the proviso about the non-Jewish majority was disregarded. The involvement of several Arab armies saved the Old City for the Palestinians but lost them territory in Galilee they might otherwise have kept. A great many Moslem and Christian civilians fled from the Jerusalem area, largely as the result of the massacre of the villagers of Deir Yassin by Menachem Begin's terrorist gang in April. Others emigrated in the hard years that followed the creation of Israel. On the other hand the large influx of Jewish immigrants made the city of Jerusalem taken as a whole become predominantly Jewish.

In what Anthony Nutting has called 'a monstrous piece of political surgery', Jerusalem was partitioned between Jews and Arabs, as a result of the mounting tension between them, in November 1947, and it was a divided city when I brought the Wings tours there. Although the United Nations resolution of 1947 said that Tel-Aviv not Jerusalem should be the capital of the Jewish section, the Israelis started moving their ministries to Jerusalem in 1949. Several of the most powerful countries had their consulates or consulates-general, not their embassies, in Jerusalem, and they regarded the city as a *corpus separatum,* that is a complete entity separate from the surrounding area and not belonging to any state, its status being 'undetermined' until a peace settlement was made. These countries were U.S.A., Great Britain, France, Spain, Italy, Greece, Belgium, and Turkey.

At the Partition the Jews had as their portion the New City which

was the main business and residential part of the town, and the Arabs
had the Old City which contained the holy places and housing for
about sixty thousand people. After the creation of Israel when the
British Mandate ended, the segregation was complete (except for some
Arabs remaining in Israel), so that the Jews could no longer reach their
Wailing Wall, and tens of thousands of Arabs were cut off from their
houses, schools, businesses, markets and means of livelihood in the
New City, their access to the Mediterranean, and many of their holy
places. The Hebrew University and Hadassah Hospital which the Jews
had built on Mount Scopus, a strategic high-point to the north-west of
the city, became an island of Jewish territory within Jordan and were
no longer used for the purposes intended after a lorry-load of doctors
and nurses were massacred by the Arabs in reprisal for Deir Yassin.

Though there was inconvenience and discomfort for the Israelis,
they had little conception of the hardship and heartache caused to

the Palestinians by the Partition: they had gained a country when
before they had none, while the Palestinians felt they had lost two-
thirds of theirs. For it was not only Jerusalem that was partitioned
but also the land of Palestine, and over a million Palestinian Arabs
left their homes, lands and means of livelihood and came flooding into
the other Arab countries, mainly Jordan. (The Hashemite Kingdom
of Jordan was actually created in 1949, combining Trans-Jordan and
the remaining third of Palestine, which included the Arab section of
Jerusalem). Jordan could not possibly absorb the large number of
refugees that sought her protection: agriculture was virtually her only
industry, and this was in private hands, not organised or modernised.
Besides, a British survey in 1938 had shown that the water on the
Arab side of the Partition line would be insufficient for their needs,
and the Israelis diverted some of what there was.

When the Palestinians in Jerusalem regained their spirit and their
will to live, they set themselves to construct a new town beside the
Old City to supplement what they had lost at the Partition: public
buildings, schools, hotels, hospitals, offices, shops and houses went up
with surprising speed in the nineteen-fifties and -sixties. They used
only the local stone, and the results were aesthetically pleasing. The
new town of Arab Jerusalem was clean, quiet and friendly: the Old
City was colourful, crowded and fascinating. Jordan had most of the
holiest places of Christendom, apart from Galilee and Nazareth, and so
they enlarged the little airport outside the city and started to develop
tourism. They succeeded in this remarkably well.

On their side, the Israelis set their faces against past sufferings
in Europe and recent troubles in Palestine, and began to build their
country in all the pride of new nationhood. They built a new Hebrew
University and Hadassah Hospital, and replaced the kibbutzim that
had been abandoned and destroyed in Jordan with many new settlements in the part of the country that became Israel. Some of the
Arab villages were destroyed, some were left deserted, and some were
partly resettled with new Jewish immigrants, and the old system of
village agriculture yielded place to a government-organized development programme. But they gave too little thought to the mounting

resentment of the displaced Arabs and 'the naked, poor and mangled Peace,' which could not be passed by for ever.

The American Colony was one of the few buildings on the Jordan side of Jerusalem that had existed outside the Old City at the time of the Partition. Another was the English Cathedral of St. George (who was a Palestinian saint), which was an improbable piece of Gothic in a Middle Eastern setting. I had stayed in the hostel there for a weekend six months before. It had happened to be Remembrance Day and the wife of one of the canons was complaining about another: 'Poppies before breakfast? That's too much!'

Passing the Cathedral when we came from the airport, we turned north alongside a wall known as the Dividing Wall (actually put up to protect people from Israeli snipers shooting across no-man's-land) and arrived at the Colony. Gabriel and Anton Nahhas were waiting for us at the gate. Anton shook my hand briefly: 'Here's Gabriel,' he said. Gabriel was wearing a blue suit and light-coloured shoes: behind his very black sun-glasses he looked dark, foreign and slightly sinister, and I knew that his glasses had little mirrors inset in them with which he watched the tourists sitting behind him in the taxi. Then I recalled his telling me he had actually had the mirrors fixed when he was teaching, so that he could see any missiles aimed at him from behind, and could unnerve his pupils by appearing to have eyes in the back of his head. Having been a schoolmistress for several years myself, I had a fellow-feeling about this, and I relaxed and accepted his ardent handshake.

That evening he took me to the Grand Hotel, Ramallah, where we had dinner and danced on an open-air floor; and the next evening over a drink in a Jerusalem café, he showed me the jewellery he had ready for the girl he would marry: a set of pearl bracelet, brooch, ring and earrings, eight gold bangles, and a wedding ring. He talked about marriage, and the 'customs and traditions' of his people and his church, and asked me to dinner with his family the next evening. I understood that they, and I, would be on approval.

Amongst the poorer families of Palestine it was regarded as the natural thing that the eldest son should bring his wife to live with the

parents and unmarried brothers and sisters, both because it was more
economical that way, and also because the eldest son was anyway duty-
bound to look after his parents. I took it that Gabriel and I would
live with the family if we married, mainly because living alone seemed
financially out of the question. It was therefore very important that
the family and I should like each other.

Gabriel wanted me to bring someone with me, and I suggested
Margaret Daley, the girl I was sharing a room with. He suggested
I should also invite her parents: Mr. Daley was a clergyman, and
Gabriel wanted them to act as a substitute for my parents, as befitted
Arab custom. A cousin of Gabriel's called Morad Gharibeh was also
there, and Mariam Khamis, another cousin with whom Morad had
been friendly many years.

Gabriel's mother, Mary, had a wonderful face, deeply-marked with
suffering, a face of strength and relentless goodness - fit subject for a
Rembrandt. Much of the credit for keeping the family's heads above
water in the hard years after 1948 must go to her, for Gabriel, though
virtually head of the family and the only bread-winner from that time,
was still a young man. She was very eager for Gabriel to marry: in
fact his bachelorhood at thirty-three was considered a disgrace, and
she had turned him out of the house just before I came saying 'Don't
come back till you've made up your mind to get married.' His father
Simon, had been shot in the shoulder by a stray bullet in the troubles of
1936 and was becoming increasingly incapacitated. Gabriel had lately
stopped him dressing in the baggy Turkish trousers worn by most of
his contemporaries in the Assyrian community, but still they did not
consider him presentable enough for foreign visitors, and he was kept
in the background. Neither parent spoke any English except the word
'good' which the mother put to very versatile use: and in fact both
were illiterate, having had no schooling at all. I shall refer to them as
Abu-Jabra and Um-Jabra, 'Gabriel's father' and 'Gabriel's mother',
as parents were always known by the name of their eldest son.

They had had eight children altogether, three sons and five daughters, but one daughter had been run over when she was small, and
another, the one next to Gabriel and his favourite, had died in tragic

circumstances in 1953. One son and one daughter had married: Khalil was living in a town north of Amman, and Victoria in Baghdad. The older daughter Azizeh had stayed at home to keep her mother company when they became refugees, and as she had had very little schooling, she spoke no English and her interests were mainly domestic. The youngest daughter Widad was an attractive and intelligent girl of nineteen, and the youngest son Mousa was still a schoolboy. They both spoke English.

We sat for nearly an hour in the sitting-room which was a small, square room with chairs placed arm-to-arm all the way round it, and Gabriel talked while his mother smiled and nodded at us. Nothing was said about a possible engagement, and the Daleys did not know it was in the air. Margaret knew only that I had been out with Gabriel in the evenings. Most of what he said that day was aimed to prove he was unrivalled as a guide for the Holy Land and had very good connections abroad. Here is the archangel blowing his trumpet:

'Once I guided a group of twenty-five Baptist ministers. They were amazed how well I knew my Bible, and they sat round in a circle with me in the middle and fired biblical questions at me. I could answer every one, giving chapter and verse. So they asked me if I would go to America to take part in the sixty-four thousand dollar quiz programme they had on television. If I won, I would take $ 10,000 and they would divide the rest among themselves. I agreed and I would have gone, but the American Embassy refused to give me a visa.'

Dinner was in the huge, vaulted inner room which was part of the original house, while the sitting-room and the bedroom next to it had been added on later. Of the family only Gabriel sat down to dinner with the guests. He asked Mr. Daley to say grace, and after that Um-Jabra and Widad started to ply us with stuffed zucchini, wrapped vine-leaves, a flat pastry with meat known as *sfiha*, objects made of cracked wheat and minced lamb known as *kibbe*, and chicken that was falling off the bone and ready to melt in the mouth.

'This is how we eat,' said Gabriel, taking a *sfiha* in his hand, folding it over and preparing to take a bite. 'We say that this', and he put the *sfiha* down and held up his right hand with fingers spread, offering it for inspection from every side, 'has been with you all the time. The knife and fork haven't.' Forgetting that we were poised to eat, he continued: 'You must know whom I mean by Glubb Pasha. He was the British officer in charge of the Jordanian army till 1956. Well, once he came to a big *mensaf* given in his honour by the municipality of Bethlehem. A *mensaf* is a banquet at which the main dish is mutton, rice and bread soaked in yoghurt. When he saw the knives and forks on the tables, in front of all the army officers and town dignitaries he said in the purest Bedouin dialect, "For shame! Take those things away and bring me water." Three soldiers came up with water, soap and a towel, and turning back his sleeve - for he was wearing Arab dress - he washed his right hand in the traditional way and then plunged it into the steaming dish before him.

'So feel at home. Help yourselves, please. There's plenty more when you've finished that. And don't worry about your stomachs: this is all cooked at home.'

The Daleys were rather abashed by the reference to their stomachs and also daunted by the quantity of food and the thought that they had to make a hearty meal to show their appreciation; but I was hungry and quite ready to do it justice. After I left, Gabriel would have said to his family admiringly, 'Did you see how much she ate?'

After dinner we returned to the sitting-room, coffee was served, and Gabriel gave Mrs. Daley an embroidered bag and Margaret a Crusader cross. It was not only hospitality that was in his blood, but any form of giving. Everyone who came to his house, almost everyone who came in his path, received a present; and an unending stream of ancient pottery, statues and glass, precious stones, jewellery, Crusader jackets, embroidered village dresses, mother-of-pearl brooches, and olive-wood Bibles, rosaries and Nativity sets passed from his hands to his guests, clients and hoped-for clients. The Assyrian kings were often depicted with the right hand extended as if offering something, and the habit had come down to Gabriel after nearly three millenia.

Not long after dinner Gabriel seemed to switch off, and I remembered that it was customary to leave after the serving of coffee. Also we had to make an early start next morning to Petra. I said Goodbye to Um-Jabra, and she kissed and patted me approvingly. She told Gabriel afterwards that 'her heart and mine had exchanged talk' and that I was 'a real lady'.

After the second visit to the rose-red city, I parted from Gabriel in Jerusalem on a very cold, grey May morning, and it was understood that I should return later in the summer and we would get married. The reason I accepted this after so short an acquaintance was in part because I had a strong feeling it was predetermined. The thread that had brought us into the same orbit was quite a tenuous one.

Even so, I might never have dragged myself away from the reassuring greenness and secrecy of our 'sceptr'd isle' to what Conrad called 'the violence of sunshine', had it not been for an unexpected summons from Wings. They wanted me to be their representative for five weeks in the Lido di Jesolo near Venice. I accepted and told my parents reticently that I would probably go back to the Middle East when the job finished. To say I was going to marry an Arab guide did not sound promising; and if I said he only became a guide because he was a refugee and there was no other work, it sounded no better. And I did not want anyone to put pressure on me.

In Jesolo I had a letter from Widad telling me how 'faithful, courtly and unbrazen' her brother Gabriel was, and how much they were looking forward to my coming out, and there were several letters from Gabriel.

I took a boat to Beirut, went through immigration and customs, and found noone to meet me on the quay. This might have been because he did not get my letter, or because he was unable to get free time. I asked the two porters who were carrying my numerous suitcases to take me to a taxi where I could buy a seat to Bethlehem. They did so, and the man in the office took a chivalrous interest in me, told me he would be taking me in his taxi himself when it filled up, and gave me the obligatory cup of Turkish coffee. As I was drinking it, the door burst open and Gabriel arrived like a tornado. He looked as if he was going to fight the taxi-man at first, but when he had established his right to me, they parted fairly amicably and I learnt that the man was one of the Assyrian community in Beirut.

Only afterwards did I hear how Gabriel had found me. He had flown from Jerusalem that morning and arrived in the dock after ten. Finding all the passengers had already disappeared, he asked the customs men if they knew where I had gone. They had no difficulty in understanding whom he meant because I had been the only unattached female on the boat, and they told him, 'She left with two seamen'.

Now Arabic is a language that is spoken by a hundred million people, and there are so many different dialects that only a scholar like Sir Richard Burton of 'Arabian Nights' fame - if he - could understand everything that was said to him in different parts of the Arab world. What Gabriel understood from the customs men was that I had struck up a shipboard friendship with not just one, but two of the crew and had gone off with them to taste the many pleasures of life in Beirut. Fuming, he followed the trail of 'the girl with two seamen' until he found me and discovered that 'seamen' is what the Lebanese call the dock porters.

We stayed in Beirut a week and while there I met Gabriel's relations on his mother's side. Um-Jabra had - literally - lost her family at the time of their persecution by the Turks. The Sultan was supposed to have said, 'It is right to suck the blood of every Christian,' and her story was a revealing illustration of the sufferings inflicted on about two million innocent Armenian and Assyrian people; later the Greeks in Turkey also suffered. We believed her family lived in Adana, but it was difficult to get exact information about her early life. The harrowing tale as told to her children and grandchildren was as follows:

Her father and eldest brother were put in prison in their hometown. The father became very ill and was thrown out into the street to die. A kindly Moslem merchant had pity on him and took him into his house, and the father begged him to bring him news of his son. But the son had also become ill, and he had been cast into the sea; and when the father heard this, he died of shock and grief. The rest of the family learned of their deaths from the merchant, and then they were driven eastwards by the Turkish soldiery in a forced migration. Um-Jabra saw her second brother burnt in a hayrick with other boys; and when the youngest brother was snatched from her arms and dashed against a wall, she ran from the horror of it all and was separated from her mother and two sisters. An Assyrian family took care of her for the rest of the terrible journey. At times they had nothing to eat except pellets made from the husks of corn they found in the dung of the Turks' horses. A British ship came to the aid of the refugees and brought them from a Turkish port - perhaps Iskenderun - to Lebanon, and from there the flight became a pilgrimage and they made their way to Bethlehem. Um-Jabra was brought up there by the Assyrian family, and in 1925 she was married to Abu-Jabra.

In 1933 the British government collected the names of the Armenians and Assyrians who had survived the persecution, and Um-Jabra discovered that her two sisters were alive and living in the Lebanon. The three of them were lucky, for many of the little girls involved in the pogrom were taken by the Turks to be servants or concubines. The elder of the sisters had married an Armenian and was living in the Armenian quarter of Beirut: the other was married to an Assyrian and lived in Tripoli, north of Beirut.

We had difficulty in finding the elder aunt's house, because the Armenian quarter seemed to spread for miles in a maze of identical narrow streets with little shops and flats above them. Eventually we came upon Gabriel's uncle quite by chance and he took us to the house. It was old and run-down, with only three small rooms. Gabriel told me when he first came there with his parents in 1933, it had been almost the only house amid fields planted with okra and squash. His uncle had owned much of the surrounding land, but he had given it away to other Armenians as they came to settle there.

The two sons, Joseph and Haratoun, worked in metal and both were newly-married. Haratoun was the more successful, and he had rented a modern flat for himself and his bride - and her mother, who seemed to be part of the bargain. The old aunt spoke only Turkish, for this was what she and her husband has spoken as children; the next generation spoke Turkish, Armenian and Arabic. Gabriel did not know very much Turkish, but he and his aunt conversed, he in Arabic and she in Turkish, and understood each other perfectly.

We were invited to the mountains for the night to stay in a cottage rented by the family for the summer, and we went for a walk after dark with Gabriel's cousins. The air was beautifully fresh and cool after the humid heat of Beirut, and Gabriel was in exultant mood.

'One day when I was walking in the desert near Petra,' he said as he pranced along, 'I came upon a lion. I went straight up to it, and it opened its mouth to swallow me. I wrapped my headdress round my arm and plunged my hand down its throat. I seized its tail with my hand and pulled and pulled till the lion came inside out.' He enacted the feat in the sparkling night air, and then I took his arm again and we returned to the cottage. 'My brave Assyrian lion-hunter,' I said, and we entered the one big room where all of us, men and women, were to sleep; and there was much joking about their having to keep Gabriel strapped down on his bed.

The Tripoli family was better-off than the Armenian one, and we spent Sunday with them. There were fish for lunch, shoals of them fresh from the sea and cooked with their heads on, and fourteen of us sat at a table in the courtyard and picked the bones clean with our hands. The eldest son of the family, Jacob, had a very good job with the Iraq Petroleum Company: he was like Gabriel, but an older, more assured Gabriel. After lunch we walked down to the little Assyrian church which was right on the sea, and there we met the bishop, who told me I was marrying one of the finest young men of the community.

It was a pleasant and interesting day, and it seems strange now to think how I started the visit. When we arrived we were shown into the sitting-room, which was only used when visitors came, and sat in the seats of honour under the photograph of Jacob's paternal grandfather, another Jacob, who wore the Turkish *tarbush* and a magnificent pair of moustaches. As first they talked in English for my benefit, then Gabriel embarked on a lively conversation in Arabic. I sat still for a few minutes, and then I suddenly got up and walked out of the room, out of the house and down the street. I walked fast, and Gabriel had to run to overtake me. When I saw his bewildered look, I relented and came back with him to the house. Jacob received me with courteous amusement; they told me the subject of their discussion, which was politics; and they hardly spoke Arabic the rest of the day. I had

committed no unforgivable social solecism: it was the Middle East I
was allowed to be a capricious woman. But this was only the first of
many trials of love I subjected Gabriel to.

During that week I probed a little into what had happened after
the disaster of 1948. 'Didn't you ever get any compensation for what
you had left behind?'

'Nothing,' he said.

'Didn't you have anything saved?' I asked.

'We had £800. This was frozen in the bank for a time. When we
were able to get it in 1951, I took it and spent it all in one weekend in
Beirut. We were so sure that we would be going back any moment to
our house and the work we had before.

'We Palestinians were like kings then: we had the brains and some
of us still had some money left. Beirut was nothing, and of course
Amman was just a village. They only became what they are because
the Israelis took Palestine.

'There was a wonderful Lebanese singer called Sabah: she still
sings, but at that time her voice was like a bell. We bought gallons of
champagne and poured it over her feet. Then some Kuwaitis started
to assert themselves - Kuwait had just discovered the oil then - and
we had a tremendous fight. We broke the whole place up from top to
bottom.'

'Your poor mother,' I said, and I thought of that small, tough
woman trying to eke out the UNRWA rations while the champagne
washed over Sabah's feet.

Gabriel and I left Beirut in a service taxi, and with mounting
spirits started towards Bethlehem and the ceremony in which we would
commit ourselves to each other before God. As we neared the Syrio-
Jordanian frontier (we could not go by the direct route from Beirut to
Jerusalem because Israel intervened), the realisation started to come
over me that not only was I going to live in a strange country but also,
probably, to die there.

'Gabriel, what will happen to us when we die?' I asked him.

There were some big white birds wheeling and circling a little way
ahead of the car. They resembled gulls but it was rather far inland

for sea-birds. Looking at them he said, 'We shall be like birds,' and it was just the reassurance I wanted. I was so glad he did not tell me in which corner of the hard, stony land our bodies would moulder.

When we reached Bethlehem, Um-Jabra opened the door, and the shrill ululation she made on seeing us was a sign to the rest of the family that their waiting was over and the celebrations could begin for the wedding of the beloved eldest son.

1. Archbishop MacInnes after the service.
2. The wedding: Delia coming from Mariam's house.
3. Gabriel guiding.
4. The wedding service.
5. Gabrial & Delia on the roof of the house: Church of the Nativity in the background.

CHAPTER FOUR

Wedding in Bethlehem

WHEN Um-Jabra greeted us with her ululation, Gabriel said to her in Arabic, 'Sh! she will think we're savages,' but he need not have bothered: I was to hear that sound very often in the coming month, a month of endless visitors and mounting excitement.

I was told on the evening of our arrival that we would become officially engaged the following afternoon. I slept in the room that was to be ours: it had been newly furnished, and cosmetics and scents were laid out ready for me on the dressing-table. The sisters thought I would not like to sleep by myself and were ready to keep me company, but I assured them I was quite used to being alone. All of them slept in the huge vaulted room that served them as bedroom and living-room. The sitting-room next to our room was only used for special visitors. These two rooms had been added on to a much older house, and both had a wonderful view over Bethlehem and the country to the north and east. To the right we looked up at the Church of the Nativity, and in front and below us was the village of Beit Sahour, 'the House of the Watchers.' The land adjoining this village is known as the Shepherds' Fields as being the most likely spot for shepherds of Jesus' time to have been watching their flocks. It would have been near here too that Boaz saw the foreign widow Ruth gleaning his corn and fell in love with her. Beit Sahour is a Christian village and many little churches dotted the

43

landscape. Beyond were the Judean hills and the high volcano-shaped mound of Herodium, one of the three fortresses or palaces that Herod the Great built overlooking the Dead Sea. Here he was buried when his long reign came to an end in 4 B.C. just after the birth of Christ. (Our dating is wrong). We could not see the Dead Sea because the rift valley fell away beyond Herodium to a depth of thirteen hundred feet below sea level, but we could see the Mountains of Moab rising up on the other side.

Gabriel surprised his family at supper by indicating that he and I would eat together: it had been their custom to serve him first, alone, and they ate together afterwards.

There is an Arabic saying that 'nothing good comes out of the sea,' and yet my strange western ways were never thought to portend anything untoward. If Gabriel wanted me as his consort as well as his wife, so it should be. The mother and sisters made a path of gold before the hot and hungry breadwinner. They washed the floors every day to make the house clean and cool. The tiles shone like mirrors; shirts, under-clothes and sheets were the purest white. When he was at home, they trod quietly, they spoke softly. They stood to serve him as he sat at table, plying him with the sheep's tongue, the lamb's legs, a tightly sewn and stuffed stomach, the hottest peppers, the heart of the lettuce, the freshest fruit, the first cup of coffee; and they sat down to eat only when he stretched out to sleep. But because Gabriel wished it, the path of gold was for me too.

At breakfast the next morning the table was laid with eggs, bread, olives, cheese, fresh tomato juice - and a bottle of Johnnie Walker. Gabriel helped himself to a generous glassful from the latter. I looked at him and then at the whisky: 'Is that what you're having?' I asked.

'Yes.' A flicker of doubt came into his face. 'Do you mind?'

'Not a bit,' I replied, and I pushed my cup toward him. 'I think I'll have some too.'

That first morning we both solemnly drank our whisky, but the bottle never appeared on the breakfast table again.

Gabriel told me afterwards that he went to see a doctor that day and told him his bride-to-be did not like him drinking. The doctor examined him, and his verdict was that the alcohol content of Gabriel's bloodstream was so high that if he stopped drinking he would die. 'What about if I go on drinking?' asked Gabriel. 'You'll also die,' said the doctor. Gabriel decided he would rather die peacefully, and so he almost completely gave up drink for many years.

I had not been told what was involved in the engagement, and it was upon me before I knew what was happening. I had a rest after lunch because the weather was rather hot, and when I appeared at four-thirty I found the main room absolutely packed with people. I tried to retreat to change into something different, but Gabriel seized me: 'Where are you going?'

'I'm going to change. I can't appear like this in front of all these people.'

'You look all right. Come on in.'

'What are they all here for anyway?' I asked.

'Don't worry about them. The priest has come to betrothe us.'

I had not realised it was to be a religious ceremony, and I did not know till I went to another engagement much later that the girl usually buys a special dress for the occasion and prepares herself as carefully as for the wedding. Gabriel was not interested in what I was wearing or what the people were going to say about me: he was only interested in getting me engaged. He had none of the usual Arab concern for 'what the people think.' He wanted to observe the traditions of his community in the religious aspect of the marriage, but he had really no respect for convention when it was not concerned with important things. He had several long, roundabout talks to me before we married about observing 'the customs and traditions', but what it boiled down to was that he did not want me to cuckold him.

Of course the rest of his family observed the whole gamut of conventions; and though Gabriel was devoted to them and very proud of their rebirth after successive disasters, this did not stop him outraging them quite often by his rebellious flouting of the customs they followed. Their first attempt to get him engaged was before the Partition when he was only twenty-one. The little Assyrian bride-to-be and all the guests were waiting for the betrothal ceremony and only

Gabriel was missing. When he turned up it was in a borrowed car with his arm round a Jewish girl. And there were many other fiascos in the succeeding years. This time the vital factor was all right. he was prepared to pledge himself to me; but he was terrified that some jealous person would tell me about his adventurous past and his family's many unsuccessful attempts to marry him off. He kept saying, 'Don't talk to anyone. Stay near me. Don't listen to what that man says.'

All those who had gathered for the ceremony were Assyrians from Bethlehem. Most of them made a meagre living as carpenters, cobblers, barbers, shopkeepers and taxi-drivers, and several of the women also worked as dressmakers. Barring Kando, the shoemaker of the Dead Sea Scrolls, the only Bethlehem Assyrians who had made money were those who had gone to America or the oil states of the Persian Gulf, but they often sent money back to their relations at home. They were a cheerful and resilient people, with no chip on their shoulder in spite of the persecution they had suffered, and as their dominant characteristics were curiosity and love of gossip, all engagements and weddings were gala occasions, and ours were no exception.

The Assyrian communities of Bethlehem and Jerusalem were divided into groups or 'tribes' from the various Turkish villages of their origin, and there was much rivalry between them - sometimes light-hearted, sometimes quite serious. Gabriel's father came from Isfis on the upper Tigris, and in the absence of my father I was represented at the betrothal by Abu Girias ('the father of George') who was the headman of Isfis. He took his duties very seriously: the jewellery that Gabriel was presenting me with was laid out on the table, and Abu Girias examined it critically and suggested it was not enough for his adopted daughter. I assured him it was quite sufficient for my needs, and the ceremony began. The priest, a young Iraqi Assyrian from Mosul, gave a short service of prayers and blessings in Aramaic, and put the wedding rings on the fourth finger of our right hands to show that we were now betrothed. A loaf of bread which he had blessed was passed round and those who were near us took and ate a small portion. There was an outburst of ululation from the older women, and everyone started talking at once and came up to shake our hands and say '*Mabruk!*' ('Congratulations!'). It was all over.

Arab and Assyrian marriages were usually arranged between the families of the man or boy and girl concerned, and though they were very rarely effected against the will of the young couple, there was sometimes a certain element of half-heartedness on one side or both.

The man's family would make enquiries about a suitable girl, and when they heard of one, would make extensive investigations into her family's background and the girl's qualities. She must first and foremost be innocent of any breath of scandal - but this was almost tautologous to saying she was a girl, at least at this time. Looks came second in importance - and youth third, because in a society such as this a pretty girl would not remain unmarried for any length of time.

A good high school education was considered desirable, and a reasonable level of domestic accomplishment was taken for granted. They preferred that the girl's family should be poorer than they, so that they should not be dominated or patronised.

When the girl seemed to be suitable, the man's family visited hers and the young people met each other. If one did not reject the other outright, the visits would continue - first from one family, then the other. Meanwhile the girl's family would be making *their* investigations, for the Arabs valued their daughters very highly and did not give them lightly. To them money was of the greatest importance, and an older man who was well-off would have much more to recommend him than a bright young man who was not. Reputation came second, and every other factor came a long way behind. These considerations were paramount not only for the parents, but also for the girl, and this was the reason why so many Arabs married foreign women. It was almost unheard-of for an Arab girl to step out of line and say she wanted to marry a man although he was poor or had a dubious reputation.

It sometimes happened that a man and girl fell in love with each other in spite of parental disapproval. Gabriel helped with one runaway match. The man concerned was Victor, the goalkeeper of their Bethlehem football team, and he fell in love with Vera, a girl who was still at a convent school. He did everything in the proper way, but Vera's parents refused him because he was Catholic and they were Greek Orthodox. They used to meet secretly by the convent gate, and with the help of Gabriel they planned an elopement. Gabriel and Victor bribed a Greek Orthodox priest, who agreed to marry them by night - which was in any case quite irregular - and in spite of Vera's being under-age. Gabriel and another member of the team picked her up at an agreed time after dark, brought her to the church where Victor was waiting, witnessed the brief marriage service and sent them off to Damascus by taxi for their honeymoon. From there they cabled Vera's parents: 'We are married. Congratulations! Victor and Vera.' The parents were reconciled to their son-in-law when they found the deed was done, and I knew Victor and Vera as an ideally happy couple, always to be found together in the shoe-shop that they ran.

After the success of this elopement, the captain of the football team, who was called Lolas, thought that he would emulate his goal-keeper. He was in love with a girl who actually got engaged to a cousin and he enlisted the whole team to stand by to kidnap her at the wedding. The girl was willing and the priest was in the secret; but the team failed to find the psychological moment to ravish the bride; the ceremony went smoothly, inexorably on, and young Lolas-Lochinvar's passion was thwarted.

Gabriel had not been inclined to get married before 1949, and when they became refugees he was no longer in a financial position to marry. He solaced himself with a series of Falstaffian adventures, once leaping from the balcony of a respected Bethlehem lady's house on to the top of her next customer, who was a police inspector. Another time he and Morad Gharibeh, who owned a lorry, visited a gipsy encampment. The gipsies of the Middle East were of Indian blood, and their women were tall and slim with a beautiful bone-structure. They used to follow the army camps, and the women would dance for their visitors, the bangles on their ankles clinking as they shook their hips and whirled enticingly round. The most seductive of the dancers on this occasion was led away to another tent by a bemedalled Saudi-Arabian officer; and Morad and Gabriel, seeing where they had gone, tied the guy-ropes to the lorry and towed the whole thing away, complete with its two disconcerted occupants.

By the late nineteen fifties Gabriel was doing quite well as a guide, well enough to marry, but the money used to slip through his fingers and he did not bring very much home to Bethlehem. The taste for drink that he had acquired in the NAAFI, the prevalence of card-playing amongst the guides, the borrowing habits of his friends and colleagues, and his general open-handedness meant that money was never with him for very long. Saving for the future or for another rainy day was the last thing he thought of.

The family hoped a wife would steady him down and give him a sense of responsibility, and they set about finding him the right one. They picked on a girl in Ramallah who seemed suitable, and Gabriel offered no obstacle. Then came the investigation of Gabriel by the girl's family. Her brother went to the town enquiring where he was. 'If you want Jabra Khano, go to the High Life grocery', he was told. This was a seedy little shop not far from the Damascus Gate where Gabriel and other guides used to drink after work or between jobs. It was not legal to consume liquor on the premises, and they used to sit at a table behind a curtain at the back of the shop. If a policeman was in the vicinity, the customers and their bottles would be tipped unceremoniously out into the small, dirty yard at the back to wait till the danger was past. On this day a great many empty bottles had accumulated on the table behind the curtain, the other guides had gone home, and Gabriel was left alone waiting for the service taxi to come and take him to Bethlehem.

'Do you know Jabra Khano?' the brother asked the shop-owner, who was of a humorous disposition.

He said, 'Know Jabra! I should think I do! Look,' drawing aside the curtain and revealing a disconsolate figure among the empties, 'Look how many bottles he has got through.'

The loyal brother did not stop to enter into conversation: he had seen enough. But when Um-Jabra and her daughters made their next visit to the girl's family, they were greeted with insults about their drunken, good-for-nothing candidate.

A similar failure met the next attempt. Two uncles of the next girl chosen went to the American Colony to make enquiries about the would-be bridegroom. They were told, 'He's in the café next door.' Gabriel had been playing cards with some colleagues, and at the moment that the uncles appeared he was called for work. He leapt up from the table and left the game. But he has due to pay the others a few shillings because he had lost the round, and they all shouted at him. 'Which is Jabra Khano?' asked the uncles. The café-owner also had a sense of humour: 'Why, he's the big gambler just running away because he's lost all his money.'

Nothing could make Gabriel cynical, but he did begin to lose hope of ever acquiring a bride. The next time they found a possible girl, they had almost to drag him by force to her house, and nothing could disguise the fact that he was as tight as an owl. In response to his mother's and sisters' encouraging winks and nods, he leered at the girl horribly through a haze of liquor as she demurely brought round the chocolates, and left no doubt in her family's mind that he was as undesirable as rumour had it. The visit was not returned.

The net was then cast wider to include even Madeba and other Christian villages on the East Bank of the Jordan where the inhabitants has not advanced very far from the Bedouin state. But if the rumour had not reached people that Jabra Khano was a wastrel, he was rejected because he was only a guide and had no prospects. Gabriel would quite like to have been married, and his enthusiasm was momentarily kindled when a young Jerusalem girl of rather compelling attractions was put forward. She was the daughter of the man who ran the Garden Tomb, and her mother was extremely fond of Gabriel. However he found she was too ready to accentuate her decolleté for his benefit from the second meeting. 'Too easy,' he said, and lost interest.

Beginning to despair of seeing her firstborn married - and from the eldest son's earliest years this is the wish that everyone had for the parents: 'May your son find happiness!' - Um-Jabra proposed a sixteen year-old Bethlehem Assyrian girl. 'I'm not starting a kindergarten,'said Gabriel. 'Well, don't come home till you decide what you *do* want,' said his mother.

It was a few days after this that I stepped out of the taxi at the

American Colony and walked unsuspectingly past him and up to the reception desk. 'It was love at first sight,' his sister Victoria explained to some Americans later. 'The Arab way.'

As soon as Gabriel became engaged, the girls who had refused him and were still unmarried started to have second thoughts, and their families made overtures to the Khanos hinting that their daughters might consider him after all. I found myself the object of many a bitterly envious glance at this time. Some of these girls never found husbands: others married men whose income was a fraction of what Gabriel's eventually became.

After the betrothal I wrote and told my parents what I was doing. I did not encourage them to come out for the wedding, which was planned for three weeks later, as I thought the social problems involved would be too daunting; but I said we hoped to make a visit to England the following year. They first cabled and then wrote their blessings and good wishes. My mother was slightly shattered by the news, but my father was quite excited about my unusual choice of husband and he carried her reservations before them.

Now we were in the thick of the wedding preparations, and when I think of this time it is mainly in terms of sound: the controlled but insistent rhythm of drums, the wild piercing shriek of the ululations; Gabriel's favourite popular song 'I love you with all my heart', and mine 'One way ticket;' even the silence of night shattering before the recorded and amplified voice of the *muezzin* calling the faithful to prayer at three in the morning: 'God is great, and there is no god but God.' For though Bethlehem had been an almost entirely Christian town from the earliest times, in 1948 a large Moslem element had arrived as a result of Israel's creation, and were housed in three large camps; to serve them a mosque had been built opposite the Church of the Nativity.

The Assyrian community visited us nightly, and one of the girls would start playing a small drum made of sheepskin stretched tightly over a pottery frame, while others danced. Victoria arrived from Bagdad, and Widad and she were the best dancers: Widad with an electric vitality and almost professional skill, Victoria with less expertise but with the posture and profile of an Assyrian princess. I came to know some of the community better: first the priest, who explained the marriage service to me with Gabriel interpreting. As a parish priest he was married, though some Orthodox priests and all bishops were celibate. Then there was Gabriel's schoolmaster, Morad Barsom, the one who called him half-angel and half-devil, who was a small, slight man with a large forceful wife. His ex-pupils held him in great respect; for he was a remarkable man and an Aramaic scholar. He also had a beautiful biblical style in English, and he helped Gabriel with his copious correspondence with past clients. Thirdly there was Elias Morad the tailor who with his attractive wife and children was better-off financially than most of the other Assyrians, and he was on the municipal council and an active member of the church. He used to talk to me in Italian, and Gabriel often asked him to reassure me about his (Gabriel's) qualities and intentions and the charms of married life. It was like being wooed by proxy. Then there was Morad Gharibeh who used to take us for drives in his lorry; and he and Mariam Khamis would join us on evenings out in Jerusalem or Ramallah. Mariam was a dressmaker, and it was she who made my wedding dress.

The material was chosen in a mammoth shopping expedition which was one of the traditional events before the wedding. All the wedding expenses were on the bridegroom's head (or his father's) including this expedition, in which his female relations helped the bride choose her trousseau. Mariam made the dress with her assistants in a day and a night. This was not really necessary, but it was Mariam's way of underlining the excitement of the occasion.

It was arranged that I should spend the night before the wedding at Mariam's family's house which was right next to the Syrian Orthodox Church: and at midnight I heard the shouts from the Khano house a hundred and fifty yards away, as the stag party reached its climax and Gabriel was lifted up to the ceiling after being shaved.

The Syrian Orthodox Church was a little way up the narrow street leading out of Manger Square, which was in front of the Church of the Nativity: the mosque with its high minaret was at the end of the street on the square. Kando, the Assyrian shoemaker who became rich from the Dead Sea Scrolls, was still at that time to be found in his little shop near the mosque, but he had used some of his wealth in 1950 to add the bell-tower to his church. The mosque was built about then too, and when Kando saw how high the minaret was to be, he added another storey to the bell-tower. The Moslems retaliated by adding extra amplification to the *muezzin*.

The wedding was at four o'clock. I was dressed by three and a great crowd of women came to pay their respects. Victoria was my matron of honour, also dressed in white, and she looked magnificent as she danced. 'This dance is for your mother,' she said, and 'This one is for your sister.' Although my family was not there, I was not allowed to forget them: no one in the East is alone.

Mariam's father, a dear old man with baggy trousers, the Arab headdress, a rather dashing white silk scarf, and the usual fine moustaches, handed me down the steps to the church with great gallantry. Gabriel was early and had already been waiting twenty minutes when I joined him at the church door. There were some tough-looking boy-scouts at the entrance who were throwers-out for the many children who were milling about, and as we passed between them Gabriel nearly tripped over my train. I steadied him with my hand and we entered the church together.

The priest led the procession up the aisle, and we were followed by Mr. Barsom and others who were to lead the singing, and some boys carrying *sistra*. These were silver discs which were rattled at significant moments of the service to attract the attention of the Holy Spirit and to banish evil; they had their origin in Egypt in the worship of Isis. We stopped after a few yards to undo a white ribbon stretched across the aisle; then we took our places with the best man Marcus and Victoria beside us, and two little girls carrying enormous candles in front. There was rather an interesting curtain between us and the altar which had a sort of Byzantine motif, and I remembered that Gabriel had explained that it symbolised the Veil of the Temple which hid the Holy Place from the Holy of Holies and whose rending at Christ's death marked the end of the Old Covenant and the beginning of the New. The curtain was jerked back and the service began.

Archbishop MacInnes, the Anglican Archbishop in Jerusalem, was there with his wife, and he was installed in a very modern chair on the altar platform. Mrs. MacInnes sat in the front row with a few other foreign guests, and the Assyrian and Christian Arab population of Bethlehem packed the other pews. Photographers' flashes punctuated the third century chants, the symbolic actions were greeted by shrill ululations from Um-Jabra's contemporaries, and there was a buzz of conversation throughout. Some of the more curious wandered about near the front to get a better view, and the priest occasionally inter-rupted himself as he intoned the beautiful Aramaic liturgy to call them curtly to order in Arabic.

I was able to follow the service by what Gabriel had told me about it and by recognising the proper names. First white ribbons were tied round our necks; (Gabriel had assured me these had no connection with a noose: in the Greek church, and later in the Syrian, golden crowns were used instead of ribbons). Then our rings were changed from the right hand to the left. My veil was lifted, and the words recalled that at this moment Jacob discovered he had been given the wrong sister, Leah, and he then had to work another seven years for Rachel. Our hands were joined, and as we sipped the communion wine, reference was made to the miracle at Cana. As the service neared its end, Morad Barsom and another rather small man with difficulty hoisted the Bible over our bowed heads, and the Archbishop read the lesson from Matthew nineteen. He was given the last word and he pronounced the blessing that released us. Everyone crowded round, kissing and congratulating us, and we gradually made our way out of the church. Outside the door we lined up with the rest of the family to receive congratulations, while sweets were distributed to all the guests.

When we had shaken about three hundred hands, we walked down the steps beside the church to where a huge limousine was waiting for us. It belonged to a member of the Jordanian parliament, the sheikh of the Ta'amreh tribe, which was the tribe that found the Dead Sea Scrolls. The car and its driver, who was also one of the Ta'amreh, were to take us to the house and then to our place of honeymoon.

Qubeibe was about seven miles north-west of Jerusalem, and there was a German hospice there set in lovely wooded grounds, a favourite honeymoon spot. It was believed by some people, including the Franciscans who had a church and seminary there, to be the biblical Emmaus. As we drove along in our limousine, a most surprising thing happened: two beautiful gazelles, their heads erect, bounded across the road immediately in front of us. They crossed from left to right, coming from the direction of Jerusalem and springing away over the stony hills to the north-west. It was the only time I ever saw gazelles except in captivity.

CHAPTER FIVE

The Little Town

TO see gazelles at large near Jerusalem was so unusual that it was regarded as a portent, and when we told Assyrian friends in Bethlehem, they said, 'Ah! you will have twin sons.'

There was great emphasis placed on having sons amongst the Palestinians, particularly in the poorer families, and the reasons were primarily economic. In a country where old-age pensions had not been thought of and it was not the commonly accepted practice for girls to go out to work, elderly parents depended on their sons to provide for them - and also, usually, to provide a home for them. The women also looked to the men to protect them, and a girl who had no brother was an object of pity. There was a great tradition of chivalry amongst the Palestinians: the more conservative men did not like to leave their womenfolk alone at night, and it was very rare for a woman to be left standing on an Arab bus.

The woman's role was very clearly defined in the Arab countries at that time, and within its limits most women were perfectly happy and fulfilled - perhaps more so than the Arab man who had to contend with all the frustrations and anomalies of the outside world, and also more than the western woman who no longer really knew what her role was. I rarely heard an Arab woman envying more emancipated members of her sex, and at times she seemed to find them slightly amusing - possibly thinking, from the number of solitary western females trailing

57

round the tourist sites, that they had gained their freedom and lost their men.

The women of the Khano household worked together in perfect harmony - indeed with a kind of telepathy - and if they put what seemed to me undue emphasis on scrubbing and bleaching, they did it because they enjoyed it and even felt it to have a ritual significance. Food, as was natural for those who had not always had enough for a daily meal, was of absolutely central importance. If a big meal was to be made for some special occasion (for instance the first Sunday lunch after the wedding), the neighbours and relations would come to help them, and work would start on the previous afternoon. On the day of the banquet the central hall would echo from early morning with chopping and pounding, the pumping and hissing of primuses and the clattering of huge pans. The acme of achievement was the *kibbe:* it was very skilled work to prepare the outer case of cracked wheat and meat and to stuff it with more meat, onions, spices and pine-nuts; a good Arab mother was known by her *kibbe*, and Um-Jabra's *kibbe* was unrivalled.

I tended to feel out of my element in the daily onslaught of cooking and cleaning, but I did my best to learn the Arabic cuisine and language while Gabriel was at work, and sometimes produced the meal of the day myself. This was not always a success, because I did not know how to make the best use of the food available, and I was daunted by the mysteries of a new kerosene stove which had no oven and whose burners used to flare up and made everything black. However the family considered me a creature apart and regarded what I cooked as intended to be the way it was, and they were absolutely delighted when I produced an outsize shepherds' pie which was cooked at the local bakery. One day I bought a packet of oxtail soup powder, and Mousa, seeing the picture of an ox on the front of it, told the others in an awestruck voice, 'They take a whole ox and put it in a great pot, and then boil it and boil it till only this powder is left.'

Gabriel and I used to go for a walk every evening, and I remember it as always brilliant moonlight. The tourists had returned to their hotels in Jerusalem, the touts had gone home, and Bethlehem was as

it must have been for hundreds of years: the narrow streets, the little
houses dating from Crusader times or before, the greetings on every
side from those we knew and those we did not, and the blind fiddler
who used to walk slap down the middle of the road at full speed, his
stick out before him, his fiddle on his back. We often accepted one of
the invitations we were given, '*Fuddulou*', 'Come in', and entering a
low doorway with a cross carved in the stone lintel, we would spend
a pleasant hour of gossip and banter. Sometimes we had more cosmic
discussions, and there was an Assyrian carpenter who amazed me by
the breadth of his knowledge of ancient history. I was always given
special treatment and served before the men with the loaded plate of
fruit and, at the end of the visit, the traditional cup of coffee.

We found that a rift had taken place as a result of the wedding,
between Abu Girias and Mariam's father. Abu Girias considered that
as headman of Isfis and my father's representative at the engagement,
he should also have represented my father at the wedding and have led
me to the church. Mariam's father upheld that because I had stayed

in his house the night before the wedding, *he* was *in loco parentis*. I do not know how long the rift lasted, but it was quite serious at the time, and the community discussed it and took sides. Both old men always called me and referred to me afterwards as '*binti*', 'my daughter'.

When I saw the results of the photographers' efforts at the wedding, I learned something I had not fully realised before. A middle-aged woman from Amman, a cousin of the family and mother of Marcus the best man, had been busy throughout the service sewing Gabriel and me together. This was a precaution against the evil eye, that is against anyone wishing ill on our marriage and seeking to separate us. Though a superstition and not part of the service, this was quite generally believed to be advisable - perhaps particularly so in our case - and the priest permitted it. When we looked under the collar of Gabriel's wedding suit some time later, we found about twenty needles put there as arrows to enter the heart of the ill-wisher; and in every photograph taken in the church, there was Um-Marcus behind us, sometimes peering rather ominously between us.

Um-Marcus also took a prominent part in the festivities after we had left for our honeymoon. Many of the guests came to the house, there was dancing, and Um-Marcus improvised chants in extravagant praise of the bridal pair and all the members of our families. A tape-recording was made, and her warbled eulogisms and accompanying ululations would have made anyone else hoarse. At one point we heard her asking what my father's name was. 'Kenneth', she was told twice, but she could not get it. She made it '*Kins*' which is Arabic for 'treasure'. '*Kins* is a stag', she shrilled, 'and Delia is the antlers', and then came an earsplitting ululation. And so she went on far into the night.

I found it was a sure way to the Assyrians' hearts to tell them I came from Isfis, and when they asked if I spoke any Arabic I would say 'No, only Isfisany'. There was quite a body of legend about Isfis passed down by the older generation, and Gabriel used to sit cross-legged on the floor as a young man listening to the stories of Abu Girias and the others. According to them the lands of Isfis stretched further than a man could ride in a day's journey on horseback, and the fish from the

river were of unimaginable size; the rice grains were like *kibbe* so that
the plants bent over unable to support their weight, and the water-
melons so large that a camel could carry only two at a time. They used
to swim in the Tigris using hollowed-out pumpkins as floats, and they
took their produce downstream on bamboo rafts supported by inflated
goatskins to trade with the towns of Iraq. Isfis even had its own saint,
St. Dodou, who was said to have done many healing miracles in the
third century, and all through the years the people would bring their
sick and lay them on his tomb. Another Assyrian saint, St. Ephraim,
also lived in the third century, and he was the composer of most of the
hymns and chants still used in the church, including those used at our
wedding. In his day and for long afterwards they were sung as popular
songs by children in the streets, and it was he who introduced music
into the Christian church.

Gabriel was named not after his grandfather as the custom was, but
after his great-uncle who was a very important man in the tribe, and
there were several Gabriels named after him among the Isfis people.

They used to laugh about an unfortunate experience Abu-Jabra
had as a boy, when he fell off the roof of a house into the huge cooking-
pot in which the meal of the day was being prepared for the whole tribe:
being a mixture of cracked wheat and tomato, it luckily provided a soft
landing.

They even found humour in the memory of their flight southward
from Turkey. When they came to Lebanon they saw a train approaching amid clouds of steam. 'It's Jesus Christ coming in glory,' rose
the cry, 'and there's the trumpet of the Archangel Gabriel', as the
train whistled shrilly. Many of them went down on their knees and
crossed themselves trembling with awe. Others said, 'That's never Jesus Christ,' but the believers told them, 'What do you expect to see
bigger than this?' One old woman doubled up with mirth as she told
me about an old man who, on hearing a clock chime for the first time,
thought it was the church bell, crossed himself and set off for morning
prayer.

The Isfis tribe settled for a time in the Christian village of Madeba
in Transjordan, and then in Salt; but they were drawn to the holy

places as irresistibly as a band of medieval pilgrims. Though the journey there was fraught with danger and hardship, some of them had already made pilgrimages from Turkey, while others had dreamed all their lives of making one. It must have been a great home-coming when they arrived in their beloved Saviour's birthplace, settled among their fellow-Christians and learned their language and their ways.

The population of Bethlehem, like that of Palestine in general, had a wide range of different origins and it was surprising how homogeneous it was. To take the Moslems first: about twenty-eight thousand refugees from other parts of Palestine came to Bethlehem in 1948 and were still living in camps outside the town. (Christians also became refugees, but many were better educated and they had more would-be patrons than the Moslems; this was before the oil boom.) There were four Moslem Bedouin tribes of Bethlehem. One was the Ta'amreh, who lived a nomadic life to the south-east of Bethlehem and normally only came into town on Saturdays to shop and barter. They were said to be descended from the widowed Tamar who slept with her father-in-law Judah by a trick and bore him twin sons. Some members of the tribe believe there was a period in which they were Christians, citing the crossed belts they wore across their chests and the cross pressed into the unbaked dough, conversion to Islam coming either with the arrival of the Arabs from the peninsula or after the triumph of Saladin. It should not be forgotten what cruel treatment was meted out to the Eastern Christians by the Crusaders.

There was a non-nomadic tribe called the Fawaghreh, used in early times by the Christians of Bethlehem as guards against Moslem marauders. A Christian town or village often had a tame tribe, as it were, to protect them. The Fawaghreh lived in the street that goes up to the Syrian Orthodox church from Manger Square.

One still saw at this time a few of the married women of Bethlehem wearing the *shatweh*, the raised hat that was like a truncated version of the tapering woman's hat of Crusader times. The unmarried woman wore simply a white veil. The distinction between married and unmarried girls avoided the unpleasantness of a young man setting his eye on someone else's wife, which might cause a family quarrel. In other villages that did not have the *shatweh*, a man could tell the married woman by the coins worn round the veil. These would be given by the husband at the wedding; and we may think of the special importance of 'the lost coin' in the New Testament. The wife might well have told her neighbours and swept the whole house to find it, because it would have been given her at her marriage and was really like a wedding ring.

There was another interesting point in the village costume: both men and women wore a long band round their waists which was actually a swaddling cloth. These were originally used both as grave-clothes and to swaddle a baby. They were a reminder of the imminent danger of death: 'in the midst of life we are in death'; and as I mentioned before, the fact that Jesus was wrapped in these (probably taken from his parents' waists) and laid on the stone slab of the cave was a 'sign' to the Shepherds, the sign of his mortality. There was a difference in their attitude ('they went on their way rejoicing') they being part of the family, and that of the Wise Men who, as Gentiles, showed by their gifts that they regarded the baby as King, God and Redeemer.

Our date for Christmas was fixed on the pagan festival of 'the birth of the unconquered sun' and the true date may not have been in winter at all. For the shepherds near Bethlehem go down into the Jordan Valley for winter and they would not have been near the town in December. We should therefore think of a date between May and October when their sheep would be grazing near Bethlehem.

The Jews were banished from Bethlehem by Hadrian, and the worship of Adonis was instituted at the Grotto of the Nativity and lasted until Constantine ordered a church to be built there. Some relics of pagan worship lasted till modern times: in Beit Jala there was a shrine to the full moon, respected by Christians and Moslems, and the villagers of Taibeh regularly put out milk for a snake, perhaps remembering a Canaanite deity.

The Bethlehemites were divided into eight communities for the purposes of municipal administration; the Fawaghreh were one and the Assyrians were another, and the rest were each formed of a number of Christian tribes which had combined centuries before under an agreed name and lived in a different 'quarter' of the town. There were the

Farahiyeh ('the Children of Joy'), the Najajri ('the Carpenters'), the
Anatri ('the Heroes'), the Tarajmeh ('the Guides' or 'Interpreters'),
the Kawasshe (from *Kawas*, the uniformed men who headed a procession with ornamented sticks which they banged on the ground to clear
a way for dignitaries), and the Khrezat, which had no meaning to my
knowledge. The communities of Armenians and Copts were too small
to qualify for representation on the council. One of the families of
the Heroes was called Bendak, which was Arabic for 'Venetian': they
must have come from Venice at the time of the Crusaders, as so many
Venetians did, to exploit the new trading opportunities. Nasri Jasser,
one of the Children of Joy, had records to show that one of his family
was mayor in 892. The mayor had to be a Catholic and his deputy
Orthodox or vice versa.

There was a certain amount of inter-marriage between the Assyrians and other Christians, though there was a tendency to marry within
the community and even within the tribe. One of the girls who would
like to have had Gabriel as a husband - and there were quite a number
at different times - was the daughter of a Bethlehemite Arab who had
emigrated to Chile and become a millionaire. Bethlehemites started
to leave for South America at the end of the nineteenth century, and
the number increased when the news came through of the Turkish
persecution of the Christians in Turkey: Palestine was under Turkish
rule and they feared the persecution might spread there. They enjoyed
unprecedented prosperity under the British Mandate, but when hard
times came again with the creation of Israel, they resumed the exodus; a few returned to Bethlehem when they had made good, but altogether there were nearly a hundred thousand Bethlehemites in North
and South America. As Abraham sent to Mesopotamia to find Isaac
a wife, so the American Bethlehemites sent their sons to find brides in
Bethlehem, and sometimes their daughters to find husbands. Gabriel
turned down the millionaire's daughter because she was older than he,
but the father's story was interesting.

His name was Abu Jarour and when he was in Bethlehem he was a
porter. Then he somehow found the money to emigrate to Chile, and
he took with him the rope of his trade. When the people he met in

Chile knew that he was from Bethlehem, they used to touch him all over to be as they thought blessed. Abu Jarour decided to make the most of his sanctity, and he told them that his rope was the one that had bound Jesus to the pillar when he was scourged. Someone then wanted to buy it for a huge sum, and he sold it. Encouraged by this unexpected bonus, he looked around for further blessings.

There was a field near Bethlehem known as Wadi Hommos, 'the Valley of Chick-peas', about which there was a legend: they say Christ one day saw a man who was sowing chick-peas in this field and asked him what he was sowing. The man told him 'Stones', and Christ said, 'Then stones you shall reap', and the chick-peas turned into stones.

Abu Jarour told the Chileans this legend and produced some small stones. The fortune he made from selling stones in the months after that only went to show that Christ's first temptation was a very real one where there were simple people - I mean turning stones into bread.

There was another example of this just opposite our house: a 'Mission', hospital and orphanage run by an American minister called the Reverend Ralph Baney. From his headquarters in the mid-west he raised millions of dollars from well-intentioned Americans in the name of the orphans, widows and cripples of Bethlehem. Everyone in Palestine and many in other parts of the world knew that he only used a fraction of this money for the 'Mission', but his position seemed to be impregnable. For a time he was blacklisted by the Jordanian government, but the work - and the contributions - went on as before, and he held sway in Bethlehem for over twenty years.

Gabriel and Baney were old enemies and they had several confrontations before we married. At one time Gabriel was also involved with a mission, of which more later. They were both in a restaurant near Bethlehem once when a Spanish dancer was to perform. Baney, who called himself 'Bishop Baney ' at that time, was entertaining the celebrities of Bethlehem at a long table: Gabriel was with some other young bloods. When the performance began, Gabriel piled three tables on top of each other in order to dominate the scene from the summit, and when the dancer came to a swirling, defiant halt, he leapt down from his eminence applauding wildly, asked the band, who were all his

friends, to play a passa-doble and whirled the dancer away. This was
too much for Baney, and he stopped them and laid claim to the girl.
Gabriel said, 'I thought you were a bishop'. 'We aren't in church now,'
replied the Bishop and swept the dancer off.

Baney's contributors were devout Fundamentalist Protestants to
whom drinking, dancing and smoking were anathema; but he somehow convinced them that he was converting the orphans and others
in his care to 'know the Lord'. Widows all over America scraped and
saved to be able to pay so many dollars a month to 'adopt' and 'keep'
an orphan, little knowing that nine or ten other people were paying
for the same child, and that the surplus went to Baney's drinks, ha-
vana cigars and women wherever he happened to be, to his estate
and trotting horses in the mid-west, and to the palms that had to be
greased. Even when a child left the orphanage, his name remained on
the books and the people went on sending money for him. Every year
the 'mothers' of the orphans would receive a letter carefully copied off
the blackboard - complete with mistakes - by some child, and a little
phial of 'Jordan water' and a small box of 'Holy Land soil'. These
commodities were also advertised for sale in Baney's magazine, which
had a wide circulation. Our house was opposite the orphanage 'trade
school', but this was always shut unless some visitors came to see it
and then it was suddenly galvanised into activity: lathes whirring,
boys hammering, the instructor shouting incomprehensibly in Arabic.

One confrontation of Gabriel's landed him in prison. It was Christ-
mastide and Baney had a group of American preachers he wished to
impress with the success of his missionary work. He sent his under-
lings round the poorer districts of Bethlehem telling the families that if
they attended the mission church for several evenings, they would get
a food basket and ten dollars at Christmas. Gabriel heard of this, and
one night when he had had rather a lot to drink, he went to the church
and found it crammed with hopeful Bethlehemites earning their food
baskets, preachers waiting for the approach of the Holy Spirit, and the
Reverend Baney. For the preachers were Pentecostalists who specialise
in the Paraclete and the gift of tongues, and Baney by now had become 'interdenominational' and was ready to adapt his service to any

sect in the cause of contributions. The 'pastor' of the church was a Moslem, and as he preached in English, Baney's secretary and *aide de camp* was talking in Arabic. But he was not interpreting the sermon, he was sending up the whole thing and telling the people to act as if they were receiving the Holy Spirit. Gabriel could not stand it: he rose unsteadily to his feet and with searing anger said to the pastor, 'If you really believe in the Holy Spirit you will speak to these people in Arabic so that they know what you are saying, because this man is just making fun of your words.' Baney immediately left the church, and five minutes later a policeman arrived and marched Gabriel off. The chief of police at that time was one of the Moslem Brotherhood, which was a very fanatical Moslem society, and when he heard that Baney was charging Gabriel with being a communist, he clapped him into prison without further ado. It was twenty-four hours before the priest and members of the community could get him out.

The food baskets, when the people finally got them, were very disappointing, being half filled with paper and containing only the cheapest and most basic kinds of food.

There was only one other foreigner I knew living in Bethlehem, but she was extremely good value. She was Mrs. Wilson, who came to Palestine in the 1920s as a bare-back rider in an English circus. She had met Mr. Wilson, a clerk in the British Consulate, married him, and they lived in a little house set in pleasant country behind Rachel's Tomb, not very far from our house. She had a fund of interesting stories about her thirty-four years in Palestine, and she told us how during the Mandate she and her husband were invited to lunch with one of the employees of a British District Officer of a rather remote area. They arrived at the employee's home, a simple village house, and when they entered they were amazed to see a fine mahogany table, with matching chairs, laid with silver, cut glass and the best china. They did not quite like to make any comment, but it came out in the course of conversation that the District Officer was away, and their host had thought it only proper to borrow his things in order to receive the Wilsons in the style to which he imagined they were accustomed.

She also told us about a confinement she had attended in Beit

Sahour. There were nine little girls, and the mother, a big woman at any time, was in labour in yet another attempt to have the longed-for son. When Mrs. Wilson arrived, she was striding up and down the room as the pains came and went, calling upon God and his saints. The midwife had only one eye and even that had not very much sight, and so when the second stage came she was obliged to put her face a few inches away from the mother in order to see what was happening, and every now and then she asked Mrs. Wilson to take a look for her. Mrs. Wilson told her of the baby's appearance: 'Push, me darling', she cried triumphantly in Arabic as she peered myopically at the emerging head; and quite soon their efforts were rewarded by the arrival of a beautiful baby boy. The mother started to thank her Maker and his with tears pouring down her cheeks, and each little girl lit a candle and came and knelt beside the cradle, looking for all the world like angels at that other Nativity.

Things were not always so peaceful in the Church of the Nativity itself. Its politics were complicated because three churches had rights there, the Catholic, the Greek Orthodox and the Armenian, and feelings ran very high among their representatives. The Syrian Orthodox Church had special permission to hold services in the Grotto at Christmas and Easter, but the church members would often go there to pray on their own. One day in the early nineteen-fifties a devout young Gabriel entered the Church in a brand-new suit in order to light a candle and say his prayers at the birthplace. Arriving at the chancel he saw there was a fight going on; the negro policeman who usually guarded the door was there, and his face instead of being black was red with blood. A Catholic priest on his way to the Milk Grotto had taken a short cut from the north to the south transept by crossing the chancel, which was Greek territory, and a battle had broken out between the priests of the two churches. Bottles, sticks, brooms, whatever came to hand were used as missiles. As Gabriel hesitated, wondering if he should leave his prayers for a more propitious moment, a chair came hurtling through the air and struck the large oil chandelier above him. The oil tipped out and poured over him: the precious new suit, earned with such sweat and toil, was ruined.

Everything in the Church of the Nativity went according to the *'status quo'*, even the sweeping of the floor or the cleaning of the windows, and one day when he was guiding Gabriel found himself in the midst of a battle about a door. The Armenians had painted the door that led into the courtyard of their monastery, but the Greeks regarded it as their door and they slapped another coat of paint over the first one. When the Armenians saw this, they sent to their monastery in Jerusalem for reinforcements, and the heftiest of the Jerusalem Armenians came speeding to the scene. One man was like a gorilla, and though he wore a priest's robe, Gabriel upheld that he was retained specially for such occasions. He produced a huge brass lamp from under his cassock and proceeded to beat the Greeks with it, and there was many a broken head among the Greeks by the time a truce was arranged.

The third battle Gabriel witnessed was between Greeks and Catholics in the midst of the Christmas celebrations in 1967. By that time Bethlehem was under Israeli occupation, and Gabriel was on the roof of the Armenian monastery with two officials from the Israeli Ministry of Tourism who were attending the festival of Peace and Goodwill for the first time. In fact they had a wonderful view of the bottles flying thick and fast over the heads of the bystanders.

When we married in 1960, Bethlehem was twelve miles by road from our part of Jerusalem, because the Israelis held the direct route which passed to the west of the Old City and was only five miles in distance. We had to take a winding, roundabout way through the Judean hills. Gabriel was dependent on service taxis and could not come home till his day's work was over. He decided that we should move to Jerusalem, and we found a small house on the slope of Mount Scopus (which is a continuation of the Mount of Olives) in an area which takes its name from the valley at the foot, *Wadi Jos*, 'The Valley of Walnuts' - though *jos* also means 'husband'.

We used to make frequent visits to Bethlehem in our first four or five years in Jerusalem. I think it was in 1963 that there was quite a sensation among the Bethlehemites about a supposed miracle. There was a carpenter living just opposite our former house, and one day when he was cutting olive-wood to make the typical Bethlehem souvenirs, a log fell into two equal pieces before he touched it with the saw. He picked them up and looking at them noticed that the grain on one piece of wood suggested the figure of a man while the other suggested a woman. He told his family and friends about it, and people started to come to his house to see the figures. He made two little shrines for them, and as the news spread people came from all over the country to see them and even to pray to them. The male figure looked as if he was in doublet and hose, while the female one seemed to be wearing a long flowing gown. There was no doubt among the Christian Arabs who saw them: they were Christ and the Madonna.

In March 1970 a comet appeared in the sky to the east of Bethlehem, and again the people interpreted it as a divine message, though no-one quite knew what the message was. For several weeks it rose as the *muezzin* echoed round the hills and valleys at three in the morning, and faded with the light of dawn. A similar comet had appeared in the summer of 1948 in the west, but they told me its tail was down while in 1970 the tail was up.

We continued to see our Assyrian friends: among them Morad Gharibeh, until estrangement set in because Gabriel would not help him with his gambling debts; (before we married, it had been Morad who pulled Gabriel out of the gaming-dens); Mariam Khamis, Morad's cousin who made my wedding-dress; 'the headman' Abu Girias, who continued to work every day in spite of hardly being able to see; the priest, whose wife was always at the cinema; Elias Morad and his family, who later became our neighbours in Jerusalem; and most of all, while he was still there, Morad Barsom. He used to sit on the high couch by the window open to the narrow street, with his legs tucked under him because they did not reach the ground, and give us the benefit of his wisdom and learning: he helped us with our plans for the future, with the drafting of important letters, with laying the foundations of our business.

In time Mariam married, and had to work hard at her dressmaking to keep a husband as well as herself and some of her family. Then in 1968 she and her husband left Bethlehem to join her brother in

America. Her mother died before she left, and her father stayed on with his eldest son. I saw him just before he died: he had broken his hip and was in Baney's hospital, which at that time was just a corridor in the orphanage building. He was obviously failing, but he recognised me and told me Mariam was coming back the next year. I doubted if he would ever see her again, and I said, 'I am your daughter too - do you remember?' 'Yes, *binti, binti*,' he said, smiling faintly. I left him with a perhaps unreasonable anger against Baney and his works.

Morad Barsom and his family also emigrated to America. For some years he had been a clerk in a government office in Amman, which meant he could only come home on Sundays and had to live in lodgings during the week. His son went to America, and - as so often happened - the rest of the family followed. But over there again there was no call for Mr. Barsom's Aramaic scholarship, his biblical English or his great wisdom except in the church and privately. After working for a time in a factory, he and some other Assyrians bought a supermarket in Los Angeles, and Mr. Barsom was in charge of the vegetable counters.

CHAPTER SIX

A Visit To Britain

WE had been in Jerusalem less than a week, when unexpectedly I had the chance to introduce Gabriel to my country and my relations, friends and acquaintances as he had introduced me to his. I received a sixty-eight-word cable from Wings telling me that their courier had been hit by a car in Beirut and had a broken arm, and asking me if I could take his place when their group arrived in Jerusalem two days later. I had the idea of asking them if Gabriel and I could join the group on their charter flight back to England. Our request was granted and I cabled my parents.

We used my parents' house in Abingdon as a base, and from there made a number of visits. When I asked Gabriel what he thought of my parents, his answer was, 'They are exactly like mine'; and in a curious way this was true. My father had no physical handicap like Abu-Jabra; Um-Jabra certainly was not born with a silver spoon in her mouth like my mother, but the end-result was not so very different. Both sets of parents had suffered in different ways: one physically, because of privation, the other mentally, because their marriage had been a long estrangement; both were fond of Gabriel and me, the mothers with the blind maternal instinct to dominate, the fathers without this compulsion and with flashes of humour. Only my father cerebrated, using his education and experience to form judgments and take decisions.

My father, Kenneth Boyd, was born in Buenos Aires, where his maternal grandfather, Owen Tudor, and others of the family, were in business importing and selling farm implements. When my father was seven, Owen Tudor retired and my grandmother left her husband, who was 'given to drink', and returned to England with her father. My father and his sister came to believe his drinking was self-defence against the number and clannishness of the Tudors, and they deeply regretted this separation. Drinking after all was very common among the men of that generation - including some of the Tudors or their husbands - and did not call for such a drastic step. When my father was sixteen, his father contracted cancer of the throat and came to England to be nursed on his death-bed by his wife.

My great-grandfather, much loved by his eight children and numerous grandchildren, lived till he was ninety-six, and I can remember as a small child talking into his ear-trumpet. After his death the Tudor clan continued to gravitate to his house, 'Heart's Delight' in Fernhurst, and we spent many big family Christmases there.

The Boyds and Tudors were very fond of acting, and as young people my father, my uncle, one of my aunts and many of their first cousins produced plays and acted them in the village hall. In the summer of 1953 my father revived this tradition and produced Andre Obey's 'Noah' in the open-air Minack Theatre on the Cornish cliffs. I played Sella wife of Noah's son Shem; and at the end of the play we went off to the East to found the Semite race. There were seventeen of us in the cast: ten 'family' and the others Oxford connections, with many loyal aunts and elderly cousins sewing, cooking and brewing cocoa off-stage. One very distant elderly cousin Ursula was resurrected from goodness-knows-where just for this occasion, did absolutely Trojan work, and then disappeared from sight again. Basil Guy, later Bishop of Gloucester, who was my father's first cousin and also my godfather, had a dual role as the Lion and the Man, and his younger son, in a part specially 'written in' for him, quite stole the show as the Tortoise.

We met most of my relatives while we were in Britain, and when we had lunch with the Basil Guys, who were then at Bedford, Basil asked Gabriel what he thought of Nasser. Gabriel replied with a well-known

fable:

'Once there was a man with a drum. He used to beat it day and night to keep the wild animals away, and it made a very big noise and all the animals were terrified. Then the day dawned when a hole came in the drum from so much beating and no more sound came from it; for it was hollow. And the wild animals came and ate the man up. Believe me, believe me, your Grace, that is what will happen to Jamal Abdul Nasser.'

Although my home had always been in Oxfordshire, first in the grounds of Radley College, where my father was a master for most of his life, and then in Abingdon, I was born in my mother's family home in South Wales. This was Merthyr Mawr, about twenty miles west of Cardiff, and my uncle lived there now. He and his family were away at the time we drove to Wales, and we went to see the house with one of my mother's sisters, Olive Nicholl, from a family outpost a few miles away.

Merthyr Mawr estate was purchased and the house built 1806–1809 by Sir John Nicholl, an illustrious judge noted for his sound judgment and inflexible impartiality. The Nicholl family had been settled in the Vale of Glamorgan for more than four hundred years even then; before that they were thought to have come from Cornwall. Their crest was a Cornish chough.

The estate was between the main Cardiff-Swansea road and the sea, and it consisted of the house and grounds, several farms, a small picturesque village with thatched Tudor cottages, and many square miles of forest and sandhill.

Another aunt left us by the park-gates, and we entered the grounds of the house by a wicket-gate. An underground stream flowed beneath us, and in places beside the path the ground had centuries before fallen away in deep 'dells' where the stream could be glimpsed in the black depths. My grandfather had made one of the dells into a water-garden, but this was now tangled and overgrown.

Emerging from the trees, we came in sight of the house. Built by Henry Wood of Bristol, its perfect proportions, its very white stone, and a setting of beech-woods behind the sloping lawns in front, made it serenely, perfectly beautiful. The very wide eaves on which the roof rested were a special feature of the house. A haha divided the lawn from a field, but this was cropped so close by browsing sheep that it looked as if the mown grass continued right down to the line of trees that marked the course of the Ogmore River.

We sat under the cedar-tree near the old bowling-green while my aunt talked about the Merthyr Mawr of her day:

'It must have been one of the last remaining traces of feudal Britain, but my father's relationship with his tenants and servants was entirely paternal. The tenants paid very little rent and the farms passed from father to son - and the gardeners' jobs too. Of course the First World War interrupted this succession in some cases, but it did not come to an end until the Second World War.

'My father was very much loved by everyone on the estate, and he never discharged a tenant. I remember there was one farmer who used consistently to get drunk on the money gained by selling his livestock in the market. He would be found in the town next morning, asleep and penniless. But my father saw to it that the family did not suffer. I was with him when he visited the man's wife and made her the tenant, so that it was her responsibility to produce the rent.

'When my father died in 1935, the tenants insisted on carrying his coffin from the house down through the park and the village to the church, which is a good three-quarters of a mile. And it was the same when my mother died in 1946.'

We wandered up to the house and looked through the long windows leading to the verandah. The ground-floor had been turned into a hospital in the Second World War and the family had moved upstairs; but though the downstairs rooms were now only used on special occasions, everything had been put back as it was before. Calf-bound books lined the walls of the library as they had when my grandfather read the Iliad in Greek every night on retiring; and the drawing-room next-door made me think of the eccentric old Lady Byass who used to thump on the piano when there were children's parties.

My mother, sister and I often came to stay with my grandparents when they were alive; my father preferred to go on climbing holidays in North Wales. My grandmother, who was known by all her grandchildren as 'Gargie', the Welsh for Granny, was lame, and my sister and I would ride around the drive and park with her in the donkey-cart or on the back of her motorised chair.

My aunt, Gabriel and I crossed the drive and climbed up Chapel Wood opposite the front-door of the house, till we came to the little ruined Perpendicular chapel in a clearing. This was said to be dedicated to St. Roque, the patron saint of dogs. But perhaps the patronage was wider: my aunt said they always came to this chapel as children when they were troubled or angry and never failed to find peace and tranquillity once more.

In front of the chapel were two Celtic stones thought to have been brought there by Sir John Nicholl. One had been used as a rubbing-post by cows. I tried to decipher the Latin: 'This man says he wants to reserve the piece of ground to be a resting-place for his body until the final Judgment Day. I hope he did not mind his headstone being moved.'

We came down from the wood where the trees were turning to red and gold and walked along the drive, dappled with sunlight through the tall beeches, passing the stable-yard, the high wall of the vegetable-garden, the steep bank of the River Ogmore, and the Lodge.

'Davy George used to live there,' I told Gabriel. 'He died only a few years ago at the age of ninety-two. He was my grandfather's coachman and then the chauffeur for his Lagonda and the "Brake" which was used on the estate. He and his wife were wonderfully hospitable: Mrs. George would invite us to tea and ply us with jellies, trifles and cakes; and right up to the time of his death Davy never failed to give us a beautiful honey-comb from his bees whenever we came to Wales.

'One of the old servants still remains: Walters, who used to be the 'tweeny. Now she does everything.'

We left the drive and emerged on a quiet road where the car was to pick us up. We walked on a little way to look at the bridge over the Ogmore: though called 'New Inn Bridge', it was in fact medieval and specially constructed for dipping sheep. There were holes in its sides about two and a half feet high, where the sheep were pushed through so that they dropped into the shallow stream. This washed the maggots from them so that they were clean enough to be shorn. The custom continued to that day.

One of my parents' neighbours whom Gabriel met was Dr. John Barns, later Professor of Egyptology at Oxford. He had told my parents when they heard of our engagement and were seeking reassurance from those who knew the Middle East: 'Assyrians make up in quality what they lack in quantity, and Armenians are the cleverest people invented'; and as he had done some work on the Dead Sea Scrolls, Gabriel one evening at his house gave us an account of the background to their discovery and some of their subsequent vicissitudes. For he knew the three people who became rich from the discovery, that is the Sheikh, the Shoemaker and the Assyrian Archbishop.

Leaning forward in his chair and pointing his story with gesticulations, he began:

'There are three Bedouin tribes who live in the Judean Wilderness and the Arabah Valley to the east and north-east of Bethlehem: they are the Ta'amreh, the Ta'amreh Sawahreh and the Eibedieh. From October to May they camp in the Valley or on the lower slopes of the Judean Hills, pitching their black goathair tents where they are sheltered from the wind, and grazing their flocks on the grass that

pushes its way through the stony ground. There is hardly any rain in
the Valley, just a little dew at night, but the goathair is in any case
waterproof. They cook on an open fire, and bake their bread, which
is unleavened, on a concave iron sheet put over the fire, or if they do
not have a piece of iron, on heated stones. The flat, uneven bread is
called "*sajj*" and it is delicious.

'In May when there is no more rain even in the hills of Palestine,
and the Valley becomes very hot, the nomads pile the tents, bedding,
pots and pans on the backs of their camels and donkeys, and move
westward to higher ground where they can still find pasturage.

'For these three tribes Bethlehem is their centre, and they come
there every Saturday to barter the produce of their animals - goat
cheese, yoghurt in liquid and dried form, a primitive sort of butter,
eggs, wool, and woven rugs - and sometimes the animals themselves -
in exchange for whatever they need for their simple life: rice, sugar,
dates, tea, coffee, material and clothes. At the time we speak of, that
is 1947, their shoes used to be made and mended by the Assyrian
shoemaker known as "Kando" (his real name is Khalil Iskander), who
sat in his little shop wearing a red *tarboosh* and long brown *kumbaz*, his
right foot constantly tapping even when it was not on the treadle. A
few yards up the narrow street towards the Assyrian church, Kando's
parents had a shop where they sold clothes and material to the Bedouin
in exchange for their produce. The Bedouin would congregate in this
street bartering, bargaining and learning the news of the week.

'Now you have all heard the story of the Bedouin boy who lost his
goat and found the Dead Sea Scrolls in the search for it. Sometimes
it is given a biblical flavour: the good shepherd left the ninety-nine to
search for the one that was lost. The true story is rather different.

'In the 1940s, before the Partition, the three tribes were smugglers.
Rice, sugar, coffee, carpets and many other things were much cheaper
in Transjordan than in Palestine, and the Bedouin would smuggle them
by night across the Jordan River where a small boat was kept for
baptismal purposes.' There were few roads and little habitation by
the River and the Dead Sea at that time; and Gabriel described how
they loaded donkeys that were waiting with other members of the tribe,

and led them past weird moonscape formations, across the salt marshes and along the deserted Valley to their camp. If it was summer they would have to climb up through the hills, perhaps where the Hinnom Valley clove a way through the Wilderness and led the travellers up to the lonely Monastery of Mar Saba, where no woman might enter. The Hinnom was another name for Gehenna which meant 'Hell' and this desolate area was pockmarked by numerous caves. It would have been dawn by the time the Bedouin reached their encampment and unloaded the donkeys. Later they met merchants from Jerusalem and sold their contraband.

Gabriel continued:

'Those were the days of the Mandate, and the British were well aware of this illegal traffic. There were mounted police patrols along the border area, but the Bedouin were very keen-sighted and they were not often caught. If they saw or heard a patrol approaching, they would find a hiding-place for the merchandise and leave it there until another occasion. The best hiding-places were the caves. The whole Jordan-Arabah Valley is full of caves. The ones near the Jordan River were until twenty-five years ago inhabited by hermits who modelled themselves on John the Baptist, whose raiment was camel-hair and his meat locusts and wild honey; but the caves in the sides of the Valley were more difficult of access, and few people ever set foot in them.

'On a very early morning in the late summer of 1947, the Ta'amreh were leading their laden donkeys between the Dead Sea and the Judean Hills when they spotted a patrol in the distance. They quickly whipped the donkeys towards a cave in the hillside, threw the goods in, and mounting the donkeys, went innocently on their way.' Gabriel put the first two fingers of his right hand astride the edge of his left hand and jogged them over the desert as he spoke.

'Later that day the Bedouin returned to the cave to retrieve the contraband, and on entering they found the first collection of Scrolls. On seeing the jars that contained them, their first thought was of gold, and they broke several jars in their eager haste to find the treasure. There were several cases in Bethlehem where people did find pots of gold when they were digging to make the foundations of a new home, and I believe the Scrolls themselves mention treasure hidden somewhere in the mountains.

'When the Bedouin found only parchment inside covered with writing that they could not decipher, they were very disappointed, but they decided to carry some of it with them. They would take it to Kando. Some people believed they wanted him to make shoes of the sheepskin, but this was a mistaken association of ideas.

'When Kando saw it, he told them to leave it with him and he would mend a few pairs of shoes for them as payment. He thought the writing was Syriac, and he wanted to see if it would be of any interest for the library of St. Mark's Syrian Orthodox Monastery in Jerusalem, where there were many very valuable ancient Syriac manuscripts. A young deacon called Butros (Peter) came to see the Scrolls in Kando's shop, and he took them to his Archbishop, Athanasius Yeshue Samuel. The Metropolitan saw that the script was Hebrew not Syriac, and he resolved to find a buyer.'

Gabriel leant back in his chair and spoke more slowly. There seemed to be a weight on him as he told the rest of the story.

'The Archbishop had no car of his own (very few people had in those days), and I usually drove him wherever he wanted to go in our taxi. I took him to many officials and scholars to show them the Scrolls, but without success. The answer was either that they were fakes - '

I gasped. 'Who on earth could fake something like that?'

' - either fakes,' he continued, 'or they were quite late and of no great value. One of the places where we drew blank was the American School of Oriental Research, but a seed of interest was sown there in a bright young scholar called John Trevor, who followed the trail of the Scrolls as well as he could in the troubled months and years that succeeded.'

Gabriel drove the Archbishop to the Hebrew University and they asked for the senior archaeologist, Professor Sukenik, the father of Yigael Yadin, who was later the Israeli Chief of Staff. When they were told he was not there, they drove to his house in Rehavia. He asked the Archbishop to leave some of the Scrolls with him for further study. While they were driving back, all hell broke loose. It was November the twenty-ninth and Partition had been declared: there was wild rejoicing on the part of the Jews, rioting and shooting on the part of the Arabs. Though Israel did not become a state till the Mandate ended in May the following year, the United Nations resolution of that day in fact saw the re-creation of a Jewish nation after two thousand years. Confusion reigned for the following months, and as far as Gabriel knew the Archbishop never received back the Scrolls he had left with the Professor. As the Professor was a Jew, and the Archbishop, as a Christian, was automatically aligned with the Arabs, it is difficult to see how they could have met after the Partition, which utterly polarised the two sides.

Professor Sukenik recorded in his diary in the entry for December 1st 1947 that he had two days before 'bought' scrolls 'in Bethlehem' from 'a dealer'. The scrolls he acquired were: Thanksgiving Psalms and Hymns; an imperfect copy of Isaiah; and 'The War of the Children of Light with the Children of Darkness'; and these are now in the Shrine of the Book.

On May the seventeenth 1948, two days after the termination of the Mandate and the official creation of Israel, Gabriel and his family were forced out of their house at gunpoint and took refuge in St. Mark's Monastery with about fifty other families. The Jewish Quarter was adjacent to the Monastery, and there was a great deal of shelling. Several shells fell in the courtyard, one of them killing Butros the Deacon. In June the Khanos and many others, including the Archbishop, fled to Madeba in Transjordan; and the Archbishop took with him the remaining Scrolls and the most valuable of the manuscripts in their Library, for whose safety he had sole responsibility. After three months in Madeba, he decided to go first to Syria to hand the manuscripts over to the Patriarch, and then to America to raise funds for his distressed people. Gabriel packed for him. All the manuscripts from the Library went into one suitcase.

'What about these?' Gabriel asked, pointing to the Scrolls. 'Put those in the other suitcase. I might as well take them with me,' replied the Archbishop.

But that was not the end of Gabriel's connection with the Scrolls.

The wheels were turning slowly in America and Israel, but nothing was known of this in Arab Jerusalem or Bethlehem. It was a little later, in the spring of 1949, that a meeting of Archbishop Samuel with Dr. Albright in New York led to the firm dating of the Scrolls, and eventually they were sold to the Israeli government. It was not the Archbishop's intention that they should end in those hands, and he was not viewed with favour in Jordan when they did.

Meanwhile the Khanos had come back to Bethlehem, and nine of them were living in one room a little way from Kando's shop. The alternative was a refugee camp. Abu-Jabra, already physically handicapped, was now affected mentally by this his second refuge; the taxi that had been his livelihood was on its last legs; the only road to Jerusalem was virtually impassable; there was no work. The golden days of the Mandate, when, as Gabriel said, you only had to scratch the earth to find money, were gone for ever. Before the Partition he often drove to Beirut for an evening out; now it was almost impossible to go between Jerusalem and Bethlehem. An iron curtain had fallen across the Middle East. There was nothing for Gabriel to do day after day but sit in the shop of Kando or his parents and watch the swollen population of the little town exchanging news of suffering and separation, and, if they could afford it, mending their shoes and buying material.

That was the time when the Bedouin discovered Cave Number Four, as it is now called. Gabriel was in Kando's shop when the finds were brought in. He fetched his mother's shopping basket and filled it with fragments, and decided to use them to retrieve their fallen fortunes. He got some addresses of American ministers who might be interested from Mrs. Lambie, a Bethlehem missionary, and sent them samples. To no avail. Many times he and a friend took the basket and walked to the Arab sector of Jerusalem along the way where the road was later built, dodging the shots from snipers in Kibbutz Ramat Rahel. They went to the American Colony which was the only hotel on the Arab side at that time, and stood outside the gate and touted their wares:

'Look, madam. Look, sir. These are very old parchments. Maybe thousands of years old. Take a piece as a souvenir. Only half a dollar for this piece. All right, sir. Don't go, sir. Forty cents, sir.'

But the visitors at the hotel were mostly journalists or people concerned with relief work, not gullible tourists who might fall for a story like that. Again there were no buyers.

The shopping basket was the only one they had. Every time Um-Jabra wanted to go to the market, she had to empty the basket of these useless fragments. Finally she said:

'What do you want with these things? They are doing no good here, and they have never brought us one piastre. Let me throw them away.'

'Never mind, Mother,' said Gabriel. 'I'll take them.' And he took them back to Kando.

It was only a short time after this that the news of the Scrolls' antiquity and unique interest burst upon an incredulous world. It was the greatest discovery of modern times. The gap was spanned between Old and New Testaments. The deepest mysteries of Judaism and Christianity were revealed for those who cared to look for them.

Mindful of their place in the twentieth century, the Scrolls also brought wealth to many people. Archbishop Samuel became rich overnight, but he could not return to Jerusalem because the Jordanian government was angry about the sale of the Scrolls to Israel. Kando and the Sheikh of the Ta'amreh became rich from the proceeds of the Scrolls of Cave Number Four, which they sold to the Jordanian government; they were housed in the Palestine Museum in Jerusalem. The Ta'amreh, who had first started to become settled when some of the tribe sent back money from Kuwait, built themselves houses between Beit Sahour and Herodium. Israel built a special part of their Museum which they called the Shrine of the Book to house their Scrolls, and it was visited by tens of thousands of people every year.

When he heard that the Scrolls were finally vindicated, Gabriel persuaded some of the Bedouin to lead him and another Bethlehemite to the area where they were found. They searched several caves without success, and then they came to one from which, as they approached, thousands of bats flew out. The stench was appalling.

'Let's go back,' said Gabriel. 'I couldn't bear to go in there.'

Later, this cave gave up its treasure to others: in an official search archaeologists found there the Copper Scroll which is now in the Amman Museum. Gabriel's time had not yet come.

'So had it not been for the bats, you would have found the Copper Scroll,' said Dr. Barns.

' - and become rich,' I said.

'Yes. But it's just as well I didn't. I was too young. God knows what I would have turned into. And I would not have found you,' Gabriel replied, looking at me.

'No,' I said. 'I was at Oxford then. You would never have found me there.'

There were two things Gabriel wanted to see in London, both of them in the British Museum: the Siniatic version of the Gospels which is in Syriac, and the Assyrian Room. We saw the ancient manuscript, and then made our way to the Assyrian Room where the frieze of a lion-hunt was on view. Lion-hunting in chariots was a favourite sport of Assyrian kings and also a symbol of royal invincibility. The ancient king and his warriors were all in profile, and I made Gabriel stand beside them. His side-view was very similar: he had the same aristocratic features, but not their look of arrogance. His expression was that of King Itur-Shamagan in the Temple of Ishtar rather than King Ashurbanipal out for blood.

Apart from these highlights, London was to Gabriel somewhat of a desert: its size, its anonymity, its lowering skies, the tenseness and haste of its occupants confused and alarmed him. Here Time was the master, there was little generosity, memories were short. Personality was limited by fashions of thought, taste and behaviour far more constricting than the 'customs and traditions' of his people. I had the same feeling of alienation as he had, and I was glad we were going back to Jordan, which was emerging as a very new country from the paths of antiquity. There was no fixed routing there that we need follow.

When we got back to Jerusalem, my father wrote:

'Gabriel has left a strange warmth of feeling behind him among all who saw him for any length of time - and it was wonderful how sympathetically he fitted in to what must have been a very strange and alien world. He has certainly charmed us all and done it with such naturalness and simplicity. You must always live up to him!'

1. *Morad Barsom & Kando.*
2. *Basil Guy with Gabriel &
Delia.*
3. *Merthyr Mawr House.*
4. *Delia's father.*
5. *The house we built in
Sha'afat.*

PART II

The Divided City

CHAPTER SEVEN

Total Immersion

FROM our house in the Wadi Jos we again had a wonderful view.
We were actually on the lower slopes of Mount Scopus which was a
continuation of the Mount of Olives. We could see the old road down
the Mount of Olives where, six days before the Passover he did not live
to see, Jesus rode to the Temple on a donkey (the mount not of kings,
but of princes) in deliberate fulfilment of an Old Testament prophecy.
At the foot of the Mount was the Garden of Gethsemane; and facing
it was the Golden Gate (which the Moslems closed centuries ago) and
the Dome of the Rock, the magnificent mosque on Mount Moriah,
former site of the Temple, built over the rock where Abraham was
supposed to have offered Isaac for sacrifice and whence, according to
the Moslems, Mohammed ascended to heaven. Between the Mounts
ran the Kidron Valley, or Valley of Jehosaphat, the traditional site of
the Final Judgment.

Gabriel used to take his clients to the Moslem cemetery outside the
Golden Gate, and looking across the Kidron Valley he would point out
the Palm Sunday route, and tell them the traditions about the Kidron
Valley and Judgment Day.

'In the Valley you see Jewish, Moslem and Christian cemeteries,
because the three great religions say that this will be the site of the
Resurrection at the end of the world. It always seems to me that if

they can agree about this most important point, they could also agree about less important things.

'The Christians say that the Golden Gate will be opened when Christ comes again, and the Moslems say that when Christ returns to the Mount of Olives, Mohammed will return to Mount Moriah. Each will hold one end of a rope stretching across the Valley, and the living and those who have risen from their graves must walk across it from one end to the other: from east to west or from west to east. Those who can walk the tightrope will be saved, and those who cannot will plunge into the abyss and be damned.

'Facing us is the Jewish cemetery: the Jews up to 1948 used to bury their dead in an upright position so that they would be ready for the appearance of the Messiah on the Mount of Olives. They have not been able to use the burial-ground since that time, and so we do not know if they would continue the practice now.'

'You see that spot?' and he used to point to a space in the Christian cemetery. 'That is reserved for me. I booked it to be sure to have somewhere to stand when the hour comes, because this Valley is going to be so crowded.'

One day a tourist from a group he was guiding asked him what was written in Arabic on the Moslem tombstones near where they were standing.

'They tell you how long the people lived. For instance this man lived from 1920 to 1926. This man from 1935 to 1945. This one only from 1955 to 1956 ... '

The tourist interrupted: 'But they all lived such a short time. They must have died as children.'

'No', said Gabriel. 'Those dates tell you how long they *really* lived, not the years of their birth and death. Some people hardly live at all.'

The ambience of the Wadi Jos was not very congenial. It had been the least desirable part of Jerusalem before it was divided: in Mandate days no one went there after dark without a gun or a bodyguard, and an open sewer used to run in the valley. The Arabs were obliged to develop this area after 1948, as the west side of Jerusalem was cut off from them and building was restricted on the Mount of Olives. A good many Hebronites who left Hebron to find better trading opportunities in Jerusalem came to live in this area. They were said to have moved because they thought their children would not need shoes in Jerusalem, as the roads were tarmacked.

The Hebronites were strict Moslems. The women sometimes came to visit my mother-in-law; but if Gabriel entered the house while they were there, they would rush across to the far corner of the sitting-room so that he should not catch a glimpse of them from the front door.

Um-Jabra tried to dominate me in the early days, and there were two reasons for this. First, she thought I was living in a strange country without family and she should be mother and sister to me. Secondly, it was a common pattern in their community and what she had experienced herself.

Abu-Jabra's mother had lived with them for years and ruled the household with a rod of iron. All the money was in her hands, and she distributed it as she saw fit. Abu-Jabra paid over to her all he earned, and she had brought some gold with her from Isfis - rumour had it she had brought a great deal. Once she changed some of it for Palestinian money. She took a hundred King George V sovereigns (which the people called 'St. Georges') to a Jewish money-changer, and he bluffed her. He gave her what he said was a good price: ninety-eight piastres (or new pence) per sovereign. What happened to the rest of the gold - if indeed there was any - remained to mystery; but the Isfis people used to say that Abu-Jabra kept his mother with him because only she knew where it was hidden. If there was any more, the secret died with her.

Half of Gabriel wanted me to be a conventional Assyrian wife: 'I wish you would be to my mother as Ruth was to Naomi,' he said once, recalling the story of how Ruth left her native land of Moab and went to Bethlehem with her mother-in-law. 'But Ruth's husband was dead,' I said; and her never mentioned that parallel again. The other half of him was actually jealous of his mother if I showed any signs of finding common ground with her.

Biblical parallels constantly occurred to me at this time; for the Khanos' way of life had changed little since the time of the Bible. I could not help thinking that the eastern Christians did not seem to have followed the signposts of the New Testament at all while the West was following them too far. This crossed my mind when I went to Bethany one day with Gabriel and a couple he was guiding. The custodian, Father Agostino, sang for us in the church with his beautiful Italian baritone voice, while his tame bulbul perched on his shoulder or on his finger. Then we saw the remains of the old house there with its oil-press, and Gabriel retold the story of Martha and Mary's different reactions on one occasion when Jesus came to visit them. Martha rushed off into the kitchen to prepare a meal, while Mary sat at his feet to listen to his conversation. When Martha criticized her sister for not helping her, Jesus gave Mary his support: 'Mary has chosen the better part; it is not to be taken from her.' A woman was to be a man's partner and companion, but not to be liberated from man altogether.

All Jesus' recorded dealings with women showed an original attitude towards them: Martha and Mary, the Samaritan Woman, Mary Magdalen, the woman taken in adultery, prostitutes he consorted with, the woman of bad reputation who anointed his feet; but only his relationship with his mother was highlighted through the centuries. Queen Helena, the mother of Constantine, who came to the Holy Land as a pilgrim in 325 and fixed the holy places for posterity, may have brought the cult of Jesus' mother back to Byzantium with her; for the Madonna featured prominently in Byzantine icons and mosaics and was worshipped widely in the eastern churches. Only when Chartres Cathedral was dedicated to the Virgin in the twelfth century did the cult spread to the West, perhaps brought there from the East by the Crusaders.

On one of the fairly rare occasions that I persuaded Gabriel to go with me to St. George's Cathedral, we heard a sermon that had the miracle at Cana as its theme. It was delivered by one of the many English clergy resident there, and was about being given wedding presents one did not really want and how to deal with the consequent embarrassment. When we got home I asked Gabriel what he thought of the sermon. He shrugged his shoulders and muttered, 'He could have said so much - about the worship of Bacchus and the ecstasy connected with it - and then there is the link with the sacrament of Communion. He didn't even mention that the water was intended for purification.'

To someone with Gabriel's biblical upbringing, the appearance in the Holy Land of the western woman must have been little short of apocalyptic. He often told the story of a group he guided overland from Beirut to Jerusalem in 1955. He had just arrived tired from Beirut with the group of Baptist ministers who had prayed so fervently and - for Gabriel - to such good effect on the Plains of Jabbok, when he was greeted with orders to return to Beirut the next day. His pay was a pound a day at that time: it only rose to thirty shillings later.

He started the story: 'I was told, "This is another Baptist group: twenty-four students from the University of Waco, Texas. You mustn't smoke or drink and be sure you give them the best service." So I took plenty of Sen-Sen with me and set off for Beirut.

'When I met the group at the airport, I could hardly believe my eyes. They were twenty-four beautiful girls, and the wife of the Dean of the University was in charge of them. Her name was Mrs. Carroll.

'I welcomed them respectfully and took them to their hotel. And the next day I showed them Baalbeck and Damascus and brought them to their hotel in Damascus. After dinner I attended their scripture reading, gave them a review of the next day's tour, told them which chapters of the Bible to read, and bade them goodnight. We had to start at six the next morning as we were going to see the Baptist Mission Hospital in Ajloun.

'I went up to the roof to have a drink. I often met other guides on their way through Damascus, but this time I had had no time in Jerusalem to see who would be there. However, when I was summoned downstairs, I thought it must be one of my friends. What was my surprise on reaching the lobby to find Mrs. Carroll, with the twenty-four girls looking more beautiful than ever, for their hair was piled up on their heads, their dresses were decolleté and their shoes high-heeled.

' "Well, Gabriel," said Mrs. Carroll, as I furtively put a Sen-Sen in my mouth to kill the smell of the whisky, "the girls want to go out.

What do you suggest?"

' "But we've seen all the main sites," I stammered through the Sen-Sen, "and the churches are all closed now. There is only the River Abana: that is quite near the hotel and I could take them there. It is mentioned in the second book of . . .".

'Then a tall blonde girl like a goddess said to me, "Gabriel, don't you know anything about Damascus? Don't you know this place?" and she held out a booklet with the word "Caravan" underlined.

'I was horrified. "But that's a night-club!" I said.

' "That's right. That's where we want to go." '

Gabriel, seeing that they really wanted him to take them to one of the liveliest night-spots in town, got down to business:

' "Wait a minute. This will cost you money. Whether you drink water or champagne, the entrance fee with one drink is three dollars each." '

They paid him there and then, and he set off into the town with his troupe behind him. Mrs. Carroll, evidently thinking there was safety in numbers, retired to bed.

At the Caravan the audience was composed almost entirely of men, most of them Kuwaitis and Iraqis. The advent of the girls caused a minor sensation.

Gabriel knew the place well, and he took the waiter on one side and explained that this was a religious group, they would like a secluded table and they would not be drinking alcohol. ' "For my drink, I'll have whisky in coca-cola." ' This not to offend their susceptibilities.

But when they were settled and the waiter came to take their orders, the answer came 'Bourbon', 'Martini', 'Screwdriver' and so on from every one of the twenty-four.

'One minute,' said Gabriel, holding up an imperious hand. 'Change my order and bring me the biggest bottle of whisky you have.'

Once that was in front of him the evening left the ground and sped into some higher sphere. When the band struck up with a tango the blonde goddess asked Gabriel to dance with her. He said he did not know how: 'I come from Jerusalem you know,' he said demurely; but she said she would teach him. As he could really tango rather well, he proved a brilliant pupil and was soon sweeping her almost off her feet.

The girls applauded enthusiastically when they returned to their seats, and one by one they took on the task of teaching him to dance. The Iraqis and Kuwaitis looked on enviously, but not one dared to approach Gabriel's harem.

At about one in the morning the music changed: the regular beat of the modern dance was cut short by the more exciting rhythm of a popular oriental song. The Kuwaitis and Iraqis clapped in time to it, and reached a crescendo as a well-known Egyptian dancer with bare midriff and transparent floating draperies, dramatically took the floor. Secure in their homage, she acknowledged their applause, and supremely conscious of her power, she worked her way seductively round the floor, her sidling steps belying the bold movements of her breast and hips and the speaking provocation of her black eyes.

The men clapped and cheered louder and louder; those who had waterpipes clanged the metal mouthpiece on their glasses; the Texas girls giggled and gossiped, and Gabriel's spirits rose ever higher as the whisky level dropped. He was telling the girls the dancer needed a partner, and half-seriously they urged him to join her. 'Go on, Gabriel,' they said, and when she paused after the third solo dance, he could resist it no longer. He leapt up, seized the tablecloth off the table, and putting it round him he went up to the Egyptian and poised himself proudly for a *pas de deux*. The band struck up again, the dancer danced with even more *elan* than before and Gabriel was a perfect foil for her. When she went up, he went down: when she went down, he went up; and all the time his hips worked as eloquently as hers. The Kuwaitis and Iraqis were beside themselves: every time the dancers paused, '*Cama'an marra!* encore, encore!' came the cry on all sides; and the couple always found some new gesture, stance or step to beguile their captive audience.

So the night passed in pleasant un-Baptist abandon until Gabriel and the girls returned to the hotel just in time for the early morning call. They slept all the way to Jerusalem.

In Jerusalem he was once more the earnest, dedicated guide as he led Mrs. Carroll and the girls around the holy places. After three days of sober sightseeing, Bible study and prayer, the girls told Gabriel they would enjoy another evening out before they left for home. 'All right,' he said. 'It will cost you three dollars each again. Yes, I'll take it now. Thank you. Thank you. Be ready at nine o'clock in the lobby.'

There were no night-clubs in Jerusalem in those days, for the Arabs thought such things unsuitable for the Holy City, but Gabriel had immediately formed an alternative plan of entertainment. He told certain boys he knew on the Mount of Olives to have twenty-five donkeys ready for them at Bethphage at nine that night.

When he came to collect the girls from the Colony, he found them once more elaborately coiffeured, decolleté and high-heeled. Mrs. Carroll saw them off as they left in taxis for an unknown destination.

'Now,' said Gabriel when they arrived at Bethphage, 'you are going to ride into Jerusalem as Jesus did on Palm Sunday. Each one to her donkey, please.'

The girls obediently chose their mounts. They could not question the suitability of the entertainment, though they must have rather regretted their tight skirts. They struggled inelegantly on to the donkeys, which were then urged on to the triumphal road by their boys. Other boys joined them as they followed the historic route northward along the ridge of the Mount and then westward down the hill, through the Valley and up to St. Stephen's Gate.

'Sing!' cried Gabriel as they reached the gate of the sleeping city. 'You must enter Jerusalem singing.' So they sang 'Jerusalem' as loudly as they could; the refrain 'Hosanna in the highest!' soared over the rooftops; the donkeys joined in; the Jerusalem boys came out to swell the vociferous ranks of the Mount of Olives boys; and tousled heads appeared at every little window.

Singing, braying and cheering, the procession made its triumphant way past the first six Stations of the Cross, out of the Damascus Gate and up the road that led St. Paul to blindness and enlightenment. The girls were exhausted when they reached the Colony, delighted with the novel but historic experience - 'It really brought the Bible to life,' they told Mrs. Carroll next day - and ready for a good night's sleep before the journey back to Texas. They gave Gabriel a handsome tip when he came to say goodbye, and so ended another successful tour.

Another time he was interrupted in his talk about the Garden of Gethsemane by a woman who kept asking the name of various flowers. His knowledge of horticulture was limited to the names of four flowers, and as he did not know what those flowers looked like, he just tossed off a name at each interruption without even looking where the woman was pointing. At the fifth question, 'Guide, what's the name of this flower?' he said, 'Madam, I not an expert on flowers. My subject is the Bible and ancient history. But the gardener is over there. His name is Moses. If you have any more questions about the flowers, I suggest you ask him.'

She let him finish his exposition in peace then, and he left them to wander in the Garden and take photographs, while he disappeared behind one of the ancient, spreading olive-trees to have a quiet smoke.

'Guide!' The word rang out imperiously in the quiet of the Garden. Gabriel almost burnt his fingers in his haste to put out his cigarette and answer the summons.

It was the same woman.

'Guide, what is the name of this flower?'

'Barbarina,' he said curtly and turned back to his refuge.

'Barbarina in you head.' This in Arabic from behind him; and as he turned his head he received a clout over the ear. It was Father Eugene Hoade, a hot-tempered Irish priest who was one of the board which tested would-be guides, and which had the power not only of giving licences but also of taking them away.

'You made it that big, didn't you?' he said in the Arabic idiom, measuring the enormity of what Gabriel had said with his two first fingers.

'Really, Father, I didn't mean any harm,' Gabriel stammered. 'I hardly know the name of any of these flowers and she would keep asking me.'

'Well, you'd better start taking botany lessons,' he said, but he was grinning as he walked off.

Later Gabriel received a letter from the woman asking him how she could obtain seeds of the barbarina-flower because she had not

been able to find them in the American shops. He did not answer. He
did not know how to tell her that 'Barbarina' was the Arabic way of
saying, 'You talk too much'.

The more discerning of Gabriel's clients deeply appreciated his
guiding, but on his home-ground it was a case of being a prophet
in his own country. The drivers, caretakers, pedlars, postcard-boys
and so on loved him because he was friendly, cheerful and generous to
them, but the other guides were jealous of him, and the Establishment
did not regard him. Yet he was the leading guide when Jordanian
tourism was in its infancy; the routing of the different tours, which
became standardised later, was first worked out by him; and he encouraged many others - cousins, friends, drivers, school-leavers, even a
postcard boy - to become guides, training them, lending them books,
and infusing them with his spirit of exuberant dedication.

We finally made up our minds to start our own agency. I had
inherited a very small capital from my Nicholl grandfather, and feeling
rather alone in the world, we drew up plans.

We still visited our friends in Bethlehem, and we asked Mr. Barsom
what he suggested for a name. After a few moments' thought he said,
'Either something about Union or something about a Star.'

'I don't like Union but Star has possibilities. What about Eastern
Star?' I said.'

'No,' Gabriel said quickly. 'That's what the female freemasons call
themselves.'

'What about Guiding Star?' said Barsom.

It was obviously the only possible name, and we started straight-
away to print our letterheads and publicity material.

One of the conditions for obtaining a licence was that we should
have a bank guarantee for £5000. Bishara Canavati, the owner of a
Bethlehem souvenir shop, agreed to guarantee us, and he and I went to
the manager of the Ottoman Bank to open an account for the agency.
We were coldly turned down.

Gabriel then went to Kando in his cobbler's shop and asked him
for his help. He fumbled in the pocket of his *kumbaz* and produced
a matchbox. He was just literate, and he wrote on the matchbox in

Arabic: 'Please help this man, Kando.' 'What shall I do with this?' asked Gabriel. 'Take it to the British Bank,' said Kando.

So Gabriel went to the British Bank of the Middle East, and when he showed the manager the matchbox, the red carpet was rolled out and we were taken on as customers; and Bishara guaranteed us.

There was another difficulty. A law had been passed just after we put in our application for a licence, that there were to be no more travel agencies. We had to enlist the services of a lawyer, and finally we were granted our licence on July 27th, 1961, the day our first child, Simon, was born.

It was after this that a strain appeared in the relations between Um-Jabra and me. I felt antipathetic waves from her about my leaving our son to go to work in the office. He was her first grandson, the eldest son of the eldest son, her husband's namesake, and one day he too would be Abu-Jabra. (For the names usually went in alternate generations: Simon the son of Gabriel, the son of Simon and so on.) We agreed only in thinking him, like Astyanax, as beautiful as a star. She thought a good mother should find nothing better to do than dandle him on her knee all day, but I was anxious to make a livelihood and a future for him. The difference of our views was accentuated when my mother arrived to visit us and the two grandmothers confronted each other over the baby's cradle.

We had decided to have Simon baptised when my mother was there, and she came equipped with an old family christening robe. The ceremony was in St. Mark's Church which was mainly a Crusader building, but parts of it were much older. There was an inscription in Aramaic near the ground by the doorway dating from the first century saying that it was the house of Mary, the mother of John Mark. This meant it might have been the Upper Room, scene of the Last Supper, though there was another site favoured by the Crusaders. When Jesus sent Peter and John to prepare the Last Supper, he told them when they entered the city they would meet a man bearing a pitcher of water. Strangely enough the part of the Old City near St. Mark's Church was the only area where one could still to that day meet a man carrying water, usually in two buckets balanced on a yoke.

Not far from the church was a café called Bishara which means 'Evangelist' or 'Angel', and there was a tradition that this was the prison where Peter was released by the angel. From there he went to the house of Mary, Mark's mother, and knocked at the outer door. Rhoda, the servant-girl who went to answer the knocking, was so overcome to recognise his voice that she forgot to open the door but ran in to tell the others Peter had come. They hastened to let him in and hear the good news of his escape. On the site of this house now stood the church and it contained an interesting picture said to be a portrait of the Virgin Mary painted on gazelle-skin by St. Luke. There was such a portrait in Constantinople in the fifth century, and there is also one in Kykko monastery in Cyprus, but it is so covered in gold it is difficult to see it; and another in Malta.

We had visualised a quiet service attended by a few close friends and relations, but Um-Jabra had been busy: the entire Assyrian communities of Bethlehem and Jerusalem were there, and also Um-Marcus, that specialist in weddings and baptisms, who, as mother of Gabriel's best man, was automatically the godmother. She was, needless to say, in excellent voice for the ululations.

Simon was only six weeks old, and with the anxiety we were facing with the agency, I was not strong enough to take this ceremony. When my precious firstborn was three times immersed screaming in the font, I wept uncontrollably. I tried to take him afterwards, but Um-Marcus seized him and dressed him - not in the old baptismal robe but in a brand-new white suit she had bought him. She was all elbows as she worked him over: I did not stand a chance.

It seemed to me as I saw the Assyrian women ululating wildly, Simon screaming, and my mother and Mrs. MacInnes standing rigidly in their place of privilege in the front row, that the embattled forces of East and West, of poor and rich, were warring for my child. Gabriel, being a mere man, stood helpless on the sidelines and awaited the outcome, while I wept because I wanted neither side to win.

Later in the afternoon, still sobbing, I let my mother dress the baby in the christening robe.

There was a significant difference between the eastern and western customs on this point. In the Orthodox Church the baby had to wear something new after his ducking. St. Paul says, 'Baptised in Christ, you have all clothed yourselves in Christ.' In the East Christ was new not old: it had to be a new garment. But the West had, as John Robinson said, 'come of age' where Christianity was concerned: the christening robe might be an old one.

We had been writing to travel agencies and old clients of Gabriel's saying that he would be visiting the United States in the autumn, and before we realised it the time had come and a painful separation was at hand. We decided I should take Simon to England with my mother and stay there till Gabriel returned.

Simon was five months old when Gabriel rejoined us after an absence in America of nearly three months. But I need not have worried that he would forget his father. As soon as he saw him, he gurgled with laughter and held his arms out to him.

CHAPTER EIGHT

Retrospect: Palestine 1926–1949

IN the intervals of Gabriel's intermittent work in the first year of our marriage, I came to know more of his past - a past which veered wildly from high comedy to deep tragedy. Appropriately enough for one whose character and whose whole life was such a mixture of light and darkness, he was born on June 16th, 1926, under the sign of Gemini. At that time he was named Joseph after one of his mother's brothers who died at the Turks' hands; but at his baptism in the River Jordan his father's wish prevailed and he was named Gabriel. While still an infant he fell ill, and his parents made a vow that if he survived they would not cut his hair till he was seven years old. They then weighed it against gold and gave the gold to the church.

In Jerusalem the family lived with many other Assyrians in the Musrara Quarter just outside the Damascus Gate, and they used to take Gabriel from his earliest years to St. Mark's Church in the Old City. The little boy with the long, curly black hair was trained day and night in the Aramaic prayers and chants and marked out as a promising candidate for the priesthood. He was ordained a deacon in three ceremonies: the fourth ceremony would fit him to take services, but he did not reach this stage.

Archbishop MacInnes once wrote Gabriel a testimonial saying 'his conduct was always exemplary' in his days at the Bishop Gobat's School, but I do not think the same can be said of him at his earlier schools, of which there was quite a number. At one time he was at two schools at once, because he got into such hot water at the Assyrian school that he went and enrolled himself at another one, and for some weeks he attended them alternately, leaving a cooling-off period after his worst pranks at each school. His spare time was divided between acting as a deacon at St. Mark's, and playing in the streets, flicking stones up the kilts of the Black Watch as they marched past, a gazelle at their head. For these were British Mandate days.

He left school at sixteen, and joining the British Army was enrolled in the Pay Corps, for it was 1942 and the Palestinians - both Arabs and Jews - were doing their bit for the war effort. He found himself in the Schneller Campus in the New City working on pay slips with a sergeant, a corporal and about fifty ATS girls. They were in a Nissen hut which was roasting hot in the middle of the day; and apart from the occasional glimpse up the ATS's skirts when he dropped a pencil, there seemed to be very little future in this work, and so our hero applied for a transfer. The officer in charge was a captain whose main occupation during his invigilation hours was stroking his handsome waxed moustaches. His reply to Gabriel's request was a curt 'No'. Gabriel's frustration increased: something had to be done, and it was not difficult to see that the Captain's Achilles' heel was his moustache, Gabriel formed his plan of action and went to the Captain's batman.

'Tell me,' he said, 'does the Captain use something on his moustache to make it so shiny and waxy?' 'Yes,' said the batman. 'He puts a cream on it every morning before going on duty.'

'May I see it? I want to get some for my father's moustache.'

'I'll get the jar,' he said and he returned after a minute with a jar containing some white cream.

'Thank you,' said Gabriel, and off he went to the chemist to get some white cream for removing hair. The he found a chance to creep into the Captain's room and fill up the jar.

The next morning Gabriel and the others were in their places as usual when the Captain made his entrance, his swagger-cane under his arm. He sat down at his desk, airily signed a few papers, then pushed his chair back and lit his pipe. Gabriel watched him surreptitiously, waiting for the big moment. With a slight flourish of his hand, the Captain prepared for the main business of the day: stroking his moustache, smoothing the ends to an erect, free-standing magnificence. First one side, then the other: the two waxed points were in his hand: he was aghast.

Gabriel leapt up from his desk. 'Are you all right, sir? Is anything the matter, sir?'

'Sit down at once and get on with your work,' said the Captain purple now in the face. The other clerks saw what had happened and dissolved into smothered laughter.

The Captain could not stand the indignity: he left the room and did not reappear. Later he obtained a transfer to another unit. Gabriel was then able to get a transfer for himself, and he joined the NAAFI.[†]

He became a canteen manager quite early on, and he was told by his friends he would never be able to balance his accounts because he had a particularly clever cook, barman and cashier who would rob him right and left. One day there was a big party, and the soldiers ate a great many sandwiches and drank quantities of liquor. He was surprised that the brandy did not seem to be running out, and he went into the kitchen. He caught the cook in the act of putting some supplies through the window, and going outside he found a pile of brandy, tea, cheese, spam and other things waiting to be collected and sold. The cook had been giving short measure on the tea and the sandwiches; and for the brandy he and the barman had put alcohol with melted sugar to colour it, and the soldiers were happily going through bottle after bottle. Gabriel might have been able to beat 'em but it would have meant keeping constant watch: he took the easier and more lucrative course and joined 'em. This also meant constant vigilance because there were regular inspections from above; and the exceptionally rapid disappearance of a large consignment of English chocolate, though nothing was ever proved against him, led

---

[†]like the American PX.

to Gabriel's being transferred into the accounts section where there was no scope for such exploits. By this time he had become a hard drinker, and he and a friend called Mohammed Audeh used to meet in the NAAFI club and drink brandy and guinness - mixed - betting on who could stay the course longest.

His father consorted more with the Palestinian Jews than the Arabs at this time and he was known as 'the Jew', because he spoke Hebrew and wore a hat. Jews took him for one of themselves, and when they saw him in an Arab quarter, they would say, 'Hey, Shimon, what are you doing here?' Golda Meir used to use his taxi at this time and she made a special point of asking for him. Gabriel drove the taxi whenever he could, making sure of having it when he wanted it by putting milk of magnesia in his father's milk so that he was temporarily incapacitated. But his own almost habitual state of intoxication resulted in his driving once right through a photographer's shop and another time into the River Jordan.

If we take history as a whole the record of the Moslems and the Eastern Christians towards the Jews has been very much better than that of the European Christians. But the Arabs' suspicion and distrust was aroused by the Balfour Declaration, and this was ratified by the Allied Powers in 1920. In the 'twenties and 'thirties there were intermittent riots and attacks by the Arabs on the Jews, but these stopped during the Second World War. At the end of the War - with large numbers of Jewish refugees coming from Europe, illegal immigrants according to the British, who suggested no alternative solution for them - the Jews formed three underground organisations in order to drive the British from their mandatory task and gain ascendancy over the Arabs. For they now aimed not just for a 'national home' but for a Jewish state that they hoped would give them a refuge from the persecution they had suffered in Europe.

This was the background then to the wild period of Gabriel's youth. One day he was trapped in a cordon of four lines of fire which the Irgun T'svai Leumi, the Jewish gang commanded by Menachem Begin, had put down in preparation for blowing up the police headquarters in the Russian Compound. He drove the car through the fire and was only just in time to escape the explosion. On another occasion he was caught in the cross-fire when the Irgun and Stern gangs attacked some government offices in Mamilla Road. He hid under the car to avoid the shots, but was pulled out by an English sergeant who jumped into the car with a private and told him to chase the car in front. The soldiers leant out of the window firing, and Gabriel was terrified because he thought it looked as if he was driving terrorists, as his car was a taxi not a military vehicle. Luckily they did not meet any more of the army.

There was a third episode when a Jewish girl asked him to drive her to a certain hospital. He gladly accepted thinking it would be an opportunity for a little flirtation. He was disappointed. She asked him to stop near the hospital, and a man got in who pointed a gun at Gabriel's head and told him to drive to Beit Hakarem. When they arrived there - it was not then built-up - about ten armed Jewish men and women appeared from the trees. They got Gabriel out, still at gunpoint, and tied him to a tree. Gabriel suggested that he too wanted independence from the British and why should they be against *him?* This is a Jewish movement, they told him. And he watched five of them pile into his car and drive off, while the others remained near him.

He learned afterwards that the message went out that car 443 was in the hands of terrorists, and the British police force was alerted. But there were three cars with the number 443 and they had different letters preceding them. The police kept flashing lights at Gabriel's car but they knew it to be his, and when they saw girls in it they just thought Gabriel was living it up. But the flashing lights prevented the would-be terrorists from doing whatever it was they intended to do. They returned to Gabriel, released him and warned him not to reveal what had happened, and on no account to furnish descriptions of those who had taken his car.

The following week he was with three young British policemen, and they told him how they had let his car pass because they recognised it as his. While they were drinking, the call went out that there were explosives at the Social Welfare Department near Prophets' Street.

They rushed off, harnessed the dynamite to their armoured car, and started to drag it out. But it went off with a deafening noise, and the pieces of their bodies were picked off the surrounding buildings.

Another evening he was with two young English soldiers in a wine cellar. They came out presently and two Jewish girls came up to the soldiers and offered to walk them back to their billet in Mahnei Yehuda. The English boys' bodies were found later that night shot in the back.

The Jewish girl that he was friendly with at the time of the abortive engagement used to spend her leave and much of her free time training in a kibbutz in Galilee, and after the Partition she must have joined the army, and he lost track of her. Some Jews got their training in the British Army. Gabriel was amazed to find when he was managing the NAAFI canteen that the armed guard at the door was a Polish Jewish doctor. He would have been far better qualified than Gabriel to manage the canteen, but he preferred to do a job that put a gun in his hand.

When the Partition took place in November 1947, the Arabs still did not believe that there would be a permanent division between Arabs and Jews. There had been troubles between them before, but the British had always brought the two sides together. Gabriel thought that the British would never leave Palestine because it was their bridge to India and the Far East. But now India was independent and the rest of the Empire was dissolving: Britain in her post-war apathy was fast shedding her burdens and responsibilities.

Two groups of Palestinian volunteers were formed after the Partition to counter the Jewish terror campaign, and some of the other Arab countries sent armies to help them. Afterwards it came out that the man in charge of the ammunition supply was an Iraqi Jew, and he was able to sabotage many of their efforts. The British administration used to sentence to life imprisonment people found in illegal possession of arms, but sometimes young Britons of the Palestine Police Force sold their guns. They would go with the buyers to some remote place, and then come back and say they had been attacked and their guns taken by force. Some of the Palestine Policemen joined the Arabs when the Force was disbanded, and some joined the Jews.

Gabriel felt slightly ambivalent in his relations with Jews and Arabs, being strictly speaking neither himself, but the immigrant and Zionist element that now began to outnumber the Palestinian Jews, drove him towards the Arab side. His attempts to take a part in the hostilities came to nothing: he bought a revolver for fifty pounds, but it exploded in his hand when he loaded and fired it. He went for training with some other young men, and an Iraqi taught them how to throw imaginary hand-grenades and lie down to avoid the explosion. But Gabriel found the Iraqi always chose to fling himself on. top of his trainees and his thoughts were evidently on something other than fighting for Palestine. 'Did you come here to train us or to f____ us ?' he asked angrily and went to spend his time in a more profitable way.

Jerusalem and the rest of Palestine were now marked off by the British into Jewish, Arab or neutral zones in order to minimise clashes and protect the British offices from the Jewish terror gangs. For not only had the police headquarters been blown up before the Partition, but also the King David Hotel which was the administrative head-quarters, and the Army Officers' Club in King George Avenue. There had also been an incident when two British sergeants were hanged and their bodies filled with explosives in retaliation for the hanging of some of those responsible for the King David incident. Now the Jews stepped up the terror against the Arabs, for they had a Jewish sector of Palestine but it had too many Arabs for their liking. Jewish immigration was steadily growing, and they wanted houses for the newcomers. They also wanted a purely Jewish state. There were three explosions in crowded Arab areas, a train was blown up and so was the Hotel Semiramis in Katamon where twenty-six Arabs were killed, most of them members of one Christian family, which was thereby almost exterminated. That happened on a wild night of thunderstorm, and the explosion went unnoticed for some time; but such episodes, and constant Jewish sniping, led many Christian families on the western side of Jerusalem to leave their fine houses and seek refuge elsewhere; thus the houses were empty for Jewish squatters, who keep them to this day.

Gabriel knew many of those killed in the various explosions, particularly that in the King David Hotel, for many Arabs and Assyrians
(and also Jews) worked with the British there. They were constantly
awake to danger at this time. Soon after an incident involving a car
full of dynamite which exploded at the Jaffa Gate, Abu-Jabra's taxi
was parked near the Gate with a sack full of oranges in it. Someone
gave the alarm that the car contained a sack of explosives. Gabriel
and his father came back to the square to find terrible confusion with
people shouting and scattering in all directions, and they rushed to
the car only to be told, 'Watch out! That's the car!'

On another occasion he was again caught up in shooting. He was driving a young widow from the Pay Corps home to Bethlehem in a convoy of cars with army vehicles at the front and rear, when shooting started from Kibbutz Ramat Rahel. Several of the cars were hit; Gabriel ducked and went on driving, but he got cramp and he went to the Beit Safafa Hospital near Bethlehem to make sure that a bullet had not gone through him.

Arabs and Jews were physically separated by the Partition but the emotional polarisation was by no means complete. An Arab Gabriel knew warned the Jews he worked with in the NAAFI that there was an Arab plan to shoot them as they came out at the end of the day, and they were able to leave by another door. The Jews were very short of food for about four years after the Partition, because they had no-one to work the land, while most of the Palestinian Arabs were small farmers and they at least had a supply of fruit and vegetables. Gabriel and other Arabs who had Jewish friends sometimes put food parcels in their post-office boxes at this time.

Gabriel worked in the post-office for a few months when he left the NAAFI in February 1948. Vast quantities of Jewish propaganda about 'Arab terrorism' passed through his hands, and he discovered then that mail misdirected to Russia was not returned.

The climax of the Jewish terror campaign came in April of that year with the massacre of over two hundred and fifty villagers of Deir Yassin, an Arab village a few miles west of Jerusalem. This precipitated a great exodus of Arabs from Western Palestine and may be regarded as the direct cause of the Palestinian problem. It was master-minded by Menachem Begin.

On May 15th Britain, crippled by the Second World War and under pressure to renounce her Empire, ended her Mandate in Palestine and left the country to its fate. The Arabs were shattered and felt they had been betrayed; the Jews were overjoyed and announced the birth - or rebirth - of the state of Israel. America was the first to recognise the new state, and she was followed by Russia, South Africa and then other countries. The Porto Rican delegate was brought to the United Nations in his pyjamas in order to make up the majority, and of the African and Asian countries, only South Africa, Liberia and the Philippines recognised Israel at first.

On May 17th a group of armed Jews came to the Khanos' house in the Musrara Quarter and told them they must leave and go to the Old City. Gabriel replied in Hebrew, 'If there is to be a Jewish state, we will be Christian Jews. We are not Arabs; we are Assyrians.' 'All Christians must go into the Old City,' the man replied. 'You can return when the fighting is over.' So they left, taking the few things they could carry.

After staying a month in St. Mark's courtyard in the midst of the battle that raged there, they went to Salt on the East Bank and stayed in the Catholic church. Then they moved on to Amman, but this was little more than a fly-blown village in the valley at the time, with only a tiny Christian minority, and they found nowhere to stay. They came to Madeba, where the Isfis tribe had stayed many years before. Abu-Jabra's brother had married a member of the family of the *muhtar*, the headman of the village, and they stayed in his house.

Here Gabriel was regarded as a *medaneh*, a townsman or city-slicker, and he later often told a story against a rich business rival who originated from Madeba: though they were staying in the best house in Madeba, its roof, made of mud and bamboo, did not prevent the unexpected arrival of a large snake falling 'plop' from the ceiling into the central dish from which they were all eating. As he related the event, his first finger, in one quick movement, would trace the snake's descent, describe its slippery coils on the table and rise up to face the astonished *medaneh*. I do not know which was funnier: the picture this conjured up of Gabriel and the snake looking at each other, or the actual sight of Gabriel gaping at his own forefinger.

The Bedouin of the district used to come into Madeba as those of Bethlehem did. Their usual method of exchange was barter, but sometimes they made an ingenuous foray into the realms of finance. One of them would come to Gabriel and say, 'I have a dinar. How many coins will you give me for it?'

'Name your price,' said Gabriel, entering into the spirit of the thing.

'I'll take ten florins or twenty shillings.'

'God give it to you,' said Gabriel, which was the usual way of refusing a price. 'I'll give you nine florins.'

If the Bedouin came away with nineteen shillings, he thought he had struck a good bargain.

It was from Madeba that they saw Archbishop Samuel off with the Scrolls, and while they were there, fighting was going on Palestine. Of other Arab countries that had come in to help the Palestinian Arabs who had no army of their own: the Transjordan army was holding Ramallah and what remained of Jerusalem; the Iraqis held the Plains of Jezreel, Nablus, Jenin and the nearby towns and villages; the Egyptians held Bethlehem, Hebron, Beersheba, Ashkelon, Ashdod, Gaza and the Negev.

Gabriel made several visits to Bethlehem from Madeba, and the Egyptians used to pick him up with other young men and take them off to dig trenches by the enemy lines. Gabriel quite often went over the lines at Beit Safafa to fetch things from their house, which was still empty then, and to visit friends 'on the other side', as we must now begin to call it.

Once he was walking his widow-friend back from some woods outside Bethlehem when some Egyptian soldiers stopped them. They had designs on the girl and they took her off, but what happened to her Gabriel never knew because he did not see her again: she had left Bethlehem when he was able to return there. He was accused of being a spy and was kept under interrogation for three days, the sweet smell of hashish in his nostrils all the time. Finally they let him go, banishing him to the East Bank and telling him not to show his face in Bethlehem.

Back in Madeba, the *muhtar* needed corn-seed to plant his land on the hills above Amman. Gabriel still had some cash he had brought from Jerusalem, and he gave the *muhtar* eighty dinars. The *muhtar* offered him eighty thousand square metres in exchange.

'Don't bother,' said Gabriel with his usual lack of acquisitiveness. 'You can pay me back with a few bushels of corn when it ripens.'

But they were not in Madeba when the corn ripened, and once more he had missed riches by a hair's breadth. For that hill later became the most select area of Jordan's capital, covered with the villas and palaces of the wealthy.

Two truces were imposed on the contending parties in Palestine in the summer of 1948. The Israelis used the pause after the first one to make themselves stronger in armaments than the Arabs; for they were obtaining arms clandestinely from Czechoslovakia, while the British, under pressure from the United Nations, suspended their supply of arms to Transjordan, Iraq and Egypt. The Israelis were then able to take a considerable amount of Arab territory, but to their great regret they were not able to take the Old City of Jerusalem. Synagogues in the Jewish Quarter were badly damaged in the fighting, but it is not always remembered that British officers were commanding the Transjordan forces there.

The cause of peace had a serious setback with the murder by the Stern Gang of Count Bernadotte, the United Nations mediator, a Swedish nobleman of exceptionally wide vision. The murderers were not brought to justice by the Israeli authorities, and one of the Gang, Itzhak Shamir, later became their Prime Minister.

On the first of October, King Abdullah of Transjordan was acclaimed by some Palestinian notables as their sovereign, and the Kingdom of Jordan was formed of Transjordan and Arab Palestine. At the end of the year the Israelis attacked and took Ashkelon from the Egyptians, and the unit of which Jamal Abdul Nasser was in command was cut off and surrounded at Faloujeh. After holding out a month, Nasser gave up and retreated to Gaza. The Israelis were then able to take the Negev and Umm Rash Rash - later Eilat - on the Gulf of Aqaba. This meant that the Egyptians in the Bethlehem-Hebron area were cut off from Egypt.

The British had a defence treaty with Jordan, and to protect Aqaba from the Israelis they sent out a battalion, which stayed a year. Gabriel thought this looked like the return of the good old days, and he went to Amman, met Mohammed Audeh and another ex-NAAFI friend and together they set off for Aqaba to see if Great Britain had need of them again. They got a lift in the back of a lorry, and thus they went, bumped to and fro, the dust penetrating to every part of their bodies, down the rough road through the desert.

They had gone about three-quarters of the way when they came to a Jordanian check-post. The Bedouins manning it searched them and found in their possession an Arabic magazine which happened to have in it a map of Palestine. 'Huh! you are spies,' they said. 'But this is an Arabic magazine,' said Gabriel. 'You must stay here and answer some questions,' said the soldiers. The lorry drove on, and for three days Gabriel and his would-be comrades-in-arms were kept at that remote outpost, living on a diet of dates flavoured with sand.

Finally they were allowed to continue with another lorry, and on reaching Aqaba made their way to the only hotel. Here men were sleeping head to toe on carpets laid out on the floor, using their shoes as pillows. Again the city-Arabs were quite out of their element, and they found it preferable to sleep on the lovely palm-fringed beach. Somehow in this little Moslem town they managed to find some liquor, and they were well under the influence when a Jordanian officer arrived to see them.

'Moufadi Beyk has arrived,' said Mohammed to the others as they lay sprawled out on the sand, giving him a title of respect. Unfortunately, as Gabriel rolled over blearily, he made a rude Arabic pun on his title, which the Beyk heard. The British Army was therefore deprived of the services of this gallant trio, and they returned jobless to Amman and Madeba.

Arrangements were made early in 1949 for a meeting between the Arab countries and Israel to take place in Rhodes. The Iraqis refused to negotiate, and the Jordanians took their place in the transactions for the northern area. At the Arabs' insistence, the negotiating parties did not meet face to face, but stayed in separate rooms while the mediator went between them.

What happened at Rhodes must be regarded as having the sanction of the western powers, since Transjordan, Egypt and Iraq were under British influence, and there were British officers in the Arab army and advisers behind the scenes. The new mediator was Dr. Ralph Bunche, a black American. Some of King Abdullah's Bedouin officers did the bargaining for the Arab side, and their standard of education was such that they thought a millimetre on a small-scale map was the same as a millimetre on the ground. They therefore blandly gave up territory that might have remained Arab.

They gave up the very fertile area just to the north of Jenin, Tulkarem and Kalqilia in such a way that the people of these towns could see their lands but could no longer farm them; and they sacrificed half the small village of Beit Safafa near Bethlehem so that the Israelis could have the railway line, while the barbed wire passed down the middle of the village separating brother from brother. Jaffa was also given up although it was to have been the Jordanians' outlet to the Mediterranean. The Egyptians who were cut off in the Hebron area were given safe conduct to Gaza, which was put under their control, being linked to their Sinai territory by a strip of land. The armistice remained in force, with many infringements and no subsequent peace settlement, until the Six-Day War of 1967.

Only three hundred thousand Arabs stayed in Israel after 1949. Those who left, in spite of the international law that people should be free to enter their own country, and of almost yearly United Nations resolutions that the refugees should be allowed back or compensated, were not permitted to return to their homes nor were they compensated. The Israelis passed a law in 1952 that Palestinian Arabs outside Israel at that time were 'absentees' and could not claim their property. Some of their shops and houses have remained shuttered and empty to this day: others have been occupied by Jews who pay rent to a Custodian of Absentee Property; and about 350 villages were totally destroyed.

The Jews in countries outside Israel, not knowing the true facts, attributed the Arabs' antagonism to unreasoning racial and religious prejudice or just natural savagery, and, begging the question, came to regard the monopoly of the land as justified because of it. The West followed their lead and often called the Semitic Arabs anti-Semites; and making the Palestinian Arab people a scapegoat for their own (westerners') ancient guilt, they laid their sins on its back and let it be driven into the desert.

The partition of his country meant years of hardship and frustration for Gabriel. Although there were opportunities for one of his dynamic vitality, most of them for different reasons slipped from his grasp, and the next decade is mainly a catalogue of might-have-beens.

CHAPTER NINE

Retrospect: Jordan 1949–1960

WHEN the armistice took place and the Egyptians left the south of Arab Palestine, or of Jordan's West Bank as we may now call it, the Khanos moved from Madeba to Bethlehem, and settled into the one-roomed house next to the senior Kando's shop. They now became Jordanian citizens. Gabriel was unemployed for some months, and it was at this time that he used to go to Jerusalem with pieces of Scroll in his mother's shopping basket. Food was shorter now than earlier, for the Arabs had lost much good agricultural land at the armistice, including the rich citrus groves of Jaffa. For years they did not see an orange, and could only dream of the orchards they had left behind for others to harvest. Then they developed Jericho and in time produced an orange unrivalled in the world. They also planted citrus near the northern border.

But if food was short, money was far shorter. For some years the Khanos saw meat only about once a fortnight, and often a meal would consist of a piece of bread and a raw onion. But Um-Jabra told her children: 'You are lucky: you have this time some-one to help you. You have the Red Cross; you have the churches. The first time we had absolutely no-one, and yet we survived. Have faith in God, and He will help us.'

There was now barbed wire down the middle of Beit Safafa village,

119

but Gabriel still used to go through it into Israel. He was always sent back by the Israelis, but not before he had secured some Israeli beef for the Jordanian sergeant at the border post. This sergeant therefore permitted him several times to reunite in the village bakery families divided by the armistice lines.

Some Arabs returned to collect things from their homes, and when they found them occupied by Jews, in a fit of angry desperation they murdered the whole family. Others stole livestock from the kibbutzim, but the Jordanians on the border used to sent them to return their loot. Later the Jordanians provided the Israelis with information about the whereabouts of these thieves, and the Israelis came and blew up their houses.

Eventually it became too dangerous to go over the lines even for one like Gabriel whose aims were mainly humanitarian; for Jordanians started to imprison or banish to the East Bank all whom they caught crossing. Jordan was proving herself the best neighbour Israel could hope to have.

The families on different sides of the armistice lines - that is, Arab families, for no Jews remained on the Jordan side - were totally cut off from each other. In time the Christians were able to meet once a year at Christmas, when the Jordanians let the Christian Arabs in Israel cross into Jordan through the Mandelbaum Gate, the crossing-point between the two sides of Jerusalem. Strangely they did not let the Moslems cross from Israel; they just let them meet their relatives at the Gate on a certain day in the year. The Israelis did not allow into Israel any Arab who was outside the country, and the Arab countries were not supposed to allow the entry of Israelis.

The Israelis complained bitterly that they could not reach their Wailing Wall while Jordan held part of Jerusalem, but the agreement about the holy places was not kept by either side: the Jews were supposed to be allowed to go to the Wall, while the Arabs were to be able to use the road between Jerusalem and Bethlehem; but the separation of the two sides was complete and neither of these concessions was put into effect. Presumably both sides valued their security too much. The Israelis could not reach the Wall, the Jewish quarter or their cemetery in Jerusalem, Rachel's Tomb in Bethlehem, or Abraham's family burial-place in Hebron; and the Christian Arabs outside Israel could not reach the Upper Room on Mount Zion, John the Baptist's birthplace in Ein Karem, Lydda, birthplace of St. George, the holy places around the Sea of Galilee, or Cana or Nazareth. The Moslems formerly set great store by the Tomb of David, but they could not visit it, not could they visit their Great Mosque at Ramleh. These were some of the consequences of the Partition.

In 1949 and 1950 Bethlehem was full to overflowing with refugees from Jerusalem and other parts of Palestine, and there were many young Assyrians of Gabriel's vintage. Their lives centred on the church. Several of them were deacons like Gabriel, and one of them, called Ephraim, who had a club-foot, had a beautiful voice and played the violin. One day when the deacons were singing the liturgy in turn, Gabriel had to sing after Ephraim. Ephraim started to giggle at Gabriel's way of jumping an octave when he could not reach a note that was either too high or too low for him, and Gabriel lost his temper, slammed the prayer-book shut and stormed out of the church.

A number of Assyrians, including Gabriel, Ephraim and Morad Barsom, were involved in a Pentecostalist Christian mission that was set up in Bethlehem from America at this time. They preached, taught, looked after the children and tried to raise money. Once some Pentecostalists came to visit them and started singing some revivalist songs. Gabriel put his hands behind his back and launched into an Arabic dance, the *dabke*. 'I like that man,' cried a minister. 'He has received the Holy Spirit.'

However, Baney was also starting his mission then, and as he looked upon his work as a profit-making business rather than a means of doing good, he would brook no competitors. He had a photograph taken of Gabriel dancing at a night-club, and sent it to the backers of the mission. This time the Holy Spirit was not given credit, and Gabriel was dismissed. The mission failed soon afterwards. Ephraim and another young Assyrian, who could pass muster as good Christians since they did not dance, drink or smoke, were taken to America by the mission people, and they were able to make a life there for them-

selves and their families. Once more Gabriel had missed the chance of
a secure future.

His next job was distributing relief for the International Red Cross.
There was a great deal of dishonesty at this time, as relief workers tried
to secure what they could to feed their own families, and even some
of the foreign workers connived at the transfer of distributions to the
Black Market; but Gabriel, though earning pathetically little and often
hungry, tried to refrain from any act of dishonesty that took food out
of the mouths of other needy people.

In 1950 the United Nations Relief and Works Agency for Palestinian Refugees was formed and started to provide rations, free education and a free health service for those who qualified as refugees. As
a temporary expedient it was an absolute blessing, and hundreds of
thousands of refugees are still dependent on it to this day; but its very
existence seemed to do something to fossilise the situation. Gabriel
felt this, and when he was taken on as a camp-leader, he led a demonstration against the refugee policy: those in the camps were in tents,
the rations were inadequate (providing only fifteen hundred calories a
day, and sixteen hundred in winter), and nothing was being done to
solve the problem. The worst thing about the UNRWA rules was that
they did not give any incentive to a refugee to earn a decent wage, even
if he was lucky enough to find any sort of job; for if he earned more
than a couple of pounds a week, the ration cards of several members
of the family were stopped. With the ration-card went free medical
treatment, and this was not something to give up lightly: once a ration
card was stopped it could not be taken back again.

Gabriel was then moved to the distribution team at a salary of four
pounds a month, and distributed in the camps the gifts of food sent
by different countries. They came overland from the port of Beirut,
and one day there was some confusion in the loading. A lorry that
was supposed to be bringing dried beans arrived full of coffee beans
instead. These were worth a fortune, and within a few hours the lorry-
driver and the UNRWA area manager had made the coffee disappear
on the Black Market and had refilled the lorry with dried beans from
the souk. Gabriel was indignant, and he wrote to headquarters in

Beirut to tell them what had happened. A letter come back to say he was a 'trouble-maker', and he was dismissed by the area manager. The lorry-driver was able to build a block of flats in Ramallah, and the area manager built himself a very nice house and continued to rise in the ranks of UNRWA.

For a short time Gabriel taught at the Assyrian school near the church, and this was when he acquired the sunglasses with the built-in mirrors. Apart from his regular teaching, he was given the job of training the choir, which always rather surprised me, but he assured me they never sang better than under his baton. But his patience was too quickly exhausted during the ordinary lessons, and his thoughts turned to other Arab countries.

By now Kuwait and Saudi-Arabia had found the oil, and the great diaspora of the Palestinian people had begun. They disappeared not only to the oil states, but also to North and South America, to Europe, to Lebanon, Egypt, Syria, Iraq and the North African countries. Wherever they went in the Arab countries, they quickly rose to the top: many did well even in the tougher going of Europe and America. Those from the towns of Palestine were better-educated than most other Arabs, and seemed even to have a greater natural ability. Perhaps the tremendous mixture of races found in their land had something to do with it; for Palestine was the crossroads of the world and a vantage-ground for viewing both East and West. They were, so to speak, well-occidented.

Shackled by responsibility for his eight dependants, Gabriel was often on the verge of desperation at this time. His bitterness was kept within bounds by Khatoun, the sister next to him. She calmed him down when he saw the world black before him, and scolded him when he managed to find some sort of alcohol and came home drunk. She was the strongest personality in the family, and she kept them united. Gabriel adored her.

One day Khatoun and the middle brother Khalil took a bus from Beithlehem along the long, rough, precipitous road through the Judean wilderness that was the only way at that time to go to Jerusalem. She wanted to take Khalil to the doctor in the Augusta Victoria Hospital, which was under UNRWA administration. It was the only decent hospital in Arab Jerusalem then. On the other side of the city, that is in the New City, there had been French, German and Italian hospitals, and the government hospital in the Russian Compound. The Jordanian government hospital was now in an old Austrian hospice: a dark, dingy building in the Old City. A French hospital was started in an even more unsuitable building, the 'House of Caiphas' or St. Peter in Gallicantu, on the steep eastern slope of Mt. Zion. A worse disadvantage than the poor buildings was the incompetence of the staff. There were few Palestinian Arab doctors at this time, and nursing was not considered a respectable profession for an Arab girl. The staff were therefore mainly unqualified. But the most disruptive element of all was dishonesty: medical supplies were stolen and sold on the Black Market, and twice the medicine store of the Augusta Victoria was burnt down to cover up large-scale thefts.

On this day they did not go to the Augusta Victoria, because Khalil gave Khatoun the slip. She did not concern herself too much because they had relations in Jerusalem, and she knew he could always find a bed there. She met friends, the wife and daughter of a Bethlehemite who had become rich in Venezuela and returned to his native town, and she decided to take the next bus back to Bethlehem with them.

The bus was only just passing the Garden of Gethsemane when it caught fire. The windows of the bus did not open and the back door was jammed shut. The driver parked the bus near the wall by the side of the road and was the first to leap out of the front door to safety. Had he parked in the middle of the road, most of the casualties would have been avoided. Some of the passengers broke the windows and climbed out that way, but the majority left by the door and fell into the drain between the bus and the wall. Then whether they went by the front of the bus or the back, they had to pass through the fire which now raged down its length.

Khatoun's nylon stockings caught alight as she fell out of the bus, but she was able to wrap her coat round her legs and put the flames out. The she and a certain Dr. Albina saw that the girl she had been with was trapped near the front of the bus, and her clothes and hair were on fire. They went back to try to save her and suffered their most severe burns in the attempt. It was of no avail: the girl, who was very beautiful, was burned to death before their eyes.

From the Garden of Gethsemane the Church of All Nations looked down on the scene impassively. On the top of its pediment were two bronze deer recalling Psalm forty-two: 'As pants the hart for cooling streams, so longs my soul for you, O God.'

When help came, Khatoun was taken to the government hospital. Her friend's mother also died in the fire, and when the father heard the news he went mad.

Khatoun lived for over two months in agony. She was given a penicillin injection every day, and her burns were covered with a dressing which was clumsily removed and replaced every two days, causing her excruciating pain. When the family saw no sign of her improving, they questioned the doctors, but always received evasive answers. Gabriel tried to get her transferred to the Augusta Victoria, but he was refused. He was not in favour with UNRWA: he was just one of the many hundreds of thousands of penniless, powerless refugees in Jordan.

On Saturday the family came to see her, and she was cheerful as she always was. On Sunday morning, the priest came to her as usual at five o'clock, and she took communion. But when the family came again on Sunday afternoon, she was dead. Only then did they see her legs, which were fleshless and green with gangrene. Gabriel believes - and I think he must be right - that the daily injections were made with expired penicillin or some other useless substance, while the good penicillin was sold.

He was beside himself with grief and rage. Widad told me how he wept and tore his clothes and tried to kill the doctors and nurses. He had to be forcibly held back and taken home.

Afterwards they learned that the doctors had told Khatoun a few days before that she would have to have her legs amputated. She had replied that she would rather die, and they had just let the gangrene spread over her body without telling her people anything.

Dr. Albina was taken to the French hospital in St. Peter in Gallicantu, and there he too died. He was a very fine doctor and a terrible loss to Bethlehem. A Mr. Mattar, who had burns more serious than Khatoun's and Albina's, was transferred to the Augusta Victoria. He recovered.

There was no-one now to steady Gabriel and give him courage. His mother was brave and tenacious, but as she had no education her vision was limited. He had to forge a way into the future alone.

Marian Khamis told me once, 'Khatoun was the best of the sisters; she was as intelligent as she was beautiful.' Gabriel told me, 'She was like you.'

He was unemployed for several more months after this, but the next turning led eventually on to the high-road of his life.

One morning in 1953, as he was going to say his morning prayers in the Grotto of the Nativity, he heard a licensed guide giving a halting and inadequate explanation of the site to some visitors. Seeing that tourists were beginning to come to Jordan and realising that his knowledge of the country was much greater than this guide's, he decided he would try to be a guide himself.

He had a wonderful memory - and whatever the shortcomings of the Arab system of education, it did train the memory remarkably well - and he could remember the Islamic religion he had been taught in the Moslem government school, and the ancient history, geography and scripture he had studied at Bishop Gobat's. This had been supplemented by his reading of the Bible, both privately and in his connection with the church.

He had to appear before a board to get his licence, but this was not a problem, because he knew more than most of the board members. He then set about reading the subject in depth. He once had quite a good collection of books on the Holy Land, but his unfortunate habit of lending them to others who wished to become guides caused it to dwindle over the years.

When I married him, I found one cupboard in the house crammed full of Bibles. There were twenty-five of them: some 'placed here (or somewhere) by the Gideons', some presented 'to Gabriel, our wonderful guide', some undesignated. He clung to his religion with the unflinching belief that it would eventually bring him safely through the fires of adversity, and the Bibles were something concrete to show for it.

He was taken on at the American Colony through George Albina, brother of the doctor, and the Mr. Mattar who survived the accident, for his brother was then manager of their tours. Gabriel put his whole heart into his work, and the gap very soon widened between the excellence of his service and the indifference of his employers. But his dedication had its reward. He was in fact building up the basis of his future clientele, and after many years his bread came back to him. Some American tourists sent him money in the difficult times that were still to come, and it is tragic to think that their help might have saved Khatoun had the accident happened a year or two later. Visitors were always welcome in the East, but they were doubly welcome in Jerusalem in those days because they represented a hope of salvation.

Gabriel's attitude was rather different to the foreign residents of the city, with some of whom he had some angry brushes. This was partly a deprived young man's natural resentment, and partly because he felt that too much money went into administration and entertainment, not enough into relief work, and hardly any into what he called 'colourful projects' for the refugees.

Many of the foreign employees of UNRWA stayed at the American Colony and with Mrs. Vester they kept a careful check on the records to be sure that Gabriel did not have more than ten days' work a month. If he was paid more than ten pounds per month, they would have been able to stop some of the family's ration cards. He therefore relied on his tips and commissions to make a living. There was one Frenchman in particular who tried hard to take away some of his cards, but the manager of the Colony backed Gabriel. Gabriel was very bitter against this man and invoked a great curse on his head.

After his tour of the Middle Eastern countries in the spring of 1954, when Gabriel was his guide in Jerusalem, Aldous Huxley wrote to a friend from Athens:

'I have never had such a sense of the tragic nature of the human situation, the horror of a history in which the great works of art, the

philosophies and the religions, are no more than islands in an endless
stream of war, poverty, frustration, squalor and disease. One sees ...
the hopelessness of the inhabitants of Jerusalem for whom the holiest
of cities is a prison of chronic despair.'

On one occasion Gabriel was returning after dark from a very long
day's guiding in Petra, when the taxi stopped at the garage that used
to be on the spot where the post-office was later built. He had had
a fair amount to drink, and getting out of the car to stretch his legs,
he did not notice the pit where mechanics worked on the underside
of cars. The ground suddenly disappeared from under his feet, and
he found himself in the oily depths of this pit. When he was pulled
out by the taxi-driver and two of the mechanics, his suit was smeared
with grease and his head and hands were black. The driver drove him
back to the Colony, and took him to the servants' quarters near the
pig-sties. There he and the night-watchman scrubbed him clean, took
his top clothes to be cleaned in the laundry and bedded him down for
the night near the pigs.

Gabriel did not regard guiding as a permanent job, and in 1954 he
made an application to work as a receptionist for Point Four, Eisen-
hower's mission to help underdeveloped countries. On entering the
office in Amman for his interview, he found a fresh-faced young American with his legs up on his desk. He did not move when Gabriel
entered but motioned him to sit down. Gabriel sat down and put *his*
legs up on the desk; and the American was obliged to conduct the
interview in this rather ludicrous manner.

When the news came that the other candidate had been preferred
to him, Gabriel went back to the interviewer and told him:

'The man you appointed can hardly read or write, but you appointed him in preference to me because he was recommended by a
government minister. I have no-one to recommend me: I am just a
refugee with a large family to support and no strings to pull, and so I
don't get the job.

'You Americans talk a lot about Communism, but it is people like
you who will make us Communists. You are living in luxury with a
huge salary, a large car, driver, servants, whatever you want. We have

nothing and there is no way we can improve ourselves'.

This speech of his must have been duly noted down in the records. For when he applied for an American visa the following year, thinking that there would never be a settlement and he must make a fresh start in life, he was turned down on the grounds that he was a Communist.

It was about this time that a young friend of his in Bethlehem, Hanna or John, became mentally unbalanced. He lost his job in UN-RWA, and though this had only meant an income of £4 a month, it was for him all the difference between hope and utter despair. He was the only son of a widow, and to make his situation more desperate he had lately fallen in love with a girl he longed to marry. Gabriel, understanding very well that it was not really his wits but his circumstances that were awry, knew how to cheer and encourage him. But he was away in Damascus once when Hanna became very ill, and he was taken to the mental hospital outside Bethlehem. Electric shock treatment was still quite new even in the West then, and though the hospital had the equipment they did not know how to use it. They gave Hanna too strong a voltage and he died under the treatment.

Afterwards, whenever he could afford it, Gabriel would take money to the destitute and inconsolable mother.

He often told me about Palestinian exiles who died in these years after 1948 - as he put it, 'from the anger'.

On October 29th, 1956, Israel attacked Egypt in what became known as the Suez crisis; and forty-three men, women and children of the Arab village of Kafr Kassim in northern Israel were shot and killed, because they did not observe a curfew which they did not know about. There was no real connection between the events, and the news of the war completely overshadowed the gratuitous massacre.

There were no tourists in Jordan for six months. In the spring of 1957 Gabriel went to Kuwait and worked for a short time for a new American oil company. But he could not stand the heat, and the venture ended in farce. His nose started bleeding and would not stop in spite of his being put into the cold storage room of a hospital. He returned to Jordan - in time for the reappearance of the first shy visitors.

It is hardly surprising that he augmented his income in any way he could in these uncertain times. If the tourists seemed to be gullible, he did not miss the chance of playing to the gallery and making a little extra money. 'Before 1948 I was the Sheikh of a rich tribe who owned many thousands of camels, goats and sheep. In 1948 we lost everything,' and his tip was doubled. And again: 'This ring belonged to the wife of the Mayor of Jaffa who is now a refugee and has had to sell her most treasured possessions,' and the ring would be sold for an inflated price and he would get a handsome commission.

The tourist traffic again stopped in 1958 owing to political turmoil in Lebanon and Jordan and the arrival of the Sixth Fleet off Lebanon. In Lebanon the trouble was between Moslems and Christians - for almost anything served to upset the delicate balance that existed there between the two religions - and in Jordan, since 1953 under the rule of Abdullah's grandson Hussein, between the government and the Leftists. To counter-balance Egypt's recent union with Syria, Jordan made a union with Iraq, where Hussein's young cousin Feisal was king and Nuri Said was prime minister. Under this regime money was pouring into Iraq from the western countries, and there were many good jobs. Gabriel set off to seek his fortune there.

But no sooner had he arrived in the capital Bagdad, than with his usual genius for attracting dramas or what he called 'cat*os*trophes', he found himself in the middle of the most savage revolution. Everyone associated with the monarch was butchered, including many Jordanians who had come to cement the Union; and Nuri Said, who nearly succeeded in escaping disguised as a woman, was recognised by his shoes and met a terrible end. Gabriel was indeed lucky to be rounded up with other Jordanians who did not have Iraqi residence cards, put into a lorry and driven back, going for about thirty hours without food or drink, through the burning desert to Jordan.

Gabriel sometimes adapted his very genuine faith in these days to fit the requirements of more opulent Christian sects than his own. It was one of the great misfortunes of Christians in the Holy Land that the western Christians who took most interest in them were the American Fundamentalists with their general obsession with 'conversion' (which E. M. Forster says is peculiarly attractive to the half-baked mind) and many individual fads in the various sects. The Palestinians, being a malleable people and in need of financial help, did not scorn this brand of religion but adapted themselves to it when they came in contact with it. Some swallowed it completely; others observed it with a greater or lesser degree of duplicity.

I have already mentioned Gabriel's short-lived excursion into Pentecostalism in 1950. In 1956 he became involved with the Christian Scientists. Their tours to the Holy Land were led by an elderly lame woman called Mrs. Hoyt. Coming to the Colony she was given Gabriel as her guide, and she immediately decided he was the man to make her reputation as a biblical expert. As they went round the holy places and archaeological sites, she got him to hold her arm and whisper his exposition in her ear, and then she would relay the information to her followers as if it came from her. In return for this help she introduced him to the works of Mary Baker Eddy, and he learned to quote them like the Bible. Finding him such an apt pupil, she made him a Reader and put him in charge of the Christian Science work in Jerusalem and Bethlehem. As it was a wealthy movement and the work brought in some very welcome contributions, Gabriel accepted the post. He did not believe in all their tenets - and the memory of Khatoun's suffering made this hardly possible - but he started to take an interest in the psychosomatic aspect of illness. But once more his reputation as a drinker and gambler undid him, and Mrs. Hoyt did not carry out her intention to dedicate him as a First Reader at the mother church in Boston. She still wanted him to guide her, and a group of hers arrived at the same time as our first Wings tour in 1960; and it was because of his flat refusal to guide Mrs. Hoyt that the Colony was displeased with him at that time.

Because of the Fundamentalist visitors ('pilgrims' was not really the word for them, since it had overtones of self-abasement), the Garden Tomb acquired more importance on the tourist beat than the Holy Sepulchre. This was a first-century tomb not far from the Damascus Gate, which the Fundamentalists, without any evidence, accepted as the tomb of christ; this in spite of the Holy Sepulchre's almost incon-

trovertible claims to be the site, and the unbroken tradition of worship
at the spot since Queen Helena's visit in 325. It was really that unbroken tradition of reverence and pilgrimage that the Fundamentalists
disliked, since they tended to distrust any brand of Christianity except
their own. They also found the simplicity of the Garden far more congenial than the unfamiliar darkness, antiquity and ornateness of the
Church of the Holy Sepulchre.

It was at the Garden Tomb, one day in 1958, that Gabriel was
'converted' by Billy Graham's right-hand man, Dr. T.W. Wilson. He
was a large, kind-hearted man from the southern States with a rugged,
humorous face, and he was leading fifty 'Youth for Christ'; Gabriel was
their guide. Gabriel was standing with the drivers a little way away
from the group, when T.W. appealed to him to come over and listen
to his preaching. He hesitated, but when T.W. called him again, he
went to join the young Americans near the tomb. This was something
which should not be regarded with too much cynicism. It really was
a turning-point in his life: he did not abandon his church, but he
was infected with T.W.'s evangelistic zeal, and henceforth regarded
himself as a missionary as much as a guide. The warm friendship and
whole-hearted patronage T.W. gave him from this time brought him
closer to his American clients and removed the traces of resentment or
antipathy from his attitude towards them.

The 'spiritual messages' he now gave at Bethlehem, Gethsemane
and Christ's tomb often deeply affected the people he addressed. His
eyes glowed like coals when he spoke with feeling, and he could very
easily bring tears to his listeners' eyes. One of the people who was very
moved by his guiding was Hastings Deering, the biggest manufacturer
in Australia. When we were married, he gave me a silver Georg Jensen
brooch of a gazelle kneeling and turning its head to look backwards.

There were several American girls with money who might have
married Gabriel and taken him back to America, and this would have
solved his problem about a visa, given him American citizenship, and
ended his struggle to survive. But it would probably have left his
family high and dry, and in any case it was not a matter in which he
was prepared to give up his ultimate integrity. A little duplicity had

been necessary for survival; but he was not going to sell his soul.

In 1968, when we had been married eight years, a Reverend and Mrs. Brooks from Florida came to see us during their stay in Jerusalem. It was their second visit: they had had Gabriel as their guide in 1959.

Something seemed to puzzle them about our marriage. 'Did Gabriel know you in 1959?' they asked me.

'No. We met in the spring of 1960,' I replied.

'Because there were several young girls in our group in 1959, and we were encouraging him to choose one to be his wife, but he told us he wanted to marry an English girl.'

'You see,' said Gabriel, delighted that I should hear this. 'I was holding the string, and I pulled and pulled and at last she came.'

'It wasn't quite like that,' I said, and I quoted William Blake's verse:

> ' "I give you the end of a golden string; Only wind it into a ball,
>
> It will lead you in at Heaven's Gate,
>
> Built in Jerusalem's wall."

'You see I wound the string up.'

Gabriel then wanted to argue that it was he who had wound it up, but we left it till later.

CHAPTER TEN

'Angels Unawares'

STORIES about Gabriel's tour of U.S.A. in the autumn of 1961 joined the repertoire of his great set-pieces, like the donkey-ride and the tale of Barbarina, which were often told in company with his own special brand of gestures and the most superlative timing. All of them stressed the strangeness of the western world seen through the eyes of one coming from the desert: in Jordan he might be a *medaneh*, but he certainly was not in America.

The suitcase he took with him was almost entirely filled with presents for the people he was going to see. On the plane he was given a form to fill, in which he was supposed to list any presents he had in his luggage. One could only bring in ten dollars' worth duty-free. He did not fill in the form, and when he came into the customs-hall at New York airport, looking around the officials to find one who might be lenient, he picked on a black man. As he waited in line for his turn, he realised he had made a mistake: the man of his choice was going through everything with a fine tooth comb. It was too late to retreat, and he muttered a brief prayer for help.

'You haven't filled in the form. Why?'

'You see, officer. I don't read or write English - I just speak it.'

'Well, have you anything to declare?'

'Just a few gifts,' he said, thinking of the rings, rosaries, worry-

beads, antiquities, embroideries, cuff-links, crosses, carvings, Bibles
and bedouin jewellery that lurked in every corner of his case. The
man opened it impatiently, but the first things he saw were the cards
Gabriel had had made for his tour. They were business cards with a difference: they were double and opened out to reveal some pressed wild
flowers picked in Jordan and stuck in a decorative design by refugee
children. Beside them was the message which Gabriel relied on to
bring us tourists by the hundred: 'The Guiding Star with its reminder
of Peace and Goodwill, invites you to follow in the steps of those pio-
neers of Christian pilgrimage, the Three Wise Men. Be Wise: let the
Guiding Star light your way to the Holy Land.' On the facing page
was his name and address.

'What's this?' asked the black, looking at one of the cards. Gabriel
explained that he had a tourist agency and was going on a promotion
tour. 'You should come,' he said. 'Everyone should visit the Holy
Land at least once in his life.'

'I'd sure like to, but I don't see that I'd ever be able to,' the man
replied rather wistfully.

'Never say that,' said Gabriel. 'I thought I'd never see the United
States - and here I am. Take a card. Perhaps one day you'll make it.
and you shall be my guest.'

'Okay then,' said the man as if he had suddenly changed his mind
about ransacking the case. 'The Guiding Star says "Go". So long
now.'

He stayed in Brooklyn with a minister called Kenneth Nelson, one
of the many people all over America who felt that Gabriel had given his
all to them on their visit to Jordan and that they would like to repay
him in their own country. On his first day, when he was still dazed from
the long journey, the time-change and the lack of sleep, Nelson took
him to Manhattan. He drove through the tunnel under the Hudson
River, informing his alarmed guest that the Queen Elizabeth or Queen
Mary might be sailing over their heads; took him to the dizzy height
of the Empire State Building; to Wall Street with its bewildering mass
of papers and the ceaseless tick-tack of the changing prices; and then
sent him down the Subway. He told him to get a train to the fourth

stop and he would meet him there. But it was the rush-hour and he could not bear another minute. He thought he would walk to the fourth stop; but as he crossed the street, an iron grasp descended on his shoulder. It was a policeman.

'They've got me,' he thought. 'They must have discovered that old file which listed me as a Communist.'

'Yes, sir,' he said fearfully to the policeman, who had produced his notebook. 'What have I done, sir?'

'Can't you read?' he asked brusquely.

'Read what?'

'That.'

'What?' asked Gabriel, looking around.

'That sign. It said "Don't Walk". Now it says "Walk". Are you stupid or something?'

Gabriel now understood what his offence was: he was a jaywalker. He groped in his pockets and pulled out his passport. 'Look, sir, I've only just arrived here on a visit. I come from Jordan. See it written here: "J-o-r-d-a-n". We don't have any cars there, you know - just camels and donkeys. They let us cross the road any where we want.'

The policeman looked at him in astonishment, studied the passport and then decided to let him off with some fatherly advice. 'If that's the case, you'd better be careful. These New York taxi-drivers, they're just crazy. They don't stop for no-one. So you watch that sign and don't move till it says "Walk".'

'Thank you, officer. Thank you very much. I'll do just as you say. Goodbye, sir.'

Kenneth Nelson picked him up and took him to the Jordanian Consulate to see what they could provide in the way of promotional material. They wrote a letter for him to present at the Arab Information Office telling them to give him any help he might require. When we went there he asked them for a film on Jordan that he could show in a church in New Jersey the next day, and they gave him one.

He had no chance of seeing the film before he went to New Jersey, but they provided him with a projector and someone to work it, and he made an introductory speech. 'Now I will show you some of the places you will visit if you take a Guiding Star tour of Jordan.' The projector whirred; the lights went out; and on the screen appeared the words, 'Fly El Al to ISRAEL'. The audience, to whom Israel and Jordan were very much the same thing, settled more comfortably to watch the film, and they could not understand what was wrong with Gabriel when he clapped his hand over the lens, said 'I think they have given me the wrong film', and made the man stop the projector. He asked for a projector for his slides and dispensed with the film altogether.

He stayed with a Mrs. Diener near Boston and she took him with some friends to a fish restaurant in the port. Gabriel ordered lobster and it so happened that the others at the table did not. When the waitress had taken the orders, she came back and dressed Gabriel in a sort of bib. Seeing that he had been singled out for what seemed to him a humiliating indignity, Gabriel became very agitated. When the waitress came up again, he nobbled her: 'Look here, young lady, I may be from the Middle East but I know how to eat. What made you think I was from the Middle East anyway?' She looked at him in amazement and then realised that it was the bib that had upset him. 'Everyone who orders lobster gets to wear that. Just look around. I hadn't an idea where you came from, and I'm not trying to insult you.' Gabriel sat down again abashed but reassured.

When we planned his tour, the only map we had of the United States was in an old Bartholomew's school atlas, and in it the cities he wanted to visit looked no distance from each other. He was quite disoriented when he found how vast the distances were, and many times he failed to keep appointments because his schedule was quite unrealistic. However, he was on time in Washington for a meeting with a Dr. Edward Bauman who wanted him to appear on his Saturday morning Bible-study programme on nationwide television. Dr. Bauman was a Methodist minister who taught the New Testament at the University of Washington, and he had several times brought groups to Jordan and been guided by Gabriel.

Gabriel had never seen television: in fact the first television he ever saw was on the monitor set for this programme. He wore Arab costume for the occasion, and the girl who put the microphone round his neck was so nervous that she could hardly get it over his head. This shook Gabriel. He had not even thought of being nervous before, but when the red light went on, the programme began and the cameras started converging on him, he hardly heard what Dr. Bauman was saying.

'Today I have a wonderful surprise for you. Almost every week on these programmes you have heard me mention Gabriel, our guide in the Holy Land. Now he is with us here in person. I asked him to dress in the costume of the country, and here he is: our Christian Arab guide, Gabriel -

'Now, Gabriel, I want you to tell everyone what are your feelings on this first visit to our country.'

Silence. Gabriel was looking at himself sideways in the monitor set and thinking how the girl's hands had shaken.

'Gabriel, it's not like you to be silent. Won't you tell us your impressions of America?'

'Well, Dr. Bauman, I've never seen television before - we don't have it in our country - and the girl who put this microphone round my neck was so nervous that she's made *me* feel nervous.'

Then Dr. Bauman started talking about Jordan and he was able to draw Gabriel out. Gradually he warmed to his subject, and in the last few minutes he mentioned the agency and produced a Guiding Star brochure. Afterwards the producer of the programme told him laughing that he had had thousands of dollars' worth of advertising time.

He made many other television appearances, and after all of them people rang up to say they wanted to see more of this dynamic Arab with the compelling eyes. He greatest hit was in Indianapolis on a programme called 'Cross-Exam'. He was put on a panel with a rabbi, a Methodist minister and a woman social worker, and they answered questions on religious and social subjects. One of the questions was on the Dead Sea Scrolls, and in the course of his answer, the rabbi said that the Scrolls proved the Jesus was an Essene and his teachings were derived from the Essene doctrine.

Gabriel leapt up from his chair, his eyes blazing with indignation: 'Are you trying to tell me that Christ was just a member of the Essene sect who broke his vows and became famous for ideas that were not really his?'

The rabbi was slightly caught off balance. 'Well, don't you think there was a connection between the Essenes and Christianity?'

'Of course there was a connection: they were expecting the Messiah to come at that particular point in history, but that is not to say that he was one of them. John the Baptist may have had a link with the Essenes. Living in the Jordan Valley as he did, it is very likely, and this may be why he baptised Christ. The Essenes put special emphasis on the washing away of sins ... '

'Yes, they had a daily bath ritual. We know that,' said the rabbi.

'It sounds as if they had some pretty modern ideas,' said the social worker who knew nothing about the subject; Gabriel sat down again; and the chairman took advantage of the breaking of the tension to go quickly on to the next question.

Gabriel was on a radio programme when he was in Baney's home-town and the centre for his money-raising activities for the Bethlehem orphanage, and he took the opportunity to attack him, charging him with misappropriating the funds and challenging him to reply to his accusation if he could. Nothing was heard from Baney, but this may have added something to the tidal wave of criticism that later engulfed him and eventually purged him from Bethlehem.

In Chicago Gabriel stayed with the Daggett Harveys, the couple who had insisted on Mrs. Vester's inviting him to her reception. They gave a cocktail party for him while he was there, and one of the distinguished guests present later came to Amman as British Ambassador. The next night they saw Verdi's 'Otello' from the central box, because Daggett Harvey was chairman of the Chicago Opera.

The third day was a Sunday, and Gabriel rang up a Reverend Ralph Gade, who had said he wanted to see him when he visited Chicago.

'Where are you staying?' asked Gade.

'With the Daggett Harveys.'

'You mean the Harveys of Harvey Restaurants?'

'Yes.'

'Well, you'd better come over here this evening and see how the ordinary American lives. We'll take you to our evening service.'

As Gade drove Gabriel to their town on the outskirts of the city, he told him the Harveys were the second richest family in Chicago and that Jean Harvey had been a Vanderbilt before she married. But his invitation to him to see the ordinary American was not quite fulfilled. Gabriel blinked his eyes and stared out of the car window: the whole neighbourhood seemed to be alive with fiery devils, long-nosed witches and pumpkin-headed ghosts. He said nothing and waited till they should be in the safety of the church. But even the sacred precincts of the white-boarded church were haunted by a ghoulish mob of little people, who did not vanish even at the advent of the man of God. Gade went up to the altar, leaving Gabriel in the front pew with his wife. Peering nervously round at the ghastly faces behind them and distinguishing the features of human children under some of the disguises, Gabriel whispered, 'Do they always dress like this for church?'

'No. Only when it's Hallowe'en,' said Mrs. Gade, thinking no further explanation was necessary, and Gabriel did not discover what it was all about until the Harveys told him that night.

On the Monday morning Gabriel got down to work. Leaving the Harveys' luxurious apartment overlooking Lake Michigan, he set off for the business centre of the town to visit some travel agents. He had only made a few calls when he found it had begun to rain. He knew Chicago was called 'Windy City' and he had his winter underwear on, but he had brought no means of keeping himself dry. He went into a department store and bought an umbrella. That was fine for the upper part of his body, but his feet were still getting wet. He went into another store and asked for some galoshes size forty-four.

'Forty-four!!' said the girl in amazement.

'Well, this is my foot. What size do you think it is?'

The girl found him some galoshes in an appropriate American size, and he left the shop which was too crowded for him to put them on.

The street was no better. It was the lunch-hour by now, and the typists' heels were hurrying clickety-clack along the pavement. Determined not to be distracted from the matter in hand, Gabriel set down his brief-case and the extended umbrella, and balancing on one foot he eased the other with difficulty into a galosh. It was rather a tight fit, and his arm shot back and struck a passer-by. Straightening up, he turned to apologise for the unintended blow.

A man was looking down into his face, and as their gaze met incredulity was followed by amazed recognition. It was Jabra! It was Kevork! They had not seen each other since 1948. They had been in the same class at school, in the same football team, they had both been in the NAAFI; they had been the closest friends. When disaster struck in 1948, they had been separated: Gabriel the Assyrian had taken refuge in Jordan; Kevork, who was Armenian, had eventually reached America. Neither had any idea what had happened to the other.

The second galosh, Gabriel's briefcase and the umbrella lay forgotten on the crowded pavement, while the two friends staged a scene worthy of some extravagant operetta reaching an improbable climax before the final curtain. The birth-mark was recognised: the nurse had revealed all: the long-lost brothers were united in a passionate embrace that effaced the multifarious vicissitudes of the last three acts. They kissed and kissed, first one cheek, then the other, as the tears mingled with the rain and coursed down their faces. Traffic on the pavement was brought almost to a standstill. The typists of the Middle West had never in their lives seen anything like this display of Middle Easter emotion. Their hurried steps were checked: they walked hesitantly past the outspread umbrella and stared unbelievingly at the two men locked in each other's arms.

'What are you doing here?' asked Kevork when they could speak.

'I'm on a business trip. I've just started a tourist agency in Jerusalem,' said Gabriel, wiping his eyes. 'Are you living here?'

'Yes, since 1949.'

'Are you married?'

'Yes, and I have a son. What about you?'

'I'm married too, and I've got a son,' said Gabriel, delighted at the coincidence.

'Shall we have lunch?' Kevork suggested.

'That will be wonderful,' and they went off together, talking without drawing breath and nearly forgetting the impedimenta on the pavement.

On various occasions Gabriel had guided the President, Dean, and various professors of the University of Kentucky in Lexington, and he was invited to stay with the President, Dr. Frank Dickey. The morning after he arrived, the wives of the leading citizens of Lexington were to enjoy an outing to the town fall-out shelters, and Gabriel was asked to join them. They were wearing their best clothes and their hair was styled in delicate shades of blue and purple as they set out chattering like a flock of starlings. In the shelters deep underground everything was arranged in the most convenient way possible - sitting-rooms, bedrooms, kitchens, bathrooms. 'Charming,' they exclaimed: 'It's real homey,' and they scattered to examine the kitchen fittings and the well-stocked cupboards, to try the bunk-beds, or to seat themselves on the comfortable chairs ready for coffee and cakes.

'I think I shall have to be getting along,' said Gabriel, backing towards the door, and not waiting to hear the outcry of protest, he bolted up into the fresh air.

He was asked to speak at the Campus church on Sunday, and he had no inhibitions about saying what he was thinking.

'Jesus in the Sermon on the Mount told his listeners. 'You cannot serve God and mammon.' If he were here in America today, he would have to tell you the same thing.

'Do you know what is written on your dollar-bill? It says "In God we trust." But you put your trust in the paper it is printed on.

'You have spent millions of dollars on fall-out shelters, but will they really keep you safe if there is an atomic war?

'Why not use your money for better causes and have faith in God? You cannot fear God and Russia.'

As he penetrated further south into America's Bible Belt, home of Billy Graham and many other famous evangelists, he received more invitations to preach. He became more hell-firish; his eyes darkened; people began to compare him to Jesus Christ - until finally I received a cable from him saying he was going no further south, he was cancelling Florida and would be with us in England two days later.

When we returned to Jerusalem, the rest of the family moved to a house at the foot of the hill, leaving Gabriel, Simon and me on our own. Before we split up, Gabriel puzzled me by asking me for reassurance. 'You will give me water, won't you?' I told him I would.

We bought a refrigerator so that I would no longer have to go to the *souk* every day to shop, but I now had to struggle with Arabic cooking, which was really invented for the extended family, with a calor-gas stove whose oven had no thermostatic control, and with a very demanding and active baby. Water was sometimes short, but at least there was more than there had been our first summer in Bethlehem, when we had had to buy all our water from passing lorries. It had to be heated on the stove or in a geyser in the bathroom. We had no telephone.

In the Wadi Jos neighbourhood I was surrounded by women heavy with child-bearing, domestic work and disapproval of me, who were infinitely better qualified than I to run an Arab house, while in the outside world there were many ways in which I could have been useful.

Since I had been in Jerusalem I had been asked to be a radio announcer, to run a hotel, to teach and to write a guide-book. But of course the office had first claim on my free time, and I helped there whenever I could. My frustration and loneliness in the house were eased by the daily appearance of a little Circassian girl called Rudina. I never knew why she started coming, but she used to leave her shoes at the door and come softly in as if entering a mosque, and her presence would lighten the drabness of the house and help pass the time till Gabriel returned.

One day when I was alone, a man unknown to me rang the bell and entered the house when I opened the door. My Arabic was not very good and at first I only knew he was saying something about '*kutub*', a book. He asked me for a pencil and paper and drew a picture of a scroll. Then I understood he wanted to sell us a scroll, and I gave a negative answer. Later Gabriel learned he was one of the Ta'amreh. Their Sheikh had quarrelled with Kando, and they were looking for an alternative buyer for the scroll they had recently found in the Dead Sea area. The man was offended that I turned him away without offering him a cup of coffee, and as a result they went back to Kando and sold the scroll to him.

We were very lucky to have acquired the services of an excellent man as manager of the office, John David. The Davids had been a wealthy Jerusalem family before 1948, owning a building in King George Avenue which is still known as the David Building though in Israeli hands. John had been working in Beirut, but he left his family to live in Jerusalem, working for us at a very low salary, on the understanding that he would later open an office in Beirut for us and be our partner. We needed someone like this to start the office on a sound footing. Though Gabriel, contrary to what he told the customs-man, could read and write English, he had not the temperament for paperwork. The inspiration behind the agency was his; the contacts were his; but he always needed someone to do the routine work. At first he divided the guiding between himself and Mousa, who had now left school and had learnt the job from him. We started to have individual tourists in the spring of 1962 - our first clients from England were the Marquis and Marchioness of Northampton - and we had about six groups - all from America - in the summer.

The ideals with which Gabriel founded the Guiding Star did not fade with the passing of time or the growth of our business. The clients must have their money's-worth. No matter how many countries a group was covering, no matter if it was of religious orientation or not, Jerusalem must be the highlight of their tour. No single client must be disappointed, however much he might have expected. Everyone must be made to feel welcome, and they must join the Arab family by breaking bread and eating salt with the people of the country. And they must leave the Holy Land with a gift or memento.

That first year he insisted that all our clients should be entertained in our house. His family did the cooking, sometimes with the help of Mrs. Morad Barsom and others from Bethlehem, and course after course was served to the minister and his flock.

In July Dr. Bauman brought a group of fifty from Washington, and Gabriel, wishing to make this a special occasion, invited thirty-three Palestinian and foreign residents of Jerusalem to join them at dinner at our house. The number was brought up to eighty-four by Basil Guy, who was in the city with another agency leading a group from his diocese.

We borrowed small tables and chairs from a friendly hotel and put them on the patio, in the central hall and in three of the four rooms. We had let some of the furniture go with the family when they moved, and as we had not then replaced it, there was enough space. And the family cooked a mammoth amount of food.

Gabriel twisted his leg when going down Lazarus' Tomb with this group, and afterwards he affected an unusual walking-stick to give him support. It was made in Bethlehem of an olive-wood branch and it had the stumps of smaller branches growing from its sides. Wielding this, he was limping histrionically when he brought the group to dinner. They were younger and livelier group than the average, and there was a great deal of banter between them and Gabriel.

He made them a speech of welcome:

'We say "*Ahlan wa sahlan*" "welcome". This is your second home.

All your lives you have heard about Jerusalem and Bethlehem, Jericho and Samaria. You have grown up with the knowledge of them. Now you are here, and I don't want you just to cross us off the list and say, "We've done the Holy Land". I want it to live with you more vividly day by day. And this is how we will become one in spirit, because you will be thinking of the people as well as the places. And we shall be thinking of you too.

'The purpose of our coming here tonight is to break bread and eat salt together. Then we shall be one family. We can trace this custom back to the days of Abraham. When he pitched his tent under the oak at Mamre, which you have seen near Hebron, three strangers came to him. Without enquiring who they were, he slaughtered a lamb and asked his wife Sarah to prepare them a meal, as I asked my wife Delia to prepare you dinner today. Only when they had eaten the meal did he discover that they were not strangers but angels, and they gave him three blessings.

'I should say that many of those here tonight are well-known to me already. I have guided Dr. Bauman for many years now, and I was on his television programme in Washington last October. Some of his group have been with him on previous tours: the others have been with us for a week now as we covered the country from north to south and from west to east. Then we have with us many good friends who are residents of Jerusalem: some are Palestinians native to this country; some are from abroad and they are working for UNRWA, the Anglican Cathedral, the American Friends of the Middle East or other organisations that give valuable help to the people here. I will introduce them to you individually later. And we are very honoured to have as our guest Bishop Guy, Bishop of Bedford, who is a relative of my wife's. I will ask him to say grace and then we can begin.'

I think Basil had expected to remain incognito and he was not wearing the purple, which had disappointed Gabriel greatly. However, he said grace and then retreated to the table he was sharing with a canon and his wife from St. George's. Gabriel and I circulated throughout the evening, first serving the food and drink, and then talking to our guests. Gabriel gave each of them a present - a five-pointed star on a mother-of-pearl pendant, or cufflinks - and then they took their leave.

When Basil came to say goodbye, Gabriel on an impulse took the walking-stick from the crook of his arm and offered it to him.

'I don't need this any more,' he said.

'What about your knee?' asked Basil.

'It's cured,' said Gabriel. 'Look' he walked a few steps without limping, and came back holding the stick out horizontally in two hands. 'I should like you to have it. It was made in Bethlehem of olive-wood.'

'Well, thank you very much,' said Basil, taking it. 'And thank you for an interesting evening. Goodbye, Delia. I'll tell your parents I saw you. Goodnight,' and he went down the path to the taxi that was waiting for him.

1. Delia and Belinda with Mark when he graduated from Oxford.
2. Simon.
3. Gabriel in the office.
4. Belinda at Birmingham University.
5. Delia.

CHAPTER ELEVEN

The Guiding Star in the Ascendant

OUR business grew rapidly after that first year, and many of our guests turned out to be indeed angels. By what Gabriel called 'mouth-to-mouth advertisement', the name of the Guiding Star spread amongst the American public and the travel world.

We once had a very well-to-do widow called Mrs. Lambrose and her forty-year-old son George as our clients, and they were delighted with their tour. 'You may be sure we will recommend your agency,' were her parting words after dinner at our house.

They decided to come again the following year, and they used a different agent, Flying Mercury of New York. When Mrs. Lambrose went to see them to confirm the arrangements, she mentioned in passing, 'I am sure you use the best agent in Jordan.' 'Well, I hope so, madam,' said the manager a little nervously. 'We use ＿＿＿＿＿.' 'Then cancel our bookings. I will go with no one but the Guiding Star.' Not wishing to lose such a well-heeled and forceful client, the man said he would use our services for their tour. Still not satisfied, Mrs. Lambrose said bluntly, 'You should send them all your business,' and she was able to pressure them into doing so.

The way we started to work with another New York travel agency,

Grand Circle Tours, was very providential. Two ladies came on a preliminary tour to Lebanon and Jordan, and Gabriel happened to be on the same plane from Beirut to Jerusalem. They were a plump, ebullient Italian girl called 'Lucky' Cantoni who was a Grand Circle employee, and a charming elderly American lady called Mrs. Lana who was the travel co-ordinator for an association of retired people which toured with Grand Circle.

Gabriel, to whom no-one was a stranger, entered into conversation with them on the plane, and when they landed in Jerusalem he helped them through customs and took them to their hotel. As no plans had been made for them, he and Mousa between them showed them the country.

The first group of retired people had already been booked for a tour of Lebanon and Jordan with a Beirut agency. But when this group was in Lebanon, Gabriel received a call from the Grand Circle office asking him to come to its rescue when it arrived in Jerusalem. It had been stranded in Beirut because the agent was in financial straits and no-one would honour his bookings. Gabriel reserved a hotel for them, met the plane and conducted the tour. Grand Circle had already paid their man for both Lebanon and Jordan, and they asked Gabriel to collect the money from him. He never succeeded in doing so: the man was broke and litigation offered no guarantee of success. We therefore paid over a thousand dollars from our pocket for this tour, but it was the beginning of a happy association with this company which sent us thousands of retired Americans over the years - even though we once nearly asphyxiated their vice-president.

This was George Subo who came over for two days to see the country and our handling of one of their groups. Gabriel drove him round Jerusalem and Bethlehem in the Vauxhall we had by then, and he wondered why George seemed to like to have his head out of the window the whole time. After he left, he discovered the reason. When one of our guides called Joseph Asad took the front passenger seat, he leapt out again saying, 'There's a terrible smell here. I think it's coming from under the seat.' They looked and found there a large fish that had been left behind when we bought fish by the River Jordan six days before.

The Billy Graham Association sent a tour to Jordan in 1962 under the leadership of T.W. Wilson. They were booked with another agent I shall call Isam. Gabriel heard from a friendly taxi-driver that T.W. was eager to see him but the Isams were trying to prevent him doing so. Gabriel went to look for him at his hotel, which was owned by a Haj or 'holy man', that is, one who had been to Mecca. He had previously had a chick-pea stall on the site of the hotel, but this did not stop him resenting others who were rising from humble beginnings, and he was firmly in the Isams' camp. His people tried to refuse Gabriel entry, but Gabriel pushed past them, seething with anger, to the dining-room where he found T.W. having dinner. There was an affecting reunion. 'Where have you been?' asked T.W. 'I kept asking for you but they said you were out of town.' 'They did not want me to see you. The hotel people tried to stop me coming in.' And he pointed out the Haj and one of the Isams glowering at them from the door of the dining-room. The man sitting next to T.W. heard this exchange and said, 'You mean they tried to stop you coming here to see your friend T.W.? Let me speak to them.'

They were called over, and this group member, who was apparently very rich, faced the Haj and demanded an explanation. 'You did not want this man to meet his friend Dr. Wilson?' The Haj said: 'Dr. Wilson is the Isams' client, and this man is their competitor. I was protecting their interests.' 'If it is not enough that we are paying for our stay here,' said the American, 'tell me how much you want for your hotel and I am ready to buy it,' and he produce a cheque-book from his hip-pocket as his forebears might have produced a gun.

The Haj started to beat a retreat when he saw Gabriel had money on his side. 'Of course that is not necessary. Enjoy your evening together,' and he left them taking the reluctant Isam with him.

The result of this confrontation was that the Isams lost the Billy Graham business to the Guiding Star.

We took the tours sponsored by Biola College in California because of a chance contact, and we gained a Lutheran agent in Missouri through a minister Gabriel had guided. There was another minister

from the Church of Christ who brought a group to Gabriel every year
from 1953; and various Baptist ministers brought us groups, including
one who was nearly washed away when he tried to baptise some of
his flock in the River Jordan. When they saw his success, Gabriel's
enemies accused him of being all things to all people - a Baptist to
the Baptists, Lutheran to the Lutherans, Catholic to the Catholics.
In fact, he had a very broad ecumenical view of Christianity, and he
did not share any one denomination's prejudices against the others. If
we had had to rely on his Syrian Orthodox connection to help us, we
would not have had one client. And I can say almost the same about
my Anglican connection. We built up an excellent business among English secular agents - Wings, Cadogan Travel, Harold Ingham, Express
Travel, Hickie Borman and Houlder Brothers - but though we knew
some of the bishops and clergy who led Anglican pilgrimages, we did
not handle any of them.

It would not have been difficult to tell the Baptists he was a Baptist or the Catholics he was a Catholic; but though he did not do that,
Gabriel achieved something much more difficult: when we had a group
of American freemasons he was accepted by them as a freemason. His
handshake seemed to give the right signal, and they thought he was
one of them and started knocking him on the back and performing
other mysterious antics. One of them whispered to him, 'Won't it be
wonderful when the Kingdom of David comes again?' He knew something of their traditions and their connections with Solomon's Temple
- Solomon's masons were free and were united in a bond of brotherhood to help each other and serve God - and had prepared for each
of the group a box of masonic symbols: the gavel and hammer, the
book (that is, the Bible) and the keystone, all carved in stone from
Solomon's Quarries and enclosed in an olive-wood box.

The same agency also sent us a hundred and seventy-five freneti-
cally purposeful ladies from the General Federation of Women's Clubs,
intent on meeting their counterparts in Jordan on a 'person-to-person,
people-to-people' basis. They were given hospitality by the Women's
Unions of Jerusalem and Bethlehem, and returned to America with a
new idea of Arab women.

In 1963 we had a group from the American Bar Association who were returning from a convention in the Far East. Gabriel met them in Beirut where we now had our own office, and one of the lawyers, a Mr. Levy, came up and said he and his wife were going to Cyprus instead of Jordan.

'Why?' asked Gabriel. 'Jordan is more interesting.'

'Well, we understand those of the Jewish faith may not enter Jordan.'

'Don't worry,' said Gabriel. 'I'll get you in.'

He did so, and when later on he was the guest of the Levys on a visit to America, Mr.Levy told him they had been treated as well on the Jordan side as in Israel, and he felt Gabriel made quite a contribution to international understanding in the work he was doing.

In 1966 we received a group of forty-five members of the National Newspaper Association, and Gabriel thought this would be a good opportunity to bring to their notice some of the anomalies of the political situation. He arranged for them to meet King Hussein in Amman, but the King only shook hands with them and then he had to go to another engagement. Gabriel took them to Beit Safafa so that they could see the barbed wire down the middle of the village street.

It was about this time that an Egyptian magazine had a unique series of photographs of a wedding that took place on either side of the barbed wire, the bride in Israel and the groom in Jordan. They could not speak to each other, because anyone communicating through the wire, whether caught by the Israelis or their fellow-Arabs, was accused of spying. Only when the girl was married could she cross through the Mandelbaum Gate into Jordan to join her husband.

An officer from the army post took it upon himself to address the journalists, but instead of telling them how the 1949 truce had affected the lives of the villagers, he puffed out his chest, tucked his swagger-cane under his armpit and launched into a technical exposition about degrees of elevation.

Gabriel interrupted: 'Sir, these are journalists, not military strategists. Can't you tell them how the village was divided so that the Israelis could have the railway and how father is now separated from son?'

A man from the Ministry of Information was with the group, and he came up to Gabriel, took his arm and drew him on one side.

'I don't think we should go into such sensitive matters. Let us just stick to the military aspect.'

But a journalist who was standing nearby heard and understood, for he was of Lebanese origin and spoke Arabic.

'Gabriel is right,' he said. 'People should know about these things. Too little is known in the western world about the situation here.'

Some of his colleagues came up to the Lebanese and asked him the subject of the argument, and a general conversation followed in which Gabriel was able to put across some of the points he wanted to make.

On their departure from Jordan the group was to cross into Israel by the Mandelbaum Gate, which was about two hundred yards north of the Damascus Gate. Quite a mythology had grown up about this crossing-point. There were actually two barriers, one on the Jordanian side and one on the Israeli, with thirty yards of no-man's-land in between. People heard that they would be covered by the guns of soldiers on both sides as they crossed, and they would have to carry their luggage through no-man's-land because the Jordanians and Israelis could not approach each other without a conflagration. The reality was that they walked peacefully from one barrier to the other with porters carrying their luggage, and Gabriel and some of the Jordanian officials used to accompany them right to the Israeli side. Gabriel always made a farewell speech that sent some of our clients into Israel weeping:

'As you go over to the other side of this divided city, I want you to stop a moment to pray for the peace of Jerusalem. The psalm says, "They shall prosper that love thee. Peace be within thy walls and plenteousness within they palaces." But it also says, "Jerusalem is built as a unity in itself." We want to see Jerusalem in peace, not in pieces.

'Whatever you may hear on the other side, don't forget that there are people on the Arab side who can look across at their homes but cannot reach them, and there are many who have not seen their homes for eighteen years. Goodbye and God be with you.'

This was how he parted from the Levys and the other lawyers and their wives, and how he bade farewell to the journalists. There was - of course - quite a delegation on the Israeli side to receive the journalists, and some of them asked who Gabriel was. One of the Jordanian police told them, 'This is Gabriel Khano of the Guiding Star Agency.' 'Oh yes,' said one of the Israeli officials when the answer was reported to him. 'I know about him. He's the son of a bastard.' He spoke in Hebrew but Gabriel understood because he had known Hebrew before 1948. He started to retreat to the Jordanian side in case he should be kidnapped and put away where he could not make such subversive speeches.

'Goodbye,' said the journalists, 'and thank you.' And they walked off into looking-glass land.

With tedious regularity all the old ladies of the Grand Circle tours would come up to me at the farewell dinner, shake me by the hand and say, 'I *so* enjoyed your husband.' After the agency's second year, before I had thought of a suitable reply to this remark - though I could think of plenty of *un*suitable replies - Gabriel started to give most of the guiding to other guides, so that he only took over if there was an important group, and we acquired a fine team of guides, many of whom had been trained by Gabriel. I had expected a dwindling of our clients' enthusiasm when Gabriel no longer guided them himself, but this did not happen. Not only were our guides so good that no-one could imagine that there could be better, but also Gabriel's speech of welcome on their arrival and his presentation of the farewell dinner translated their tour on to a different plane from any other they had ever experienced.

Arriving at Jerusalem airport under the auspices of the Guiding Star was unlike arriving at any other airport in the world. Gabriel met the plane on the tarmac, and if it was a very special tour, he would present the tour leader's wife with what he called a 'banquet' of flowers. The leader, acting on previous instructions, gave Gabriel the tour members' passports which he had collected. The group then walked straight through immigration and customs without pausing, and boarded the taxis which were waiting at the door. In a few minutes their luggage followed, and Gabriel with the stamped passports.

The favourable first impression of Jordan gained by this smooth arrival was confirmed by the sympathetic friendliness of guides, taxi-drivers, hotel staff, shopkeepers (though here we had to be selective), and the local guests we invited to the farewell dinners. 'Let us build this country and serve this nation,' King Hussein constantly urged his subjects in Arabic and English; and we had the exciting feeling of belonging to a small, rapidly-developing country to which we were making quite an important contribution.

We could not take our tourists to Galilee because that was in Israel, but we could take them up the Jerusalem-Nazareth road as far as Samaria. It was a beautiful drive, and rich in biblical history. I often joined the tours when Gabriel was guiding. He would stop the cars to point out Nob where David defied the Law and ate the shewbread of the Temple; the hill of Gibeah where Saul had his palace; facing it the commanding site of Nabi Samuel or Mountjoy; Rama where Samuel was born, and where the voice of Rachel was heard 'weeping for her generation which was not'; Mizpah ('observance'), where Jacob and Laban set up the stone of benediction: 'May God watch between thee and me when we are separated from one another'; and Beeroth, where the tourists liked to photograph the village women at the well. It was probably here that travellers returning to Galilee after the big festivals at the Temple stopped to draw water as the sun was setting, for it was 'a day's journey' from Jerusalem. Here Joseph and Mary found that the twelve-year-old Jesus was missing and had to go back to the Temple to find him. Jesus had probably had there his Bar Mitzvah that introduced him to adult life with its religious obligations. Gabriel told us that in those days the women and children walked on one side of the road and the men on the other. At twelve Jesus had reached the age when he could be with either men or women; and Joseph may have thought he was still with the women, while Mary thought that he had joined the men. Only when they all met together at the well did they realise that he was not there at all.

Continuing north along the ancient Road of the Patriarchs, one saw Bethel and Shiloh in the distance, and then came to the point where the road wound steeply down into the Plains of the Dancers. Here the men of the tribe of Benjamin, because the Israelites had sworn not to give them their daughters, lay in wait in the vineyards for the daughters of Shiloh. When they came there to dance at an annual festival, the Benjamites fell on them and each one carried off a girl to be his wife.

The plain was a wonderful sight when we went there once in spring-time; the wheat was an unbelievable vivid green which set off the rich purple and red dresses of the women in the fields; men returned from the market in rickety mule-carts; donkeys ambled past with a boy or two on their backs; children waved; there was an aura of timelessness: God and man were at one.

We were in Samaria. The Jews of biblical times despised and hated the Samaritans since they were of mixed descent from Jews who had intermarried with colonists brought there by their Assyrian conquerors; and there were certain important differences in their religious beliefs: the Samaritans recognised only the first five books of the Bible, the Pentateuch, and they had their temple on Mount Gerizim above Shechem, while the Jews held that the only site for the temple was Mount Moriah in Jerusalem. Though Samaria was predominantly Moslem now, there were some of the Samaritan sect still living in present-day Nablus at the foot of Gerizim, and they celebrated the week of Passover on the top of the hill, the high-place where their temple once stood. The Jews stopped making sacrifices when Herod's Temple was destroyed by Titus in 70 A.D., but the Samaritans still sacrifice a passover lamb to this day. In Jesus' time the Jews would either bypass Samaria on their way north or go through it at night so as not to encounter the people; but the fourth chapter of St. John's gospel tells how Jesus entered Samaria in daylight and arrived at Jacob's Well at noon, parched with thirst.

We did the same thing, and before Gabriel started on his exposition, he lowered the bucket from the well-head and brought up the clear, cold water from a hundred and ten feet below for us to drink. Then he skipped briefly over the less savoury elements of the Old Testament references to Shechem and came to the account of Jesus' visit to the Well.

'The authenticity of this site had never been called in question: this was the well Jacob dug on the parcel of land he bought for a hundred sheep; and after massacring the men of Shechem by a trick, he and his sons were able to control this important point on the north-south caravan-route.

'We learn from St. John that when Jesus came here he found a Samaritan woman drawing water and he asked her to give him some of it to drink. She was very surprised at his speaking to her and said so: not only was he a man and she a woman unknown to him, but also he was a Jew and she a Samaritan. He told her that if she knew who he was she would ask him for living water that she might never thirst again; and as for the old dispute about the site of the Temple, true worshippers would one day worship neither on Gerizim nor in Jerusalem, but in spirit and in truth. He then told her that she had had five husbands and her present man was not her husband.

'The woman was amazed that he seemed to know all about her and went back to her village - Sychar, which means "drunkenness" - and told her people about this unusual man. She believed he might be the Christ. The people came to the well to see him, and he stayed with them for two days.

'Jesus did not need to be divine to know the woman had a bad reputation: he could tell this because she came to the well at noon instead of evening when the other women would come. But he was unique among the Jews in mixing with the Samaritans, and later when he told the Parable of the Good Samaritan, it was like a present-day Jew telling his people about a charitable Arab.'

The Greek priest who was in charge of the Well was an old friend of Gabriel's, and Gabriel had told me what a hard drinker he was; but when he invited us to his lodgings one very hot summer day when I was eight months pregnant, I was not prepared for his incredulous amusement that I should refuse a glass of neat whisky. He assumed because I refused this tempting offer that I could not possibly want anything, and I had to face further amusement and incredulity when I plucked up courage to ask for a glass of water.

From the Well we drove into Nablus to visit the Samaritan community, the smallest sect in the world. There were two hundred and seventy-five of them there and a hundred and twenty-five in Holon in Israel. It was said the total number never varied from four hundred: if a Samaritan baby was born, another Samaritan died. There was no intermarriage with the Arabs or Jews, and they were very inbred. Some of them worked in government offices, but their main means of support was the tourist fees and charity. They never missed an opportunity to tell their visitors that they were going to build a community school, but though contribution were sometimes forthcoming there was still no school. Here, as often, Gabriel was torn between loyalty to his fellow-countrymen and the flock he was temporarily responsible for - sometimes backing the Samaritans in their appeal and sometimes telling his tourists that they were nothing but professional beggars.

The three high priests and two younger priests received us at the door of their Synagogue and took us in to show us their ancient copy of the Pentateuch, the five books of the Mosaic Law. Each of the high priests had a different key and no-one could enter the synagogue without the three keys. The three of them represented the three tribes: Manasseh, Ephraim and Joseph. Sadakah, the chief high priest, produced the ancient scroll and unrolled it with care. We looked at it with a reverence which was only slightly impaired when we noticed that some torn pages had been stuck with sellotape. Sadakah told us it dated from a few years after the time Moses received the Tablets of the Law on Mount Sinai, but Gabriel told us afterwards it might be four hundred years old, not more.

One of the younger priests was Sadakah's son, Selloum, and I was very struck by his resemblance to Gabriel. As with Gabriel, the eyes were the most striking feature, but while Gabriel's were limpid and bright, Selloum's were opaque and strained. His were the eyes of a sick man, one poised on the narrow borderline between brilliant intelligence and insanity. These segregated, inbred people could see beyond the ordinary limits, but they were not masters of their destiny.

Gabriel's friendship with the Samaritans - and he seemed to exercise quite a fascination on Selloum - survived one rather bizarre episode before we married. It was when he took some tourists up to Mount Gerizim for the last day of Passover. The whole community camped on the hill-top for the week of the Festival, and that day the celebration was to reach a climax with the offering of the burnt sacrifice.

While the tourists mingled with the crowd of people who had gathered to see the annual event, Gabriel went into one of the tents to have a brief rest. A delicious smell wafted over to him. It was the sacrifice: a tender young lamb roasted to a turn was there resting on a low table till a later stage in the ceremony. The temptation was irresistible. He looked under the flap of the tent and attracted the attention of one of the drivers. 'Here, take this' - he handed him a succulent piece of flesh - 'and tell the others.'

The drivers collected by the side of the tent, and Gabriel passed the meat out between mouthfuls, till there was nothing left but a few bones.

They had only just finished when Sadakah and some attendants came to take the lamb. When he saw the sad remains, he was horrified. Gabriel had lain down on one of the mattresses at his approach and was pretending to be asleep. Sadakah shook him and asked what was the meaning of this sacrilege.

'What sacrilege?' asked Gabriel, wide-eyed and innocent.

'This,' said Sadakah, pointing to the bones.

'Well,' said Gabriel, 'I was asleep of course, but I think an angel must have come down and taken the sacrifice up to heaven.'

There was no answer to that, and though the priests were thrown into great agitation and realised quite well what must have happened, they thought no worse of Gabriel. He had just proved himself smarter than they that time.

Sadakah had his office as administrator of the community in a small room by the gate of their precinct in the town, and beyond it was another small room. Here he exercised his talent for fortune telling and magic, and Gabriel once came here with a young man who thought his wife was a victim of the evil eye. She was in hospital suffering from a mental disorder.

When Sadakah learned their business, he took them into the inner

room, spread a cloth on the table and tipped some sand on to it from
a sack. He smoothed it and drew patterns on it, studied it and told
them his conclusions: someone wished the marriage to fail and had
cast a spell on the wife in order to separate the couple. To undo the
spell he needed certain things of the wife's and he told the husband to
come back another day bringing them.

They duly returned with a shoe, a handkerchief and a hair, and
these Sadakah put on a sieve together with some salt, an onion and
some incense. Then he brought a bowl of water and some lead. Melting
the lead, he poured it into the bowl and watched as the lead hissed
and hardened into weird shapes in the cold water.

He prescribed three things to cure the girl. First he gave the husband a little bag containing some powder and a piece of paper with
writing on it. This was known as the 'hijab' and was supposed to
keep off the evil magic if the girl carried it with her. Secondly the
husband was to throw some water on the ground when she returned
from hospital, so that she had to step over it when she first entered
the house. Finally he should bring her to Sadakah and he would give
her a love-potion to cement the marriage.

The girl recovered and the marriage survived, but whether from
the efficacy of the counter-spell I do not know.

Gabriel had many Moslem friends, and he respected the basic
tenets of the Islamic religion, pointing out that it was a synthesis
of Judaism and Christianity. For Mohammed had as his mentors the
Arabian Jews on the one hand, and on the other Buheira, an Assyrian
priest he came to know in Basra. All three religions worshipped the
same God - 'Allah' to Arabs, both Christian and Moslem, and for that
matter to Arabic-speaking Jews. For both Jews and Moslems the meat
of the pig was unclean, because their religions originated in the desert
where it was common-sense not to eat pork - at least until the advent
of the refrigerator. But Islam did not name its adherents as chosen of
God: the emphasis was on its followers' submission to God rather than
their special status; and they regarded Jesus as a prophet - unlike the
Jews who, having been much persecuted in his name, never arrived
at any objective assessment of his importance. The main difference

between Moslems and Christians in the East was in the attitude to marriage ties, but even in this the educated Moslem was not very far from his Christian fellow-countryman.

Gabriel often used to listen to the broadcasts of a certain famous *sheikh* (religious leader in this case, not tribal chief) reading the Koran; he could, when he chose, speak the pure classical Arabic of the Koran; and when he was in the West, where few people knew there was such a thing as a Christian Arab, he sometimes felt closer to the Moslems than to his fellow-Christians.

When he came to England on one occasion to do some business, he brought a beautiful Bokhara rug as a present for my sister. It had not cost him a great deal because he had bought it from an Iranian '*haj*' or pilgrim on his way back from Mecca. On his arrival in the customs-hall of London airport, a stiff-looking customs officer handed him the sheet of paper listing dutiable articles, and glancing at it Gabriel said he had nothing to declare. The man opened his suitcase, and the first thing he saw was the rug on the top. As he lifted it out with raised eyebrows, Gabriel looked at his watch.

'Excuse me!' he said, taking the rug. 'It is my time for prayer. Can you tell me which is south-east?'

'What are you doing?' asked the officer, horrified. 'You can't pray here!' but Gabriel had already laid the rug on the floor and was starting to take off his shoes.

The officer could not get rid of him quickly enough.

'Here, take your suitcase and go and pray over there,' he said, pointing to a far corner.

'No, I'll pray here,' said Gabriel.

'Over there, I say,' the man told him angrily, and Gabriel picked up the rug in one hand and the suitcase in the other, and made off for the gate where my father was waiting for him.

By May 1967 we were feeling the worst of our struggles were over: we had two sons and a daughter, Simon, Mark and Belinda, and the Guiding Star was at its zenith, giving us the best clientele in Jerusalem. Cadogan Travel was sending us groups from the National Trust and National Art Collections Fund, whose passenger-lists were liable to

include names like the Duke of Wellington; and that spring we were
using a hundred and fifty of the two hundred rooms of the most ex-
pensive hotel, the Intercontinental. Rival agents were left far behind,
and our business was the envy of the town.

But soon after the middle of May the rumblings of war were distinctly to be heard: Egypt blockaded the Straits of Tiran and there was
a build-up of arms and hectic diplomatic activity throughout the mid-
East; and though none of us really thought this would affect Jerusalem,
Gabriel sent Victoria, me and the children out to Beirut on the twenty-
fifth of the month. Four days later he left with the last of the tourists
and joined us in a bungalow complex by the sea. We were there when
War broke out with Israel's demolishing of the Egyptian air force, and
after a brief conflict that involved Egypt, Syria and Jordan, we were
faced on June 11th with the realisation that yet another conqueror
had taken Jerusalem and six days of war had left our house and business in Occupied Territory. Gabriel's eventful life had entered another
dramatic and difficult phase, and this time I was involved too.

CHAPTER TWELVE

The Defeat

THE Six Day War proved Nasser's big drum to be utterly hollow; and though the Jordanian army was often referred to as a 'crack' army, the Israelis had no difficulty in finishing it in a few days; while even the Syrians, perched on the Golan Heights, did not hold their ground but retreated before the Israeli advance. Sinai and the Gaza Strip were taken from Egypt, the Golan Heights from Syria, and what remained to the Arabs of Palestine - that is the West Bank - was taken from Jordan.

The division between Palestinian and Transjordanian - which had by no means disappeared during the nineteen years of their union under the Hashemite reign - was carved deeper by the War, and subsequent events did nothing to bind them together. The Jordanian government's earlier tendency to encourage investment on the East rather than the West Bank was now viewed as a deep-laid plot, and the Palestinians thought they had made no very serious effort to keep Palestine.

There was a man who decided to leave for the East Bank after the War, and he tried to take some of his furniture with him over the bridge across the River Jordan.

'What are you doing?' asked the Jordanian guards. 'You can't bring that stuff over here.'

'You mean to say you sold them the West Bank *furnished?*' asked the exasperated evacuee.

Gabriel was quite convinced that the main part of the Jordanian army left the West Bank for Amman the day before the War broke out.

'The headquarters was at Bethel, and the commander used to keep a special flock of milking goats there, because he could not start the day until he had had a glass of their milk mixed with the raw yolk of an egg and a spoonful of pure honey. Then he was ready for whatever demands the next twenty-four hours might make on him.' He made a sweeping downward gesticulation to illustrate the utter hopelessness of the Palestinian lot: 'Even his goats were evacuated,' he said.

A set-piece of his which seemed to sum up the whole tragi-comedy of the Jordanian attempts to defend their country was his account of his experience in the National Guard.

In six months of 'training' in 1954, he never touched a gun but learned only to march in step, to stand smartly to attention and to salute his superiors with the maximum of ceremony. Some months after he finished his training, the Israelis attacked Jordan a few miles west of Bethlehem at Battir. There had been some infiltration of individual Palestinians through the Israeli lines to steal from the kibbutzim or to collect valuables they had left buried in their gardens or orchards, and the Israeli army had arrived to mete out punishment. An urgent knocking awoke the Khano household in Bethlehem. Um-Jabra ran from the high vaulted room where they slept to open the door. A man stood there.

'Does Yousef Jabra Khano live here?'

'Yes.'

'He must come with me. There has been an enemy invasion.'

'Oh no!' cried him mother. 'Please don't take him! He is the eldest son and the only one working. Let someone else go in his place.'

'No. He must come immediately.'

Um-Jabra ran to tell Gabriel, and he dressed hurriedly in some old clothes (they had no uniform) and went with the messenger to the police-station. His family, now all awake, sat up the rest of the night trembling with fear and praying for his safety.

At the police-station a group of green-looking young men had gathered, and an officer proceeded to equip each of them with a gun of 1918 vintage and a cloth belt stuck with bullets. They were told that they must bring back the empty shell of each bullet they fired. They were then bundled into the back of a lorry and driven off to where the enemy was making an uninterrupted foray into Jordanian territory. When the lorry stopped, they were turned out into the darkness and told to range themselves over the uneven terraced land and stop the Israeli advance.

Gabriel crouched behind a terrace-wall. He could hear the groaning of tanks approaching them, and presently he heard a shot and the rat-tat-rat of automatic fire replying to it. He unlocked his gun and struggled to extract a bullet from the stiff belt. The groaning of the tanks grew louder, and there was a rumbling sound as a terrace-wall collapsed. There was more firing and a loud cry 'ah-ah-ah-ah!' fading away to nothing as one of his fellows was shot. Then came the deafening noise of mortar-fire. More terraces collapsed, more shots rang out, more automatic fire replied. Gabriel had only just managed to get the bullet out of the belt and was trying with trembling fingers to insert it in the gun. Then a cry went up to heaven, '*Hut moyeh! Hut moyeh!*'

'Bring water?' said Gabriel to himself. 'What do they want with water?' Perhaps for a wounded comrade, he thought, and he edged along to where he had heard a shot fired nearby.

'What do they want water for?' he shouted to his neighbour above the din.

'To cool the guns' was the reply. 'Look how hot mine is after firing a few shots. If there was some water, I could wet my handkerchief and cool the gun with it. As it is, I must wait till it cools down - otherwise it will spit sideways.'

By now the tanks were quite close. 'I'm going,' said Gabriel. 'What about you?'

They moved away obliquely from the line of the tanks' advance, and clutching their weapons ran as fast as they could until the sinister groaning and the gunfire were only heard faintly in the distance.

'How many shots did you fire?' asked Gabriel's companion when they had regained their breath.

'None,' said Gabriel.

'Well, you'd better fire some, so that you can produce the empty shells.'

'All right,' said Gabriel, and with help he managed to load the gun. He held it up to his chest.

'Mind out!' said the other.

'What's the matter?'

'Don't hold it like that. You have to watch out for the kick-back. Look, hold it tight against your shoulder like this. Now!'

There was a crack and Gabriel staggered backwards. He had fired his first shot since the revolver exploded in his hand in 1947. He grovelled on the ground to find the empty shell, stuffed it back in the belt, and repeated the struggle to extract the next bullet.

The Israelis destroyed the police-post at Husan, blew up some cottages and advanced as far as Solomon's Pools before retiring without so much as a scratch on their paintwork. The Jordanian unit from the post at Kfar Etzion arrived when everything was over.

Jordan had four hundred and eighty kilometres of frontier with Israel, and this was how she was equipped to defend it. Whenever after the Six-Day War there was some mention of the Arabs' belligerence, I would say to Gabriel or anyone else who was in the private joke, '*Hut moyeh! - Hut moyeh!*' 'Bring water!'

In November 1966 Israel made an entirely unprovoked attack on the little village of Samua. Much of the village was destroyed and many were killed, while the Jordanian soldiers who might have repelled the attack were lost in the wilds of Judaea, having taken a wrong turning in Bethlehem.

For several weeks after this incident, Palestinians demonstrated in the West Bank asking to be trained and armed in order to defend their country. The demonstrations were put down with some harshness and King Hussein's only conciliatory action was to collect a few more young men for National Guard training.

When Gabriel was in the shop of Elias Morad the tailor some months after the 1967 War, he noticed that one of the young men who worked for him was acting very strangely. He kept running down from the upper storey of the shop, muttering 'Shoot! Shoot! You'd better run. Run! Run!' He asked Elias about him and heard his story.

He had been one of the young men trained for six months after Samua, and when the War broke out he was sent to Tulkarem by the northern border with Israel. His situation was much like Gabriel's in 1954. The Israeli tanks were advancing, and though there was some shelling from Jordanian artillery, the shells had no effect at all on their advance and sometimes fell short on their own defence lines. The National Guard with their ancient guns had even less effect on the approaching monsters; and when the officer in charge saw that they were achieving nothing, he told them that they might as well run away and save their skins. George, the tailor's boy, and some others fled south as far as Jacob's Well, and there they asked for sanctuary.

There was a new custodian since the days of the whisky-addict: a very fine upstanding young priest who had made great improvements in the precinct which enclosed the Well. He took the fugitives in, dressed them in monks' habits and set them to do tasks about the grounds: drawing water, feeding the chickens and tending the garden.

When the Israelis came, they were suspicious to see so many young monks, but the priest assured them these were novices he was training to take care of the holy places.

The experience upset George's mental balance, and he could not settle again to his work in Elias' shop. By some means he managed to gain entry to Britain, and as far as we know he is still there.

The people of Palestine still vividly remembered what they had heard about young men in Gaza being taken off by the Israelis and shot at the time of the Suez War, and many of them were terrified when the Israeli troops came to their houses on the second day of the 1967 War.

Zacha'ar, the young man whom Gabriel referred to as the 'Transport Officer' for the agency, as he supplied us with taxis, was one of these. He hid under his bed when the Israelis arrived at his father's house in the Wadi Jos, and when they found him there he came out shaking with fear.

His father pleaded with them: 'He's my only son. Please don't take him away!' and Zacha'ar took up the same theme. Edging away from the soldiers' guns and crossing one leg over the other, he held up his first finger and twisted it to and fro to show the solitariness of his filial status. 'The only one,' he said pathetically. 'The only one.' But they took him to the driveway of the Palestine Museum where he found many other young male civilians from the area and he was nearly killed by a Jordanian shell fired from the army-post near the Augusta Victoria. They were taken to the Russian Compound where they were questioned; and then for two days they were driven around Israel in lorries so that the Israelis could insult them and exult in their defeat.

The driver Ata, who took us to Petra, also lived in the Wadi Jos in a small house which he shared with his brother's family. He was in his vest and his specially-constructed underpants when the knock came on the door. His sister-in-law went to answer it and came to Ata saying, 'There are some soldiers to see you.' She assumed they were Iraqi soldiers and so did Ata.

Very much master of the household, he strode, or perhaps I should say waddled, to the door. *'Aish bidcum?* What do you want?' he asked them with an imperious gesture.

They replied in Hebrew, and Ata bolted back into the house quivering in every ample limb.

'Why did you send *me* to the door and not your husband?' he asked his sister-in-law, his voice squeaky with terror.

Without being invited, the soldiers entered the house and started searching around to see if there were any more dangerous-looking males than Ata.

Ata tried a few words of Hebrew on them.

'You speak English?' they asked, unimpressed.

'*Leetle*,' said Ata, bunching his fingers together as if he was demonstrating the smallness of some fruit such as a blackcurrant; and with this promising start, he tried to tell them by signs and an occasional word of a rather international character like 'taxi' and 'chauffeur' that he had nineteen years before been a driver for the big Jewish taxi company, Kesher and Nesher. The soldiers were still not impressed because they had hardly been born then and almost certainly did not live in Palestine at that time; and they left without bothering with Ata or his numerous family further.

One of our guides, Salah Darwish who gave me my peasant name Um-el-Abid, lived near the Palestine Museum, and as he had a semi-basement flat, many of the neighbours had joined his family to shelter from the bombing and shelling. There were no proper shelters in the whole West Bank.

When Israeli soldiers banged on the door and ordered them to open, Salah let them in.

'Hands up!'

Everyone obeyed. Terrified, Salah's children clutched at his trousers as a sergeant led him on a tour of the house.

Seeing several shelves of books in the sitting-room - for Salah was quite well-read on Middle Eastern subjects - the sergeant turned to him.

'Don't you believe that the Messiah will come from Israel?'

Salah looked at the man's gun which was pointing right at him.

'Well, since you ask me - yes, if you like.'

After looking under the beds and in cupboards, the soldiers went to the door. The sergeant warned the people they would not be hurt unless they sheltered some of the Jordanian army.

Before leaving he seemed to think that some other statement was necessary.

'We wouldn't be here if your King Hussein hadn't joined Nasser,' he said.

Only another Palestinian could understand to the full the sardonic bitterness behind Salah's quiet reply. 'He didn't consult me,' he said.

Others were more aggressive in their attitude. There was an Armenian who lived on Ammunition Hill where the Israelis made their entry into Arab Jerusalem, who spent the thirty-one hours of bombing, shelling and shooting in consuming bottle after bottle of *arak*. True to the Bedouins' name for it, 'Tigress' milk', this potent drink turned him into a veritable tiger; and when the Israelis came to his door, he was ready to take them all on with his bare fists.

'Jamalabdulnasher will show you,' he said as they laid hands on him. 'You just wait till he comesh.'

They took him to the Damascus Gate, lined him up with some others and shot them.

No damage was done to the Israeli side of Jerusalem, and though Mount Scopus was shelled for several hours, we could see no sign of damage there and Gabriel was convinced the shells were blanks. On the Arab side the beautiful Crusader Church of St. Anne was damaged, and the top floor of the Augusta Victoria Hospital was completely destroyed. There were some old British Nissen huts next to the hospital, and the Israelis apparently thought this was an important Jordanian army camp. There were a few soldiers there, but many of the huts were used by the Social Welfare. A blind Assyrian couple were bombed out of one, and they came to live next door to us. The husband was a violinist and a very good Aramaic scholar.

In Bethlehem loudspeakers went round warning people that they should leave the town within an hour or it would be destroyed, but those in the centre of the town only left their houses to go and shelter in the churches. Some of those who did try to flee across the hills were bombed with napalm. The bombing and shelling on the town killed two Bethlehemites we knew. One was a young silversmith who was one of the best craftsmen in the country; and the other was a young man of the Cattan family who was married to an American girl. He was protecting their little girl when a shell came and took off the top of his head. One shell fell outside the Syrian Orthodox Church and killed a Moslem, who continued walking into a nearby pharmacy with only half a head, causing the pharmacist to faint. Several shells hit the Church of Nativity but they did not do much damage. Mohammed Audeh, Gabriel's friend of NAAFI days, was killed as he was running with his baby daughter in his arms from his house outside Jerusalem to a nearby cave. The baby survived and was picked up by some people who were fleeing to the East Bank. It was some time before the mother discovered that her daughter was safe in the town of Zerqa, north of Amman.

Another person we knew well who was killed was Suleiman Mattar, who as Warden of the Garden Tomb, had access to the ear of almost every visitor to Jerusalem. For the Garden was the Mecca of every Fundamentalist Protestant. Both Mr. and Mrs. Mattar were well-known and popular in the United States. He was a refugee from Nazareth and occasionally he said so.

The Mattars were sheltering from the shelling in the tomb itself when they heard banging at the garden door. Mr. Mattar went to see who it was and was immediately shot by an Israeli soldier. Whether he had had precise instructions to do this or it was a haphazard killing, we will never know for sure. Mr. Mattar was replaced as caretaker by a Dutchman who for several years made the Garden Tomb his platform for anti-Arab diatribes. Later with others of the same ilk he founded the ill-omened 'Christian Embassy'.

No sooner was a cease-fire set up than Moshe Dayan came in a police jeep to Bethlehem to collect Big Kando and his brother George. He took them to the Hilton Hotel in Tel Aviv and kept them there for two weeks. By the end of that time it was agreed that a scroll they had in their possession should become the property of the Israelis. It came to be known as the Temple Scroll because it dealt with Temple ritual. The Kandos had had it since 1962: it was the scroll that the Bedouin asked me to buy.

During the short duration of the War, while we were by the sea in Lebanon and sharing our anxiety for our relations, friends and property with an American family, Gabriel announced he would have to go to Jordan to fight. I insisted that with his history his first duty could only be to his family, and this hardly included wielding a 1918 gun in the face of Centurion tanks and Mirage bombers.

It was not difficult to convince him that this was so; but with the cease-fire the question was how we were to get back. What had been to us an iron curtain had been pushed forward to encompass more territory, more Palestinian towns and villages, and more Palestinians. Those who were inside wanting to get out were leaving in a steady stream over the River Jordan, but those outside wanting to get in were unable to do so. It looked as if it was going to be 1948 all over again.

1. Gabriel's mother in Jericho.
2. Gabriel and Delia at home.
3. Belinda and Mark Garbett at their wedding.
4. Belinda's children, Lucy and Alexander.

PART III

The Unified City

CHAPTER THIRTEEN

The Return

GABRIEL sent me and the children from Beirut to England on the first available plane, and then he and Victoria tried to return home. They were given no hope by the Red Cross in Beirut; and they got a taxi through Damascus, where people looked stunned and confused, to Amman, where the situation was desperate. Refugees, now seeking refuge for a second time, were sleeping in the streets, while more were arriving daily, sometimes walking bare-foot from the bridge over the Jordan. Most of them came from the camps in Jericho. The hysteria that made them leave was catching, and the Israelis did nothing to calm it; in fact they even provided transport to the Bridge. While Gabriel was there, belated reinforcements from Iraq were wiped out by Israeli planes near Salt.

Gabriel heard that there were to be some forms for people to fill in if they wished to return, but the Israelis wanted to print them in Hebrew and the Jordanians were asking for them to be in Arabic Thinking he might have success in returning from a neutral country and hoping at least to get some news of his family, he went back to Beirut, renewed his passport at the Jordanian Embassy and obtained a visa for Switzerland.

The European headquarters of Grand Circle was in Lucerne, and he went there and was warmly received by Mr. and Mrs. Wendel and other friends we had made in the six years of our co-operation. They told him the New York office had been anxious about us, and they made a telephone call to reassure them of our welfare. They also phoned their Israeli agent in Haifa and the next day received news that the Khano family were all well and unhurt.

They then took Gabriel to see the Israeli Ambassador in Zurich and asked him if he could help Gabriel return to Jerusalem. The answer was negative. 'Tell your King Hussein to come and make peace with us. Then you can go back,' were his parting words.

When they returned to the office in Lucerne, there were two men there, and when Gabriel was introduced as the Director of the Guiding Star Agency in Jerusalem, they looked appalled. Afterwards he was told about the previous conversation.

The men were Israeli travel agents, and like many of their colleagues they had left Israel immediately after the War in order to visit travel offices abroad and take the business of Palestinian agents in East Jerusalem (as it now came to be called). The Grand Circle manager told them they had used Guiding Star for six years without one complaint and they had no reason to change.

'But the Palestinian agents cannot operate now,' one of the two had said. 'They have all closed down and their business will be absorbed by the Israeli agents.'

'Well, I can only tell you that the Guiding Star has always given us excellent service, and until we hear from them that they cannot operate we shall continue to regard them as our agent.' The other Israeli was starting to say, 'They probably bribed the tour conductors to give good reports,' not realising that one of the regular tour conductors was Mrs. Wendel who was also a director of the company - when Gabriel arrived with Mr. and Mrs. Wendel and was introduced.

The Israelis were - to put it mildly - taken aback.

'How did you get here?' one asked.

'By plane,' said Gabriel. 'How did you get here?'

'Well, by plane, but -'

'You came by plane and I came by plane. That seems fair. Have you any more questions?'

'No' was the doubtful reply and they excused themselves and left.

But I am sure the two of them on their return to Israel made indignant
enquiries why a Palestinian tourist agent had been allowed out of the
country.

Gabriel decided to go back to Lebanon and then to Jordan to see
if there was any change in the situation, and to stop in Rome on the
way to collect some money he was owed by an Italian agent. When he
came to pay his hotel bill in Lucerne, he found a tax had been added
to it.

'What is this?' he asked.

'This is a tax to help Israel recover from the war against the Arabs.'
What Gabriel said in reply was quite reasonable, but he said it with
such desperation and in such loud tones that a crowd of people gathered in the lobby. They were hostile as people always are when they
see some-one with his back to the wall, but when they realised he was
an Arab 'they were', as Gabriel told me afterwards, 'ready to cut me
to pieces'. He could not get a porter to carry his luggage. No-one
would call him a taxi. He had to walk with his suitcase to the Grand
Circle office, and from there Gerry Wendel took him to the station.
But he did not pay the tax.

He met the same sort of discrimination at the hotel in Rome. The
agent - an amiable young man whose only English was 'chin-chin' -
rescued him, paid him what he owed and sent him off to Beirut.

But not even the Arab countries wanted the Palestinians. Lebanon
had decided she would not accept any more refugees, and Gabriel was
told at the immigration desk that he must go back to Rome in the
same plane. Now his desperation broke bounds. He told them he had
no money and could not return. They insisted he must. He told them
he had an office in Beirut with Lebanese employees; he told them he
had paid hundreds of thousands of Lebanese pounds to their hotels,
buses and guides. They still refused him entry. He jumped on one of
the officials, seized the pistol at his waist and put it to his own head.

'Let me kill myself now if this is what it means to be a Palestinian,'
he said.

If he had done this in one of the European countries, I dread to
think what would have happened to him; but Arab blood was still

thicker than water. The officials relented and gave him twenty-four hours in Lebanon.

He did not need to stay that long. He collected Victoria from their aunt's house in the Armenian Quarter, and together they went to Amman.

Gabriel and I had decided in a telephone conversation that I should go to Israel and see what the situation was like in Jerusalem and explore the possibilities there of getting Gabriel back to his home and his business. As I had a British passport, there was no problem about my entry.

Khalil met me, and I found the family well and that our United Nations neighbour had prevented Israeli soldiers entering and looting our house. Our Vauxhall had been taken, but Khalil had later seen it being used to tow a half-track vehicle. Although he had eventually been able to claim it, neither he nor I were allowed to drive it because the car licence was in Gabriel's name. I stayed at the Palace Hotel which was owned by friends, but their car had been stolen and the telephone was not working, and so I had no means of transport into the town. I therefore had a long, hot trail round the government offices trying to find some way of getting Gabriel back.

They were luckily still taking a census of the Arabs, and I got a census-paper which I was able to exchange for an identity-card, which was an indication that I was a resident of Jerusalem. Armed with this, I went to the Ministry of Interior to apply for Gabriel's return. There was a form in Hebrew, but the bearded Orthodox Jew who gave it to me was co-operative enough to fill it up for me. When that was done, he leaned back in his chair with satisfaction and put the form on top of a tall pile of similar forms. I asked him when we should hear further. 'Oh, I should say in a couple of months,' he said, as if he was choosing a figure at random.

'But he lives here. His business is here. He has to be back sooner than that.'

'I cannot do anything more,' he said. 'All these applications have to be looked into carefully.'

In fact we never heard any more about this application, and it is by

no means certain if it would ever have had the required result. There
was a servant at St. George's who was reunited with his family only
after four years and endless string-pulling, while many thousands of
others failed to get permission ever to return and had to make a life for
themselves in exile, either, if they could afford it, finding somewhere
to live in another country, or, if they could not, resigning themselves
to a tent-life in the new UNRWA camps near Amman.

After ten frustrating days in Jerusalem, I flew to Cyprus where I
asked the Israeli consul if he could help. He was extremely sceptical
that Gabriel would ever be able to return, though he gave the impression that he was not quite with the government in this matter of
taking territory and then excluding the residents.

I took a plane to Beirut and met Gabriel who had been able to
enter Lebanon with a permit from Jordan. I told him I had filled in a
form in Hebrew in Jerusalem, and he told me he had filled in a form in
Arabic in Amman. He said that he and Victoria had been to the Bridge
hoping to cross it unnoticed amidst the stream of refugees coming the
other way. They had heard that the Israeli soldiers sometimes accepted
bribes to let people cross; and Victoria had nearly succeeded in coming
to an understanding with a young soldier in the middle of the Bridge,
when his officer appeared and she had to retreat.

Gabriel said he was going back to Amman to wait for news of the
forms and to do whatever else had to be done, and begging him to be
careful I returned to the children in England.

He heard that there was to be an exchange of children from the
schools of the Zion Sisters in Jerusalem and Amman, and as he was
very friendly with the sisters, he and Victoria tried with their con-
nivance to mingle with the sisters, the children and the tearful parents
receiving them, and so penetrate to the other side of the Bridge. To
no avail.

Then he heard that some sick people were to be repatriated, and
he went to see Mrs. Cattan who was the head of the Red Crescent in
Amman and a friend of his. She agreed to include him.

A few days later three ambulances sped down the road from Amman containing sixteen critically ill Palestinians, an Italian Franciscan

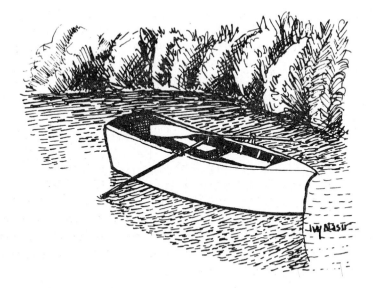

priest who had cancer, and Gabriel. Although usually a fairly healthy specimen, he was on this occasion pale and drugged from an injection Mrs. Cattan had given him, and he both felt and looked ghastly as the ambulances dropped down into the stifling heat of the Jordan Valley.

They had a long, hot wait near the Bridge while the Red Crescent and the International Red Cross argued with the Israelis, and the outcome was that only the Franciscan priest was allowed across. When Gabriel heard, he leapt out of the ambulance before he became genuinely ill. There was a team from BBC television photographing the refugees crossing from West to East for the edification of the British public, and he entered into conversation with one of the team who happened to be an Assyrian. Then he returned to Amman where he and Victoria had been staying with his uncle's Madeban in-laws.

These people never stopped cursing the Palestinians who had - so they said - brought the War and all the inconvenience of the refugees on their heads; and Gabriel, sickened by their attitude, decided to give up trying to get over by the Bridge and to risk crossing the river some way to the north. There had been quite a lot of 'illegal' crossing there, and the odds seemed slightly to favour the chance of a successful return rather than being sent back or shot. He wrote to tell me he was going to make the attempt, laid in a supply of presents and, in the early hours of the morning of August the fifteenth, took a taxi with Victoria, an elderly Assyrian woman who had fled from Bethlehem and now wished to return, and two others, to the little village of Moukhada some way up the Jordan Valley.

There they found some *fellahin* waiting for the first light to cross the river. There were farms on the other side, and they hoped to be able to blend into the landscape when they reached them. The villagers told Gabriel that people crossing a few days before had been shot at by an Israeli patrol, and they said they would tell him when the early morning patrol passed. Another hazard was that the Israelis sometimes released the water higher up the river so that the level suddenly rose and washed away the smaller and weaker of those crossing, but this was a risk that had to be faced.

When the villagers told them that the patrol had passed, dawn was just breaking and they were able to see the quiet flow of the Jordan. The water was only to their thighs, and Gabriel was not obliged to try out his rather uncertain swimming.

They had not walked more than fifteen yards into occupied territory when a half-track vehicle came grinding along. It was manned by some fair-haired young men who did not look remotely Jewish. When they spoke in English, Gabriel replied in Hebrew but they did not understand. He guessed that they must be English Gentile volunteers who had come to help beleaguered Israel against the Arab menace. He therefore told them in English that he was a travel agent who had been away on business and had now to return to his office in Jerusalem. He opened his suitcase and produced some travel literature to prove it. When Victoria offered them two cartons of foreign cigarettes, they accepted them and agreed to let Gabriel's party continue, telling them if they saw another patrol not to say anything about this meeting; but the *fellahin* they sent back across the river.

The party was increased to six along the way, as they were joined by another man. They soon came to the first check-post. They had to pass it to get on to the road, and bribery was their only hope. Luckily

it was effective: the Israeli soldiers accepted some money and several
Parker pens, and they continued into the farming area.

Most of the cottages were deserted because their owners had fled,
and near one they found a ten-year-old Vauxhall. The key was in it,
and they got in and the other man started it up. They had not gone
very far when they saw a lorry-load of soldiers bumping down the lane
from the main road.

'Stop the car!' Gabriel ordered, 'and we'll tell them we are looking
for some lost cattle.'

When the Israelis stopped and questioned them, Gabriel replied
in Hebrew that they were from a nearby farm and they were looking
for their livestock. By this time they were quite dusty and dishevelled
enough to pass as country people, but the soldiers asked them for the
permit that had been given to all the Palestinians remaining in the
area by the Israeli military governor. Gabriel answered that they had
never heard anything about such a permit, and the soldiers got back
into the lorry and drove on.

The fugitives had only driven to the next farm when another Israeli
lorry appeared. Once more they leapt out of the car, except for the
Assyrian woman who had about two kilos of jewellery under her seat.
She had taken it with her when she fled and was now bringing it back.
From long experience the Palestinians - particularly the Assyrians -
had learnt to keep their assets in this portable form. So she stayed in
the car, and this time Gabriel told the others to start scratching in the
adjoining field. It happened that it was a field of potatoes, and when
the soldiers asked them what they were doing they answered that they
were harvesting potatoes.

'You come with us,' said the one in charge. He spoke Hebrew
and very broken English. He tried to get the old woman out of the
car, but Victoria told him, 'She's sick,' because of the jewellery. The
old woman just kept saying 'Aunt, aunt. Mamma, mamma,' rubbing
her two first fingers together to make him believe she was Victoria's
mother's sister.

The soldiers left her there and took the others a little way off to
a big tent which seemed to be full of water-melons and cantaloups.

There were many soldiers there, and their questioner asked Gabriel and Victoria if they were married. He looked sceptical when they said they were brother and sister, and he showed them a list of Palestinians who he said belonged to the Palestine Liberation Organisation.

'We have their names,' he said.

Gabriel and Victoria said nothing.

'Will you say "Viva Israel! Jamal Abdul Nasser - !" ' and he spat.

Neither my hero nor his sister were prepared to be martyrs to the Palestinian cause, and when they saw no alternative they did as they were asked.

Then the Israeli took Victoria aside. 'I have girl. You give her present?' Victoria started to say, 'I have nothing ... ' Then she saw he was looking at a brooch she was wearing. 'Here, take this,' she said, and they were allowed to return to the car and the old woman who had been praying all the time they were away. They would like to have asked for a water-melon before they left, but thought they had better not.

When they came to the main road, they found a check-post manned by two soldiers. By this time they had no hand-outs left and not much money, and the Assyrian woman did not intend to part with any of her jewellery if she could help it.

Seeing that the soldiers looked like Eastern Jews, Victoria jumped out of the car saying '*Moyeh! moyeh!*' 'Water! water!' and one of the two offered her his water-bottle. The other travellers were also parched with thirst, and all of them drank till the bottle was empty. Meanwhile Gabriel noticed that the second soldier was holding a transistor which was playing Turkish songs, and he started speaking to him in Turkish. For the older generation of Assyrians and Armenians had been brought up with Turkish as their first language, and Gabriel had a smattering of it. The soldier was a new immigrant from Turkey, and he was happy to find someone who spoke his language. Victoria after quenching her thirst started a flirtatious conversation with the soldier of the water-bottle, a very dark young man with eyes like a shy fawn's. He told her he came from Yemen.

'Ah!' she said. 'I know why they put you in this remote spot. If you were in Jerusalem with eyes like that all the girls would be running after you.'

He laughed and blushed; and before the conversation could turn to less desirable subjects, Gabriel and his companions got back into the car and drove off waving to their new-found friends.

As they went along the road to Jericho, they saw several Palestinian cars coming towards them. The people were waving at them, apparently to make them go back, and Gabriel stopped a car and spoke to the occupants.

'What's going on? Can't we get to Jericho this way?'

'Not unless you have permits from the military governor' was the reply. 'Anyone caught without one will be put in a lorry and sent across the bridge.'

'Where are you going now?' Gabriel asked.

'We are going to try and get to Jerusalem via Nablus.'

'Will they ask for permits there?'

'We have been told we will need permits from Ramallah to enter Jerusalem.'

'I see. God be with you then.'

'God be with you.'

Gabriel's party turned about and drove northward deciding to leave the question of permits till they reached Ramallah - if they were able to reach it. There Gabriel thought he would ask the help of the owner of one of the Jerusalem hotels.

They did not drive through the town of Nablus but approached the main Jerusalem-Nablus road by the side-road that came out by Jacob's Well. They were following the valley known as Wadi Bedan, where the underground stream that fed Jacob's Well emerged and flowed along beside the road.

As they came near Jacob's Well, they saw a check-post close to the stream. They stopped the car, debating what to do: either they could risk passing the post, or they could abandon the car and climb over the mountains of Samaria. As they argued, several buses overtook them, and they were amazed to see that they were all full of female soldiers. The buses stopped at the check-post, and the girls, clad in miniscule

khaki skirts, emerged and made for the cooling waters. The guards
were distracted from their watch on the road by this bevy of beauty,
and they left their post to join the girls as they splashed the water on
their arms and faces.

'Let me drive,' said Gabriel, and taking the wheel, he drove to
the post, accelerated furiously as he passed it, and sped like a rocket
towards the main road.

On their left just before they reached the main road was about a
quarter of a mile square of refugee camp. Lines of little one-roomed
mud houses were divided by narrow, dusty lanes just wide enough for
the car. With a squealing of brakes, Gabriel turned into the camp,
telling the others that if they were followed, they should leave the
car, separate and lose themselves in the maze of lanes and huts. They
looked back at the cloud of dust behind them, but they saw no-one except some startled refugees peering from their doorways. They stopped
the car for a few minutes to let the dust settle and the engine cool,
and when they were quite sure they were all right, they turned on to
the main road and drove southward to Ramallah.

They were amazed to find Ramallah swarming with Israelis buying
up the imported goods, which were by their standards fantastically
cheap. The people who had supposedly been terrified of being exterminated by the Arabs two months before were now mixing with them
without any fear. Gabriel made enquiries about the permit and found
that day the regulation had changed; it was now no longer necessary
for Palestinians to have a permit to go to Jerusalem from Ramallah,
but only to come to Ramallah from Jerusalem.

They drove to Jerusalem, passing through Beit Hanina, where
Gabriel was relieved to see our house still standing; and after leaving the others at their homes, the brother and sister were reunited
with the rest of the family in Wadi Jos. By this time it was dark,
being eight in the evening of the hot August day, they were absolutely
filthy from the journey, and they had had nothing to eat since they
left Moukhada at dawn, and the only drink they had had was from
the Yemenite's water-bottle.

A week later I received Gabriel's letter from Jerusalem, and shortly

afterwards the children and I joined him there. But Victoria and he
were not yet in Jerusalem where the Israeli records were concerned
and they started a long and tedious endeavour to establish their right
to be there.

The census of the Palestinians was over and there was no way of
getting on to it now. Victoria went from office to office trying to find
the right man to apply to for an identity card, and eventually made
the acquaintance of a Mr. Tof at the Ministry of the Interior. *Tof* in
Hebrew means 'good'; and though he did not help us very much on
this occasion, we found afterwards that he was usually disposed to be
helpful in unravelling the endless convolutions of Israeli red tape: in
fact, that he was as another Palestinian's English wife put it, 'Tof by
name and *tof* by nature.'

Victoria took Gabriel and his passport to Mr. Tof, and Gabriel
gave a long, involved explanation of how he came to be in Bethlehem
at the time of the census. ('Heard that one before,' said an Australian
friend when we told him the story.) To make is more waterproof, he
said he was also ill in bed.

'I see,' said Mr. Tof. 'Well, perhaps it will be possible to arrange
something. Let me see your passport.'

Gabriel handed him his passport, and Mr. Tof glanced at the first
pages. Then he looked up sharply.

'But this was issued in Beirut on June 16th of this year, and you
have just been telling me you were in Bethlehem.'

'Oh, but - I ... ' Gabriel was appalled and wracked his brain for a
way out. 'Well, yes, I'm afraid you're right,' he ended feebly.

'Then I'm afraid there is nothing I can do for you.'

They retreated in confusion, and Gabriel cursed himself for his
stupidity in not producing his previous passport. They might have
succeeded if he had. But at least Tof had not handed them over to
the police.

Victoria then went to ask the help of Dr. Soriano. He had been their
family doctor before the creation of Israel, and had saved Gabriel's life
when he had pneumonia at the age of fourteen. He also used sometimes
to pull Gabriel out of the drinking dens in his NAAFI days. He was now

Chief Medical Officer in the Israeli government. He seemed delighted to meet one of the family again and asked after Gabriel. Victoria told him the whole story of his and her 'illegal' return to their home-town, and he suggested she should come back with Gabriel another day.

When they went to see him together, he asked Gabriel a lot of questions about his family and his business. Then he said he would do his best to help them, but it might take time.

In January 1968, as a result of Dr. Soriano's intervention and after prolonged investigations had been made, Gabriel and Victoria acquired the usual Palestinian identity cards that stated that they were residents of the country but were not entitled to the privileges enjoyed by immigrants.

CHAPTER FOURTEEN

Changing Gear

AFTER the first couple of years under the Israelis, when people constantly asked each other, 'When do you think they will leave?' (relying on the United Nations resolution which said that they should withdraw from 'occupied territory'), hope dwindled and resistance began. There were violent incidents, sometimes executed by those outside the country, sometimes by those inside; 'strikes' in the towns, when shops closed; and demonstrations in the schools and universities. Both strikes and demonstrations were dealt with harshly. The Israeli soldiers came to acquire a rough, almost dehumanised manner, and I found it difficult to imagine being the parents of such sad young human beings. I was almost as sorry for them carrying out the dreary round of harassment and repression as for the young Palestinians to whom the only political expression possible was defiant chanting, tyre burning and stone-throwing. The confrontations led nowhere and were unrelieved by any normal contact between the youth of the two sides - though I believe there was a day when some Israeli troops crossed over and demonstrated alongside the Bir Zeit University students.

In general, though, the most common sort of 'resistance' in East Jerusalem and the West bank was what is called *sabr*', a favourite Arab virtue. This means 'endurance', sticking it out until the eventual happy ending that must surely come at last.

I was almost consciously exercising this virtue one day at the Allenby Bridge, one of the two that the Israelis so misleadingly named 'Open Bridges' between Israel and Jordan, scene of many endless days of unbearable heat, tedium and frustration. 'Till, when, O God?' was my unspoken cry as I sat on a bench waiting for my turn in the next in the long series of searches. My face must have reflected what I was thinking; for I noticed one of the Israeli guards staring at me. He was evidently surprised to see a middle-aged Englishwoman going through the same routine as the Arab *fellahin*. (Like them I travelled on an Israeli identity card.) He had a striking countenance, beautiful and full of feeling, and I saw he was wearing a white skullcap. We often lost things or had them confiscated or broken at the Bridge, but that was the only day I ever gained anything: when I unpacked my suitcase at home, I found in it a white skullcap.

There was improvement in the financial lot of some (not all) Palestinians, but this advantage was offset by their inability under an alien rule to evolve in their own way or to control their destinies; and they worked for the Israelis not only as labourers, factory-workers, shop-hands and hotel staff, but also in some cases as informers and agents.

Gabriel was four times summoned by the police for interrogation, but it seemed they did not find in him a weak spot they could turn to their advantage.

The venues were graded upwards, starting with a police-station and working up through a couple of cafés till the fourth session was held in the elegant lounge of the King David Hotel. There were three men to question him: one from the Shin Bet (the security police), a sociologist from the Hebrew University, and a Lebanese Jewish businessman from Tel Aviv. The Lebanese spoke perfect Arabic and he was the spokesman. None of them knew that Gabriel spoke Hebrew, and they discussed the questions between themselves in Hebrew before putting them to Gabriel in Arabic. He was therefore prepared for each question as it came.

They showed themselves to be very well informed about our business and our contacts in other Arab countries, but they evidently wanted Gabriel to increase their store of information. Their line was that Israel had licensed the agency and our guides and was giving assistance to improve our tourist traffic. Gabriel pointed out that we had had an excellent clientele before 1967 and that what we had now was in no way due to any help we had received from Israel: the boot might even be on the other foot.

They expanded on the theme that Israelis and Palestinians in Jerusalem now shared a common destiny and anything that was for the Israelis' security was also for ours and our children's. Gabriel made the best answer he could and after some further conversation along these lines, his interlocutors again lapsed into Hebrew and came to the decision to adjourn the meeting till another day.

'We don't seem to be getting anywhere like this. Let's leave it for today and see if we can come up with anything else.' And turning to Gabriel, in Arabic: 'Well, we know you are a busy man. I expect you will want to be on your way.'

They had been drinking coffee, and as they got up Gabriel said in his excellent Hebrew:

'It was so good of you to spare me your time, gentlemen, and please don't hesitate to call me again when you would like another talk. And next time you must be my guests.'

The Israelis retreated in slight disorder, and he was not summoned again.

Ata, our rotund taxi-driver from the now far-off days of Petra, did not fare well under the new administration. One day when he returned from a visit to Amman, he was seized as soon as he reached the Israeli side of the Allenby Bridge.

'Here he is! Here's Abu Fatah!' (the Father of the Fatah, the main resistance group).

'What have I got to do with the Fatah?' asked Ata, as once he had protested to the Syrian police of his innocence of plotting with King Hussein against Syria. But that charge had turned out to be a joke: this one was serious.

'Come with us. We want to ask you some questions.'

'Ask me about rice, sugar, tea, coffee, pine-nuts, almonds,' he muttered grumpily, 'or about my taxi, but don't ask me about the Fatah.'

They hauled him away, put him in a police jeep and blind-folded hi.
Then they drove him about forty miles to the police-station in Hebron.
After they had interrogated him there for ten days, they released him.

He always parked the taxi outside Herod's Gate, and one day he
was there when a bomb was thrown. The police arrived on the scene
and took him off with some other bystanders to the dreaded Room
Number Six in the Russian Compound. For two days they questioned
him and beat him severely on the arms and legs; but he could only
tell them he had seen a man running away after the explosion. By
the time they found the suspect two days later Ata was quite badly
injured, and subsequently he only drove his taxi part-time and did not
undertake long journeys.

To add to his troubles, his son ran away with a Christian girl and
left his first wife and children in Ata's house. Ata said gloomily, 'He
just waves when he sees me and says "Peace be unto you" and leaves
me to keep his family.'

During the comparatively workless years 1967–1970, Gabriel affected the water-pipe, hubble-bubble or hookah. He would sit in the
office like the caterpillar on the mushroom, his arms folded, one hand
holding the end of the pipe against his lips, drawing the smoke through
the tube as the water bubbled up to purify it. He had to be very careful that his hubble-bubble did not come into the wrong hands, because
once a taxi-driver mixed hashish with the tobacco. After that he always sent it with a trusted office-boy to a member of the Moslem
Brotherhood who could be relied on to use only the purest weed.

There were several Israelis, usually Jews from the Arab countries,
who regularly dropped in to the office for a chat, and one day as he
pulled at his water-pipe, Gabriel put forward to these new acquaintances his own particular peace plan. The politicians were always coming out with new peace plans at this time and he thought he should
have one:

'The only time the Jews ever had peace was in the time of Solomon.
And how did Solomon achieve this enviable state of affairs? Whenever
a neighbouring tribe made trouble for him, he took the King's or the
sheikh's daughter to be one of his wives. He even took the Pharoah's

daughter: Pharoah gave her as a dowry the Canaanite city of Gezer after very considerately slaying all the inhabitants; and Solomon treated her with great honour.

'It is still the custom in this part of the world that when a man takes a bride from a certain family or tribe, the families will live in peace and come to each other's help in time of trouble. And so Solomon, because of his seven hundred wives, was on good terms with all his neighbours and his borders were utterly secure.

'Now if Golda Meir ... ' His audience already saw where his argument was taking him, and there were reactions ranging from amusement to umbrage, 'If Golda Meir married the seventeen Arab leaders starting with Sadat, we might see some stability in the area. I think it's the only solution.' I remembered this years later when Sadat made his historic visit to Jerusalem and Golda was brought out of retirement to meet him. The interlude when the newly-made grandfather and the archetypal Jewish momma laughed and flirted in perfect accord was quite spine-tingling; and we could not help thinking as we watched it on television that it was all so simple on the unofficial, human level. But Golda Meir had known the Arabs well before 1948 and she never made use of this familiarity when she was Prime Minister, but remained resolutely anti-Arab. And Palestinians never forgot her famous saying in 1969, 'The Palestinians do not exist.' I believe many, many people died because of that remark.

We were invited by some Jews who originally came from Baghdad to attend the Bar-Mitzva ceremony when their twelve-year-old son was admitted to manhood and membership of the synagogue.

They hired a huge hall for the occasion, and it was filled with people sitting at tables. We were part of an Assyrian party of eleven that included the Archbishop, who came from Mosul in Iraq. After the brief ceremony at which the boy read the Torah, a vast quantity of food was served. For like the Arabs, oriental Jews were lavish in their hospitality - very much more so than Israelis from the West. But the real business of the evening was the Kurdish dancing. Music blared out and the guests surged on to the floor. Soon it was impossible to hear oneself speak for the music, the clapping and the laughter, and we just sat and watched the dancers packed tightly on the floor.

Gabriel told me when we left the din of the hall, that his community used to do a great deal of this Kurdish dancing, or '*kurvandi*', before 1948. One of his favourite ejaculations in Assyrian company was Kurdish: '*Pacosajari!*' and the older generation used to tell him the Kurds were a fine people, brave, proud and gay, and though Moslems, men and women mixed freely. Tall and well-built, they looked splendid in their colourful costumes when they took part in the lively dances. There seemed to have been an affinity between these three minorities in or near Iraq: the Kurds, the Jews (who had probably been in Mesopotamia from the time of the Exile) and the Assyrians. Abu-Girias, Abu-Jabra and the others once danced the Kurvandi with as much zest as these Iraqi Jews, their baggy Turkish trousers swinging as they jumped and stamped their feet. But since 1948 they had not done it any more.

The two brothers who gave the party, who were carpenters by trade, found amongst the Assyrians a congenial expansiveness and warmth, and they often visited the community in Jerusalem and Bethlehem, especially if there was any sort of party, and they would bring tapes of Kurdish music with them. They spoke Arabic and even had a smattering of Aramaic, and they were completely at home.

One of these brothers was in a house in Bethlehem when Saida, Gabriel's uncle's widow, was visiting.

'Where do you live, Raouf?' she asked.

'In Kiryat Yuval,' replied Raouf.

'Kiryat Yuval! Where's that?' said Saida.

'In West Jerusalem,' said Raouf.

'West Jerusalem!' exclaimed the old woman in horror. 'Dear boy, aren't you afraid to live amongst all those Jews?'

Raouf often repeated the story in his loud throaty voice: 'Raouf, aren't you afraid to live amongst all those Jews?' And he would give a great guffaw of laughter.

Many Israelis were already casting covetous looks at the Palestinian houses in East Jerusalem. Once when we were walking in the new suburb of Beit Hanina where we lived at the time, we heard one soldier say to another, 'If we keep Jerusalem, all these nice houses will soon be empty and we shall be able to take them.'

Some of those houses had been built by Palestinians who had property in West Jerusalem but had finally given up hope of ever regaining it.

Formerly there had been hundreds of thousands of Moslem and Christian Arab pilgrims coming to Arab Jerusalem for the great religious festivals: now there were few, as only relations of those living under Israeli administration could easily acquire permits to come. 'Religious freedom' was a frequent boast of the Israelis when talking of the reunified city but it was no more a fact now than it had been before 1967.

To Christian Arabs Easter was 'the Big Feast' and they had once thronged to Jerusalem from all parts of the Arab world: the Catholics for our Easter and the Orthodox for theirs. The climax of the Orthodox Easter was the ceremony of the Saturday Fire on the eve of Easter day. The ancient walls of the rotunda of the Holy Sepulchre seemed hardly able to contain the seething, ecstatic mob of believers from the Greek, Russian, Coptic, Armenian and Syriac churches. The ceremony commemorated the flash of light that stunned the guards at Christ's tomb at the time of the resurrection. The fire was supposed to happen by spontaneous combustion inside the aedicule, and the Greek Patriarch passed it to the heads of the other churches, and thence from two holes in the side of the aedicule to the frenzied pilgrims. Greeks, Cypriots, East Europeans, Lebanese, Syrians, Iraqis, Egyptians, Palestinians and Jordanians stretched out candles to receive the holy flame, and Gabriel said he had seen men and women clasping a bunch of lighted tapers in their hands, passing the flames over their faces without singeing a whisker or an eyelash. In the eleventh century when the mad Caliph Hakim forebade the Christians to go into the Sepulchre, they gathered in the courtyard in front of the church, and the holy fire was said to have flashed out of a column, beside the entrance. The cracked column was still pointed out.

For Moslems Jerusalem was one of the obligatory stopping-places on the *Haj* (the pilgrimage to Mecca), and when the great mosques

of the Dome of the Rock and the Aksa were within Jordan, many
thousands of Moslem pilgrims used to come to the city by bus and lorry.
At the feasts of Ramadan and The Sacrifice, the whole Kidron Valley
would be filled with buses, while the Haram, the Mosque enclosure,
was a sea of suppliants making obeisance as one man to God.

Christmas in Bethlehem was a very sad affair after the Israelis took
the town. There was a blanket of security precautions through which
few Christian Arabs penetrated; and Christmas Eve, once a festival for
Christians from East and West alike, was now dominated by soldiers
and flocks of mocking kibbutzniks; and the Western pilgrims who were
not deterred by the security, formed a very false impression of the little
Christian town.

In contrast to the dwindling of Christian and Islamic worship in
the Holy Land, there was an upsurge of Jewish worship focussing on
the Wailing (or Western) Wall. This was part of the retaining wall of
the Temple that was destroyed in 70 A.D., on the side next to where
the Holy of Holies had stood. Here the Jews prayed for the restoration

of the Kingdom of David, the rebuilding of the Temple and the coming of the Messiah.

The Jews now once more had a sovereign state, while the Christians, who had for many centuries held temporal power in different parts of the world, had always emphasised the importance of a spiritual 'kingdom'. It remained to be seen if a state would fulfil the hopes of the Jewish people; whether they would resume sacrifices if the temple was rebuilt; and whether the very disparate elements in the state would ever agree on a Messiah.

The strict orthodox sect, the Hassidim, did not recognise the State of Israel because the Messiah had not yet arrived: other Israelis stressed Jewish culture and achievements and paid scant attention to the religion. Some of the more 'religious' seemed to forget what they were praying for and to find significance in what they were praying *at*: for a wall could be used to keep some people out and others in. The kibbutz system provided a social *aggiornamento* and a new ethic. Liberal Jews coming to Israel did not always apply their standards to the situation they found there, and though Zionism was originally socialistic, the country under Begin and Shamir swung ever further to the Right.

Contact with Israelis came to us gradually, because the cocktail parties given by the expatriate community were segregated: Arabs one day and Israelis the next: and one had the uneasy feeling that the hosts, rather than being impartial, showed themselves partial first to one side then to the other. When we eventually got to know Israelis, it was through our business, and friendly relations were formed on this infrastructure; and Gabriel made several friends among the Jews from Arab countries. As the business increased, his warmth and humanity, and his flamboyance, won through and he became known to and liked by a wide circle of ordinary Jews such as the porters at the airport and even the soldiers at the checkpoints.

Our first visit to Israel proper, with visitors from England, was saddening. Ein Karem, a picturesque village a few miles west of Jerusalem, probable birthplace of John the Baptist, had had a flourishing Christian community from early times till 1948. On St. John's

Day it used to be a focal point for Christians all over Palestine, one Ein Karem family alone having about three hundred members. They would come in groups of thirty or so and sit under the fruit- and olive-trees in the valley and on the hillside so that scarcely an inch of ground was left. The boy-scout band came from the Salesian monastery in Bethlehem, and when it was not playing someone in each group produced a drum or *aud* and the others clapped in time to it with cheerful abandon. There was a fun-fair: rather primitive swings and little merry-go-rounds for the children, and a big wheel with wooden boxes for seats which creaked and groaned ominously as it was turned by a handle. The women lit primus-stoves and heated huge pots of stuffed courgettes and vine-leaves which they had prepared at home, while the men of the party smoked their water-pipes and youths peddled nuts, sweets, sesame rolls and cheap toys. It was sort of Palestinian Derby Day.

All that ended in 1948, and when we went there it was a very different place. Most of the Palestinian inhabitants had fled and their homes had been reoccupied by Jews. When we walked from one ancient church to the other (one commemorating the birth of the saint and the other the Visitation), I noticed that some houses were still empty, their interiors a sad jumble of broken furniture; out of another typical little Arab house came a couple who might have belonged to Chelsea or Greenwich Village; there were no children playing by the well; and without the Christian community the two churches were just museums.

I learned from Zvi Vilnay's 'Guide to Israel' that prickly pears usually marked the sites of destroyed Arab villages, and I noticed these signs as we drove to Jaffa. They say a prickly pear can never be destroyed, and it seemed ironic that so many villages had been totally wiped out except for these relics; for *sabra*, the Hebrew word for prickly pear, means a Jew who is born in Israel.

Jaffa took its name from the Aramaic Yafo which means 'beautiful' and the Palestinians used to call it 'the bride of the sea'. It was difficult to see the reason for this now. It had been the main port of the Holy Land from Old Testament times till 1948, but now it was replaced by

Haifa and Ashdod, and it had been allowed to decline in a pathetic way. There were still waste areas from the war of 1948; there were several streets of shuttered shops belonging to those who had fled at that time; and hardly a house or shop had seen a lick of paint since. We lost our way in run-down streets with shabby houses and asked help from some raucous Jews from the Arab world; the smell of hashish pervaded the air.

We were directed to the old city which had been sold and turned into an artists' quarter; nearby were some new night-clubs 'with a touch of the exotic East', as the advertisements claimed, for visitors from nearby Tel Aviv. Study of a map led us to a closed gate in a wall near the old harbour. It was the traditional house of Simon the Tanner where St. Peter used to stay. We arrived there at the same time as a boy and girl who were apparently American Jewish students. An old woman answered the ringing of the bell; she had a frightened air and spoke to us in Hebrew; but when Gabriel replied in Arabic and told her we were from Jerusalem, she almost wept. She was Armenian, and she said she was the only Christian left in the whole area. A rich Armenian had become richer from selling the old city, and there was some reason to suppose that Simon the Tanner's house would die with this woman.

In the little compound we entered, her tiny mud house was immediately above the sea, and next to it a small mosque which she told us dated from soon after the Crusaders. Earlier it had been a church. Steps led up to the roof, and Gabriel reminded us of the story in Acts ten:

'Peter went to pray on the roof at midday, and he had a vision of a sail-cloth filled with all manner of four-footed beasts. He understood that he should no longer be afraid to mix and eat with Gentiles, and that all sorts of different peoples and races would have a place in the Kingdom of Heaven. As he woke from his trance, three men came to him from Cornelius the Roman centurion and he returned with them next day to Caesarea, the Procurator's capital. When Cornelius told him he had a divine message that he should send for Peter, the apostle said, "It is true then that God has no favourites".'

'Let's get our of here.' Something brushed past me, and I saw it was the student couple whom we had forgotten about. They left clutching each other as if we had designs on them.

We bade the old woman goodbye and walked to St. Peter's Church. There we met an old Franciscan priest. He did not want to speak to us at first; but when he knew we were Christians from Jerusalem, he invited us to his monastery. We drove him there and he talked about the plight of Jaffa.

'There are about six thousand Arabs left here, and we have four hundred Arab children at our school. We have to do what we can. Are these your children? God keep them.' He spoke almost perfect Arabic, though he was, I think, Italian. 'Our churches and holy places have all but disappeared in these twenty years, and you will see the same thing happen in Jerusalem and Bethlehem. There will soon be no Holy Land any more because its life-blood, the human element, is draining away.'

In the course of our business, as our areas of operation now included Israel proper, we came to work with a number of Israeli hotels and restaurants; and because of our equal standing and common interest as business people, our relations with manager and staff were those of mutual respect.

We were, however, subjected to a certain amount of pressure at the office by the authorities. Very early in the occupation we were told if we did not put 'Jerusalem, Israel' on our letter-heads, our licence might not be renewed; our guides were warned they should not 'talk politics' to the tourists; and the fact that the guiding course was in Hebrew meant hardly any new Palestinian guides were licensed - except for a few Israeli Arabs from Nazareth. There was a number of occasions on which Jews in an otherwise Gentile group made trouble for us, and once a large proportion of our business was threatened by an American Jew, who claimed to have been recently converted to Christianity, who was a member of a group of 'Messianic Christians'. When we sifted the evidence, his complaint seemed to be based on the fact that the guide had greeted them with the words, 'Welcome to the Holy Land' rather than 'Welcome to the State of Israel'.

One night we had a group of tourists in an Arab restaurant, and
Gabriel made his usual speech about eating bread and salt together
and their being angels not strangers. He described the *hors d'oeuvres*
that were before them:

'This is sliced cucumbers in yoghurt with a little mint and garlic
to flavour it. It is the most cooling dish for summer. The whitish base
of the other salads is sesame paste (the ground sesame seed) which
is mixed with lemon juice, garlic and a little water. This one has
grilled and pulped aubergine in it; this one chopped parsley; this one
cucumbers and tomatoes. This one is made with boiled and pounded
chick-peas and we call it *hommos* or Jerusalem cement: one plateful
with a loaf of bread satisfies you for twenty-four hours, and that is how
we make money.'

The people laughed and Gabriel looked at me as he continued:

'These are our pickled olives. I think you guide took you to Gethsemane and described the working of the olive-press. The poor donkey
or mule is blindfolded so that he doesn't get dizzy, and he has to go
round and round to press out the oil for his greedy master or mistress.

'And this is our bread -' he held up the flat *pitta*. 'You see it comes
apart without a knife - very good for making sandwiches. You break
it like this and dip it.'

Four people sitting at a nearby table but not part of the group,
had been listening to Gabriel's description of the food and had ordered some for themselves. Gabriel noticed that they were discussing
which dish was which, and he went over and showed them. They were
delighted:

'Gee, we really appreciate you people. This is sure a great country
Don't worry about that trouble you have been having. We're going
to send you *billions* of dollars so that you can drive out all those
peasants.'

'Which peasants are you thinking of?' asked Gabriel.

'All those no-good Arabs one sees around.' He pronounced the first
'a' of Arabs long.

They were Greek Americans and belonged to the Greek Orthodox
Church. Gabriel explained to them quietly that he was an Orthodox

Christian too and he was living in the country where he was born, but he called himself an Arab because his first language was Arabic. And the other Arabs were just ordinary people like him living in their own country. But this only seemed to confuse the visitors.

With such ignorance and prejudice in the minds of many western people, it seemed that Jerusalem, which St. Paul once called 'the mother of us all', was not going to be a true mother to all her children.

CHAPTER FIFTEEN

The Villages

WE built ourselves a house in the middle seventies, and from the time it was finished we were once more with Gabriel's family, as we had a large flat on the upper floor and his parents and brother Khalil had smaller flats on the lower floor. This proximity did not have the same disadvantages as when the children were small and I was still feeling strange and unsure of myself. There was much to be said for being close but not together: the children loved being with their cousins and their grandmother; we could share our visitors if we wished to; we had a common store-room; the family helped me in many ways domestically so that working in the office and entertaining was not difficult; and I came to like knowing that the house was not empty when we were out.

Unfortunately in the building of the house the planning regulations were infringed and the blame fell on Gabriel, who was at a disadvantage in not reading Hebrew. There was a court case; he was fined heavily and condemned to a three months' 'outside' prison sentence. Although he pleaded that he was needed in the tourist business which was so necessary to the country's economy, from April 6th to July 4th 1977 (when we had already been living in the house six months), he was kept all morning at a police station near the Jaffa Gate and given jobs of varying uncongeniality. One of his tasks was to put up Israeli flags for their Independence Day, which took place while I was in England finding schools for the boys.

However, his Hebrew improved during this term and he made useful friendships with some of the police officers. The commandant sent to the house a magnificent bouquet of flowers for his birthday in June, and the evening of his final day three of the officers gave a lavish party for him.

It was at a private house and Gabriel thought it was to be a stag party. But when he arrived alone, they insisted he went back to fetch me. I was interested to see Jews at home enjoying themselves in the Arab, or even more the Assyrian way, and I found my grievance against Gabriel's former captors seeping away. They treated me absolutely royally. The young people of the household spoke Hebrew, but because all the adults there came from the Arab countries, they talked Arabic most of the time, ate Arabic food, and one elderly woman dominated the conversation telling, in a broad Iraqi accent, even broader stories which would have delighted an Assyrian audience. Gabriel said she was an exact replica of his father's sister in her prime, and his hearty laughter fed her fertile inspiration.

Our new house was just off the road that we took north from Jerusalem, in Sha'afat, a pleasant Arab suburb which was the modern extension of an ancient village. Our neighbours were a mixture of *fellahin* (villagers), *medineh* (townspeople) and foreigners: an American consul had the house next door. We had a very fine view. To the south-west we saw the ever-spreading city, the skyline stabbed by several very high buildings, and the highway curling through the hills towards Tel Aviv. Following the central ridge of Palestine away from the city, one's eye was held by a tower, which belonged to the Mosque of the Prophet Samuel, now standing completely alone because the village had been destroyed. This was the highest point of the area and was called by the Crusaders Mountjoy, because here pilgrims coming from Jaffa had their first sight of Jerusalem. They went down on their knees and prayed and wept for joy.

About half a mile to the north of the house was the shell of the palace King Hussein started to build before the Six-Day War but was not able to finish. It stood on the site of ancient Gibeah where King Saul once had a palace, remains of which had been revealed by excavations just before construction began. Beyond one could see Ramah, and in the distance the modern town of Ramallah which was, before 1967, becoming a favourite resort for visitors from other Arab countries because of its elevated position.

If we went up on our roof, we could see the Old City through the gap where the road passed between the Israeli developments of French Hill and Ramat Eshkol; and the towers of the Franciscan Monastery of St. Saviour and the Lutheran Church of the Redeemer stood out. Eastwards we could see the Judean Hills and, blue in the distance beyond the Jordan Valley, the Mountains of Moab.

The situation of the village of Sha'afat, which was on the other side of the main road to us, gave it a claim to be the biblical Nob, where David persuaded the priest Abimelech to let him and his hungry men eat consecrated bread. This incident was quoted by Jesus to silence the Pharisees' carping objection to his disciples' 'breaking the Sabbath' by rubbing the ears of corn as they walked through the fields; and it looked forward to the time when consecrated bread was to be shared by all, not just the priests.

There was quite a lot of cultivated land belonging to the villagers, the Sha'afati, on both sides of the main road, and though there were many owners of the various strips, they would all rotate their crops in such a way as to grow corn in the same year. The first summer we were in our house was the year for corn, and after Gabriel had done his morning stint at the police station and had caught up with the office work in the afternoon, we used to enjoy going out to watch the harvest. (This took place in the month of June).

One typical day we went for a walk in the late afternoon, crossing the main road and coming to the level unbuilt area about a third of a mile square that was this year one huge cornfield: but being divided between several owners, the crop on the various plots was at different stages. Some of it was still being put to the sickle by heavy matrons, their long embroidered dresses hitched up at the waist leaving colourful pantaloons or petticoats to protect their legs; as they gathered the cornstalks in sheaves they knocked the ends to remove the dust and soil. On some patches the sheaves were being loaded on a lorry or truck by a group of young boys, sons or neighbours of the owner. Those who could not afford a vehicle weighed little donkeys down with a huge bundle on either side and drove them away to the thresher.

Most patches were already stubble, and on these shepherds, accompanied by small boys and sometimes a dog, were grazing their flocks. The sheep and goats were together, for only in the biblical parable were they divided: in real life in the Holy Land they ran together, and the difference between them was that the sheep was valued mainly for its meat, the goat for its milk - though the milk, meat, wool or hair, dung and skin of the animals all had their uses. There was also a difference in character, and this was the point of the parable: the sheep were docile and the goats headstrong; and the goat had a reputation for wantonness. Occasionally a boy would be seen with a sheep or goat on a rope - his private property. Many of the she-goats had their full udders protected by a bag. The leader of each flock had a bell.

On one patch of stubble a solitary *fellaha* was stacking the sheaves ready to be harvested the next day; on another a *hajjeh* was sitting by a completed stack with a plastic water-jar. We entered into conversation with her, and she said she was there to keep the animals from eating her corn. We asked her about the threshing, and she complained that the machine they had for the village cost five pounds an hour to hire, and it would take three or four hours to do her load.

Over the stubble area and on the paths skirting the field there was other activity unconnected with the harvest: a couple of girls walking arm in arm; several groups of boys studying for their end-of-year examinations, either sitting in the shade learning by heart from a book, or walking up and down reciting; a cluster of younger boys flying a kite, two others astride a donkey, spurring it home to the village.

Boys greeted us in Arabic or English; an acquaintance called from a nearby house to invite us to coffee; but we wanted to see one of the shepherds about bringing us some manure for the garden. We succeeded in striking a bargain with the *muhtar* (headman) of the village to have thirty sacks the following week. Everyone had assured us that goat and sheep manure were the best.

At the end of the cornfield a *fellaha* with wire-framed glasses leaned against a wall as she worked on a piece of material. It was a dark-blue panel for the side of a dress which she was embroidering in yellow with a piece of white muslin to set it off. When we asked her about the panel, she said it was very good imported material which was drip-dry and cost three pounds a metre.

'How can my wife learn to do that?' asked Gabriel.

'I can teach her. She can easily learn. If she has the eyes and the head, she will soon be doing it like everyone else.'

Another *fellaha* came to see what the conversation was about, then skipped off with surprising nimbleness to clout over the head a goat which had climbed up the wall and started to eat the leaves of an olive-tree.

We turned along the path to the village where a crowd of children in their best clothes and the beat of drums from a courtyard told us a wedding-party was in progress. The wedding car, decorated with ribbons, cotton wool and balloons, waited nearby to take the bridal couple to their honeymoon; but cars did not usually come into the village as the streets were narrow and fully taken up by pedestrian traffic. Shops were still doing business although the sun would soon be setting; there was a cluster of people round a stall where a man was frying *fellafel*, small rissoles made of pounded lentils and chick-peas; men sat by the edge of the road smoking their water-pipes or playing tric-trac. Between two houses an empty plot had been used to grow corn and a few animals were grazing the stubble: none of the land was wasted. From the street we could feel the intense heat of a bakery. Here the houses were old, some dating from Crusader times or earlier, the modern houses being built just outside the main village, along the highway or beyond it.

There was, however, one new dwelling in the centre of the village. A hut of corrugated iron reminded us of the demolition of a house on this spot four years before. Dozens of villagers had helped the owner and his family put up this shack, and it was ready for habitation only a few hours after their home was blown up by the Israeli troops.

We came out on higher ground and saw what looked like the remains of a town wall above us; then we dropped down to join a narrow
road that swept round and up to the back of the village. At the top
of the rise the ground levelled out and we saw a large threshing-floor
spread out before us. It might have been the top of Mount Moriah
- now the lovely, tranquil enclosure of the Dome of Rock and Aksa
Mosque - at the time when Jebusites used it as a threshing-floor for
the Jerusalem area. Corn sheaves were stacked on every side waiting
for the return of the tractor the next day. For a machine had taken
over the task of the mule, and where formerly the blindfolded animal
had circled endlessly so that the board he pulled might beat out the
grain, there was now a mechanised thresher.

'*All' 'afieh!*' we said. 'God give you strength for your labours!'

'*Allah 'aficum!*' was the reply. 'And you too!'

At the far end of the area winnowing was in progress, and we
greeted the winnower with the usual phrase for someone at work, and
he gave us the set reply. He had a wooden fork and was throwing the
corn in the air so that the strong west wind blew the light chaff to one
side, while the heavier kernels fell straight down to the growing pile
beneath. The winnowing simile (used by John the Baptist), like that of
the sheep and the goats, is often misinterpreted. George Eliot in Adam
Bede got it right: the kernels, the heart of the corn were a person's
good qualities; the chaff the unwanted but nevertheless irreducible
component, the bad qualities, which it only needed a good puff to
remove once the ear was ripe. And even those husks had their uses:
they fed Gabriel's parents in their forced migration; the Prodigal Son
in his time of tribulation; and they were often used for animal fodder.
The late afternoon was the best time for the task, as a strong breeze
always arose about four o'clock. Our neighbour Abu Mahmoud was
one of the group of men watching the winnower, and he greeted us
warmly. He held out a handful of the firm, ripe corn and told us it
would be ground by the mill in the village. For it was done by machine
now, not by hand. He said they produced enough corn for the village
and for many other bakeries in the district.

'You must come and see the *taboun* and try our bread,' he said. And we went with him to see the very old type of bread-oven.

A family were sitting under a mulberry tree a short distance away, and greeting them we were shown a low stone building in the corner of the garden in front of their house. From a pile of hot ashes inside, Abu Mahmoud lifted a large lid to reveal a deep container that was fixed there. The woman of the house went to fetch a loaf which had just been cooked, and returned it to the oven and replaced the lid to reheat it. After a few minutes they pulled it out again and we broke off a piece each. It was very hot, and roughly the shape of a knobbly disc which meant there was a generous portion of crisp crust to the spongy inside part. Abu Mahmoud told us it took four hours to heat the oven, but once it was hot the bread was cooked in quarter of an hour. The fuel they used was dung, and there were small stones on the floor of the vessel that gave the dough its knobbly shape.

With the cycle from the reaping of the grain to the baking of the bread, we had almost made a full circle and it was now only a few yards back to the cornfield. As we walked across the field in the now-fading light, we met the flocks being led to their folds by their shepherds; for the Palestinian shepherd, in biblical style, led his flock: he did not drive it. The call to prayer from the village mosque mingled with the sound of the sheep bells and the bleating of the animals, and the last glow of the sun was reflected crimson in the windows of distant houses.

Before we reached the main road with its urgent streams of north-south traffic, we crossed the old Roman road, at this point a quiet track though later merging for a time with the modern highway. It occurred to us that the Sha'afatis were still performing the same essential function, supplying the staff of life, as when Jesus and his friends passed this way between Galilee and Jerusalem; and we hoped nothing would prevent them from continuing to do so in years to come.

It was soon after we moved to this living Palestinian village that we visited a dead one, that was abandoned by all its inhabitants in 1948.

We took the day off from the tourist world to go with several members of a prominent Palestinian family to see their former village

Lifta, just west of Jerusalem. We left the Tel Aviv road by a narrow lane and saw spread before us the Valley of Aijalon, which ran from Gibeon in the north to Bethlehem in the south. The village lay a little way down the scarp on our side, reminding me of some little town in the Tuscan hills, belonging to an age that had lasted with not much change for thirteen centuries until its abrupt end in April 1948. When the killing took place at nearby Deir Yassin and the survivors were led, in their blood-stained clothes, through the streets of Jerusalem, the terrified people of Lifta fled with the few belongings they could take with them, thinking they would return when the danger was over. But the British pulled out, the State of Israel was created, and they were not able to return. The majority of the fugitives were housed in what was supposed to be a temporary camp in Ramallah, and many were still there at the time of our expedition. The family we were with had built a house in East Jerusalem, but Jewish development was now all the time encroaching on and threatening them there. As for Lifta, Jews lived in some of the houses at first, but later they were resettled in some modern flats on the hill above. Lifta was now a ghost village.

We left the cars and walked down, and David, the member of the family who was acting as guide, showed us a cave on the hill up to the left where the abundant spring started, flowing under the ground until it emerged lower down at the village well. The well was almost certainly the one referred to in the Book of Joshua as the Waters of Nephtoah, and some of us thought it would be appropriate to drink from it. But David shouted to stop us, as the spring appeared from a little tunnel above the well and this had been filled with stones and old tin cans. At the fountain the water was gushing out of a pipe on to another pile of rubbish including old bath-tubs, perambulators and suchlike. I was surprised nothing had been done to stop the water going to waste. David told us there had once been a long tiled trough and a paved area in front; here the women would gather in their embroidered dresses - the everyday dress of a strong black material with red cross-stitch, the festive dress of fine green silk with gold thread among the. red; and as they filled their earthenware jars with the sparkling water, they would sing the traditional Palestinian songs and return home with graceful, swaying gait, the full pots on their heads.

Next to the well was the bathhouse, where sometimes the men and sometimes the women of a family, would take a communal bath. The roof had fallen in, and we looked down at the still shining tiles inside and pictured the bathers scooping the heated water out of buckets and pouring it over each other's backs. Glancing back up the hill, Leila, David's cousin, who was only a child when they left home, remembered how the wedding parties would come down from the upper to the lower village with clapping, singing, laughter and shrill ululations.

We walked along the path to the main part of the village, glancing down to our left where a lush carpet of vegetation, fed by the spring water, was shaded deeply by the tangling branches of some old fig-trees. The houses, when we came to them, were only one deep on the left of the path, but on the right they climbed up the hill irregularly so that they were three or four deep. They were not the simple two or three-roomed cottages of the typical village, but fine old houses of dignity and character. The people of Lifta were stone-masons, and their own village must have seen some of their best work. David's father had been a mason, and David told us that the mortar they used was mixed with oil. It seemed to be holding well, but when we went into the houses we found a gaping hole in the centre of every ceiling and floor. This was not war damage because Lifta was not taken by war and there was not even a bullet-hole in the outer stone-work. Evidently the keystone of every vault had been removed to make it impossible for the houses ever to be lived in again. The mosque had been destroyed.

In earlier foreign take-overs, the village had fared very much better: when the Crusaders captured Jerusalem, they made a pact with the people of Lifta that they might live in peace. During the ascendancy of the Crusaders in this region and for the four hundred years of Turkish rule, they kept their homes and their lands, and were able to follow their own customs, traditions and religion.

Climbing up steps, we went into huge rooms with wide triple-arched windows looking out on to the magnificent view below; in front of the window there was usually a stone seat, and sometimes in one wall a

stone fire-place. There was an interesting type of store-cupboard in
one of these large rooms: it ran the width of the room, and I could see
it had once extended the full height too. It was made of clay mixed
with hay, and there were alcoves near the ground where the rice etc.
ran out. As there were no shops, each house had an underground
store-room, where provisions were kept to last them through the year:
flour, rice, olive-oil, kerosene, beans, lentils, dried fruit and herbs,
some of them harvested from the land, and the rest brought down to
the village by donkey; probably the store-rooms were part of earlier
houses, and those standing over them were built later. Two houses
had Arab paintings on the inside walls, and one still had tiles on the
floor.

We saw the house of the great sheikh, the religious and political
leader of the village, where the elders would meet to discuss problems
and settle disagreements, and David told us if there was a dispute between the neighbouring villages, they would bring it to this sheikh for
arbitration because of Lifta's superior standing in the region. 'Yabba',
Leila's father, was from one of Lifta's five leading families, and the
head of the family was always one of the elders.

We came at last to their house: Yabba's grandfather, the great-grandfather of Leila and David, had had four sons, and each son had one large room for himself and his wife and children, living in the extended family in accordance with the custom of the time. On the path in front of the house lay a stone about four feet long, inscribed with a quotation from the Koran and the information that the house (or maybe the one that stood there earlier) was started in the year of the Hegira 316 and finished in 318 - that is, about 928–930 A.D. David and Leila told me the stone had been above the doorway of the house. They would like to have taken it to their present house, and they even discussed how they might get a camel to carry it up the hill; but on a later visit we found the stone had been removed and we traced it to a modern house higher up the hill where some Jews lived, and it now formed the lintel of their gate.

Reaching the limit of the houses, we looked down at the fertile valley, and David showed us that the land was divided into strips with little ridges of piled stones between. These were the strips belonging to the different families of Lifta, and it was they who had laboured to clear the ground; but the trees they had planted, mainly olives which had so much importance for Palestinians, were gone and new fruit-trees planted in their place.

When we left the village, a middle-aged workman caught us up as we climbed up the hill, and Leila entered into conversation with him. He was a Palestinian Jew who had lived in Palestine with the Arabs before Israel was created and the great influx of Jewish immigrants. Leila told him in Hebrew that they had been looking at their old village; and he said it was such a beautiful village, why did the people leave it? Leila explained that they had had to. 'Couldn't they come back and restore it?' he asked. They would be glad to but it was not allowed. A few years before, an attempt by Arab refugees near Haifa to rebuild and resettle their village had been thwarted by the government. The old man sighed, and muttering about the unaccountable ways of his rulers, went on through the grass, still dew-laden at midday because shaded from the sun, towards the top of the hill, where there was a towering mound of earth along the skyline and a sinister hum of bull-

dozers beyond.

As we returned to Yabba's house in East Jerusalem, a truckload of small girls from a kibbutz passed us: they were chanting rhythmically in Hebrew, 'Jerusalem is ours, Jerusalem is ours'. On the porch of the house we found Yamma, an old woman in Arab dress, waiting, as she did every noon and evening, till all the members of the household were home. It occurred to me as she served us coffee under the pine-trees they had planted when they moved there, that there was no sense in which Jerusalem belonged to the young kibbutzniks and not also to her. When the pressures of an alien domination became too great, Yabba often thought of emigrating, but the problem of transplanting Yamma had so far deterred him. Though her sons were doctors, lawyers and teachers, she was, and would always remain, a typical *fellaha* or woman of Lifta - and Lifta was now part of Jerusalem.

CHAPTER SIXTEEN

He who Pays the Piper

THE Guiding Star clientele changed after 1967. Any tours of an official or semi-official nature were of course taken care of by an Israeli agent, with active support from the Ministry of Tourism; and for about 18 years most of our tours were groups of American Fundamentalists organised by their minister in such a way that he made a financial profit from them. This came to be with a number of ministers a primary consideration; several gave up their churches and went into travel full-time; and the result was a real boom in this type of business, from which we also benefitted.

Religious capital was made by the ministers from the Six-Day War. Translated into Old Testament terms (and they were very keen on the Old Testament), the outcome of the War was God's reward to his Chosen: Jehovah mighty in battle had smitten the Egyptian and Syrian hordes and laid low the Philistines; David had once more slain Goliath, the Israelites had returned to the Promised Land, and the desert was blossoming as the rose; biblical place-names produced the required frisson. The New Testament was also used but mainly its eschatological passages: there was a confusion between the reunified Jerusalem and the New Jerusalem of Revelations; and the Holy City, being regarded as no longer 'trodden down by the Gentiles', was about to witness Christ's second coming; the Jews would then accept him as their Messiah and he would rule the world from Jerusalem for a thousand years. There was a difference of opinion about the effect this would have on travel: some ministers told us, 'We will see you again soon if Christ comes'. and some said, 'We will see you again soon *unless* Christ comes'. Plentiful examples were found of the 'signs' that would precede the end of the world, and to supplement them faith healing sessions were staged. Armageddon was eagerly awaited.

The growth of the evangelical movement in America was something underrated by those outside it. Reverend Jones, who caused the mass suicide of nearly a thousand Americans in Guyana in 1978, was an extreme case, but we saw other evangelists who exercised a quite frightening power over their followers: they formed their opinions by the constant use of cliches, directed their votes in national elections, and dominated their lives. To help them they had at their disposal the communications media, especially television; they used every sort of electronic device and advertising stunt; some actually used brainwashing techniques. Their church organisations were run on big business lines, and some had not only missions abroad, but also universities, real estate and factories in America.

We did not blame the founder of Christianity for the actions of his ministers (on the contrary he had quite a lot to say about people like them), but Gabriel became very disheartened with some of the American clergy we had to deal with. His disillusionment with the Eastern clergy - or some of them - went back a long way; but though they too sometimes exploited their position, I would not consider them dangerous. If they gained money which was given them for the church, they did not use it to gain more money, spreading their influence in the process, but, if they were not conscientious, they used it to indulge themselves or they stored it away in jars.

When Gabriel was a young man in his early twenties, and he went to the Church of the Nativity every morning, two Arab priests of the Greek Orthodox Church, Father Canoun and Father Khoury, noticed his devoutness and regularity at church and came up to him one day as he went in to pray.

'We have a very sad case here,' they said. 'There is a poor woman

from Beit Jala whose baby is very sick. He must be baptised today lest
he should die in sin. Please, as you hope for God's grace, be godfather
to this helpless babe.'

'Who? I? a godfather? Well, if there is no-one else ... '

'She has no-one in the world to help her. Show the goodness of
you heart and you will be richly rewarded by the Almighty.'

They led the way into the little chapel off the courtyard outside
the church, and there was a woman with a fairly healthy-looking baby
in her arms. The baby was duly handed over to Gabriel, who did not
know how to hold it and was wondering what deadly disease it was
suffering from. He had grave doubts about the wisdom of immersing it
in the font in its delicate condition, but he assumed that the spiritual
benefits would outweigh any adverse physical effects; the two priests
prayed over it so fervently that he was sure everything would turn out
for the best, and the lustiness of its screams was also reassuring.

When the service was over, Gabriel imagined his responsibilities
were finished and he made to leave. But his usefulness to the priests
had not yet begun.

'Now,' said Father Khoury, 'as godfather you must of course give us
breakfast, and be sure you make it a breakfast worthy of this blessed
occasion.'

Gabriel, thinking this was part of his duty, took the priests and
the mother and baby home to his mother and asked her to prepare
breakfast. She was pleased to think he was helping a poor woman
to save her innocent child from the limbo of the unbaptised, and she
bustled about to produce the best possible spread from the slender
resources at their disposal.

The priests made a hearty meal and leaned back replete. 'Now
there is just the matter of our payment,' said Father Canoun, wiping
his mouth and beard.

Gabriel did not like to question their asking for money; no doubt
they needed it for God's work, so he paid them what was to him at
that time a vast sum, and they went about their business.

After this they used to turn up from time to time and remind him
of his responsibility for his godson and ask him to give the mother

financial help so that she could bring him up in the proper way. It was only after several years that he realised he had been duped.

An incident that happened to him in the Church of Holy Sepulchre first opened his eyes to the ways of the Orthodox priests. It was in his early guiding days. A Greek priest with an offering plate used to stand near the Sepulchre and waylay the tourists or pilgrims who came there, and they would contribute. The first time Gabriel took some clients there, he contributed himself, explained to them the different parts of the church and their significance, and then with deep reverence approached the Tomb itself. He let the people go into first the outer, and then the inner chamber of the marble aedicule, and gave them time to pray or light a candle, or just stand and meditate. When they came out, he backed out of the entrance of the Tomb so as not to show disrespect, his hands clasped behind him, and as he did so he felt something touch his hands. As he turned round to see what it was, there was a sound of coins falling on the floor. The priest, unaware that he was a guide new to the business, had been giving him fifty per cent of the takings. Gabriel stared aghast as the priest picked up the money and explained the rules in a fierce whisper.

The procedure was the same at the Church of the Nativity except that the priests there were more ambitious and usually had a five-dollar bill or even a five-pound note suggestively displayed on the plate. As Father Canoun now knew that Gabriel knew all, he regarded him as a potential ally rather than a dupe, and he would process past him swinging the censer to and fro so that its smoke nearly choked the tourists, intoning as he went: '*Kyrie, eleison! kyrie, eleison!* Bring them to Semir's' - (this in Arabic) - '*Kyrie, eleison!* Bring them up afterwards. *Kyrie, eleison!*' Semir was his son who had a souvenir shop near the church.

The matter of the shared contributions worried Gabriel, and he went to tell his Archbishop about it. The Archbishop said, 'Take you share; if you don't, the priests will keep it all. But do not use it for yourself; give it to some needy family.' He did this but he also advised his clients that there was no need for them to contribute at all.

The Reverend Baney was dismissed from the board of the Beth-

lehem Mission in 1973: the Mission was reorganised and money contributed put to proper use. But in his later years Baney was often
to be seen in Jerusalem trying to interest tourists in starting a new
orphanage.

We went on several business trips to the United States in the seventies, and during our spare time we saw many members of the large
Assyrian diaspora. Archbishop Samuel of the Dead Sea Scrolls had
gone to live in New Jersey, and a number of Assyrians had settled
near him and built him a church. We were in the area when a huge
luncheon party took place at which some Arab representatives were
guests. It was quite a moving moment when the Palestine delegate
to the United Nations rose to address the party and they gave him a
standing ovation. I had not realised till then how much the Assyrians,
even in exile, identified with the people who had sheltered them in
their time of trouble.

In Washington we met an Assyrian called George who reminisced
with Gabriel about the old happy-go-lucky days of the Mandate. The
Café Europe in Zion Square was a favourite spot for Jewish notables,
especially on Saturday nights, but Arabs were not welcome. When
Gabriel and his friends managed to get in, they would create a certain amount of confusion, and one Saturday night in 1946 they had
a spectacular success. Gabriel, George and four other young bloods -
two Assyrians and two Greeks - were dressed to kill, but the doorman
would not let them in.

Next to the café was a shelter and in it lived an Egyptain Jewish watchmaker who had no home. By day he sat on the pavement
mending watches on a box, and by night he slept in the shelter with
his box as a pillow. Gabriel and party went into the shelter at about
eleven-thirty that night and snatched the box from under the man's
head. He started up shouting and cursing and groped his way after
them. His sight was bad and he could not see who was who even in the
lighted street. They dodged behind the doorman, and the watchmaker
seized him thinking he was one of the marauders. In the confusion the
young bloods all managed to get into the Café, and the doorman came
after them with the short-sighted watchmaker behind him shouting in

Egyptian Arabic, '*Nashala! nashala!*' ('Thieves! thieves!') 'God is great! My box! they've taken my box.' The pandemonium was complete. Tables were overturned with the crash of shattered china; chairs were broken; diners were tripped up; food hurtled through the air and broke the chandeliers; the watchmaker still hunted desperately for his box.

The police were called, and they arrived and took the young men away to the station. But the young English policemen were friends of Gabriel's and the others, and they felt a certain amount of sympathy about their being barred from the Café; after an hour they let them go.

When we went to Los Angeles, we felt as if we had reached the end of the world in space if not in time. The smog-covered city seemed about to tip off into the Pacific its two and a half million inhabitants and the three million cars, so that it could be the setting for 'After the Deluge'. The place-names, Hollywood, Beverly Hills, Sunset Boulevard, powerfully evoked Bette Davis, a cigarette stuck to her lower lip, uttering in her gin-soaked voice words of emptiness and despair as she gazed out at the westering sun on the sea-line. There was nothing beyond.

Though to us they seemed to have the end of the world right on their doorstep, yet the Fundamentalists of California were desperately keen to come to the Middle East to find it there. The hospitality of our past clients was overwhelming, but I managed to extricate Gabriel and myself so that we could see Morad Barsom who, like Gabriel, had a talent for the paradoxical and he was living in Hollywood.

He came to fetch us from the Statler Hilton in a car driven by one of his married daughters. He stepped out of the car and was still in the gutter when Gabriel caught him in his embrace. His shrunken body seemed pathetically small in Gabriel's arms, for Gabriel, like me, had put on weight in middle age. All three of us wept at this reunion after eight years, and we drove back to his daughter's house where the rest of the family and several other Assyrians were gathered.

One of these was Ephraim the club-footed violinist and he was so delighted to see Gabriel that he kept slapping his outstretched right hand down on to Gabriel's to show their harmony in some shared memory or joke. 'Do you remember the mission and the preacher who thought you had received the Holy Spirit when you started to dance at the revival meeting?' Smack! their hands met amid the burst of laughter; and then Gabriel jumped up and tripped around the room with his hands behind his back as he had then.

When the laughter died down, Gabriel asked Ephraim what had happened to the missionaries who brought him over to college in America.

'I never saw them again after I finished,' said Ephraim.

I noticed later, when he drove us home, that he had a Bible above the dashboard of his car. 'My bread and butter,' he said patting it. He did not put their supermarket in the same category.

But that evening was Barsom's, and when I told him I was writing a book and he was in it, he looked pleased. 'Don't be afraid to describe me as I am,' he said. 'I don't mind.' And he spread wide his hands so that I noticed for the first time he had a slight hump in the middle of his thin back. This was probably the result of malnutrition as a baby during the Turkish persecution. He bore no resemblance to Gabriel, nor to the Assyrians of the ancient friezes - except that he had the Semitic nose. The width and height of his cheekbones reminded me that Mongolian conquerors had reached as far as Mesopotamia in the thirteenth century and perhaps intermarried with the people there; and the deep lines down his cheeks gave him a look of distaste that grew more marked every twenty minutes or so when he helped himself to a cigarette. He looked at me with a slight gesture of disgust: 'I cannot help it,' he said.

'I've stopped,' said Gabriel. 'I don't even play with worry-beads now. I used to have two: one for the business and one for the wife.' Worry-beads were an abbreviated form of the Moslem prayer-beads: instead of having ninety-nine beads (for the ninety-nine names of Allah), they had thirty-three. Hundreds of sets of worry-beads must have passed through Gabriel's hands: some made of coloured glass, some of amber, some of ivory, some blessed in Mecca, but all had been given away to those who admired them; for this was the Arab custom.

He had bought a gold lighter on the plane, and he used it now to
light Barsom's cigarette. On an impulse he set it down on the table
and said, 'This if for you.' It was the only payment we ever gave him
for a name - the Guiding Star - that was worth thousands of pounds
to us.

Barsom started to talk about the Assyrians: 'You see, we are from
the same stock as Abraham, but we are the main stem while the Jews
are the scion of a scion. The name "Israel" was given to Jacob when
he wrestled with the angel of God on the Plains of Jabbok.' (I remembered the Baptist ministers.) 'It means in Aramaic "the one who
bound God." Then the word "Jew" as you know means a member of
the tribe of Judah, one of the sons of Jacob.

'Those who were led by Moses out of Egypt may have been of
mixed race: Moshe (Moses) is a common name among the Nile-dwellers
even today, and "Hebrew" is from an Aramaic word meaning "the one
who crosses". The people of the Exodus were called "Hebrews" either
because they crossed the Sinai Desert or because they crossed the River
Jordan.

'We Assyrians are the parents and the Jews are our children, but
if we claimed that parentage, we should be laughed at. It would be
like a poor shabby old man claiming a big business tycoon as his son:
no-one would believe us.'

Big Kando had once said something similar to a reporter from
the Daily Telegraph: 'The Jews and Arabs are our bastards,' he said,
jogging his foot up and down.

I told Barsom my theory that if the Jews were still expecting their
Messiah from the line of Judah, they should be looking for him in the
Bedouin Ta'amreh, since only in them could the line of Judah still be
traced. 'That's true', he said.

Back in Jerusalem a letter waited for us from a minister called
Hirter from the deep South of America to say that he was coming with
sixty-eight members of his church to make a film about Hell. He said
he needed Gabriel as a consultant for the entire nine days of the tour
except when he was eating or sleeping. But there was a contretemps
when Gabriel presented himself to Brother Hirter in Jericho after the

group crossed from Jordan over the Allenby Bridge. It turned out he had been referring to Gabriel Matta, who had been with him two years before; he was Gabriel's cousin and a very good guide who had endeared himself to dozens of Inter-Church groups before he came to work for us in 1969.

Matta was busy with another group as it was the height of the tourist season, and it was arranged that Gabriel (Khano) should select locations and give advice about the shooting of the film and then hand the tour over to someone else.

We had a good deal of experience with films after 1967; and Gabriel had organised some very tricky scenes for various directors, including a wedding in which our secretary and her fiance were the happy couple and Gabriel's barber was the Master of Ceremonies; a sensational chase through the Old City; a location for the Garden Tomb for a minister who was not welcome at the Garden Tomb; and - this was the trickiest, sociologically speaking - a Moslem funeral complete with shrouded corpse.

In a brief morning Gabriel arranged for Hirter's Hell to be represented by a Gehenna smouldering with the eternal smoke of some burning tyres, chose the other sites and left Hirter speechless with admiration and gratitude.

For guide he had the remarkable Jamal and this choice proved a brilliant one. From the start his histrionic ability was so obvious that Brother Hirter enrolled him to take the leading part in almost every episode of 'Hell', and he was to be seen in long robes with flowing hair and beard specially made for him in the Old City, stretching his arms to heaven as he portrayed Moses on Mount Sinai, Nebuchadnezzar being carried off to perdition by two demons, and Dives writhing in agony in the flames.

The group's religious fervour mounted as the film progressed, and they had organised prayer meetings in their hotel. Brother Hirter announced one evening that he was going to take them to the Wailing Wall to pray for the Second Coming; but it rained and he decided to pray in the hotel lounge instead. At nine-thirty the exasperated receptionist rang us up at home and said they were praying so hard no-one could hear themselves think.

'If Christ ever thought of coming back,' said the man, whom we knew well, 'he'd soon change his mind when he saw what's going on here.'

We went over and found them in full spate. 'Hallelujahs' and 'Amens' resounded round the room and flew out of the windows to the city walls across the street. This considerably annoyed a party of Italian Catholic fathers who wanted to go to bed but feared sleep would be impossible. One American woman was completely overcome and started shrieking faintly as tears poured down her face.

The owner of the hotel was a doctor, and he interrupted Brother Hirter's supplication to ask him if the lady needed attention.

'She's saved, man, saved,' was the reply. 'Don't you know what that means?'

'Well, I'm a doctor and I thought she might need help.'

Brother Hirter was affronted. 'You may be a doctor, but are you SAVED?'

The doctor, a lapsed Moslem, knew the remedy for hysteria was a good slap, and he had no wish to enter into a religious discussion in this fevered atmosphere. But he had other clients to consider. 'Look, sir, there are other Christians in this hotel who wish to retire and get some sleep.'

'Other Christians? You mean those whited sepulchres in the black robes? They're not Christians: they're Catholics! You should know, doctor, that Rome is the Babylon of the modern world.'

And with that he turned away and started praying more energetically than ever, drawing from his people the 'Hallelujahs', now piano, now forte, like a skilled conductor.

The next day Brother Hirter's mother-in-law could not find her passport, and as no-one - not even her daughter - seemed very sure what her name was, Gabriel had to spend the whole morning getting her another passport. Luckily the Israeli police were able to tell him exactly who she was. She was very grateful for his help and tipped him ten dollars.

Jamal made altogether about three thousand dollars from this tour, in the form of Hirter's official tip, extra tips from his people, guiding fees, acting fees, 'expenses' for the film, commissions from the shops, and contributions to convert the infidel.

He kept the pace up all over the country, 'finding' some home-made manna in the Sinai Desert, which, surprisingly enough, the people ate without any ill-effects, and making them continue with their praying all through the long coach-rides. Some of them could not take it, and they bent down to smoke behind the high seats, bobbing up every few minutes to say 'Praise the Lord', and then bending down again for another good drag. The climax came on the Plain of Armageddon, site of 'the last battle', where Brother Hirter surpassed himself in his preaching: he had the people screaming, sobbing and throwing themselves on the ground, and Jamal jumping up and down like a jack-in-the-box, throwing up his arms and hallelujahing at each jump.

Jamal took over for the final curtain at the airport.

When the suitcases had been weighed in, he gathered the flock around him and said: 'I do not want you to leave this sacred land without one more prayer. We have such a wonderful affinity to each other, and I want you to pray for the man who has made this blessed fellowship possible. Brother Brown, will you lead us in prayer for Gabriel Khano of the Guiding Star.' And he made them stand round in a circle holding hands; Brother Brown led them in a lengthy devotion while they rolled their heads and emitted frequent 'Hallelujahs' and 'Amens'. This caused great surprise to their fellow-travellers at the airport and utter consternation to the security guards who thought it was a pro-Arab demonstration.

Brother Hirter showed 'Hell' in churches all over the United States, and it terrified hundreds of thousands into accepting Christ and making contributions.

When he returned a year or two later to make a film about Heaven, it seemed hi success and perhaps Jamal's quackery had had an unfortunate effect on his thought processes. Jamal and Gabriel Matta guided his group, and when they were near Nazareth Gabriel Matta had a heart attack. The bus driver took him with all speed to a hospital and the group missed some of their sightseeing. Brother Hirter was

indignant and told us he never wanted Matta to guide him again: 'He
told the bus driver to take him to Nazareth because he wanted his
dinner.' We protested, 'But he had a heart attack: he might have died
if he hadn't had treatment.' 'No,' said Brother Hirter, 'he wanted his
dinner.' In fact Matta could not guide for nearly a year after this. But
Hirter never lost his admiration for Jamal.

We were involved with another film which was sponsored by Billy
Graham and written by a certain Jim Collier.

The story as Jim conceived it was of an air hostess who had had an
unhappy love affair in America and she came to Jerusalem where she
found a new life. The new life was the result of her 'accepting Christ'
but - as a sort of side-plot - she attracted the attentions and eventually
the love of a young guide, whom she married. We did what we could to
help with the details of this rather unwieldy theme, suggesting Arabic
phrases and local colour. In ordinary conversation Jim made quite apt
remarks like 'I think the tourists are more impressed by the size of the
radishes than by the holy places', but the dialogue in his script was
very staid.

Gabriel introduced him to Kando who now had an antiquities shop
in Jerusalem: at that time Moshe Dayan often went there, working on
his collection. Jim loved the Old City and he planned that the hero
was to come by a rare antiquity, perhaps a coin, and then there was
to be a chase through the crowded *souks* as two young thugs from Tel
Aviv tried to take the precious thing from him.

One day Jim arrived in the office early with a new request: he
wanted Gabriel to introduce him to a fortune-teller so that the heroine
in the film could have her fortune told. After asking round the Old
City, Gabriel found an old woman who was noted for her reading of
the coffee-cup. He and Jim sat in one of the little shops that opened
on the narrow, covered street and drank their coffee. Gabriel swirled
the thick grounds round and turned the cup down on the saucer, so
that most of the sludge ran out. After five minutes the old woman
took the cup and studied the patterns left by the residue round the
sides.

'I see buried treasure,' she said. 'But it is buried deep: a hundred and eighty centimetres below the ground. For the ground is not stony: there is soil right down to the place where the treasure is - rich, brown soil. But the soil is wet and it is not clear if the gold is spoilt. It has been under the ground for a long time.

'Then I see a paper bringing news, about someone who is both near and far. It has either already come or it is on its way.'

When they returned to the office, Gabriel found a cable from my mother to say that my father had died in his sleep after a short illness.

Jim Collier returned to America to continue work on the script, and when it was nearly finished he presented it to be approved. But Billy Graham did not approve it: he told Jim he did not think this sort of story was appropriate and he asked him instead to make a film about prophecy.

The film that was actually made was put together by an American team with the help of an Israeli team. They stayed on the other side of Jerusalem and we hardly saw them for the entire six weeks they were making it. You might say the air was thick with prophecies: every prophecy from the Old Testament that might be thought to exalt modern Israel was thrillingly intoned and illustrated in full colour. The fact that the Guiding Star was thanked in the credits I think was due solely to our help with the earlier attempt.

We had Jim to dinner after seeing the film, and asked him how he came to make it. His reply was that he had not expected his Arab friends to see it.

Then he said, 'Perhaps it had its value. I was watching Golda Meir at the premiere, and when it came to the Hallelujah Chorus at the end, tears poured down her cheeks. Perhaps it was some compensation for the persecution inflicted by us Christians on Jews in the past.'

Gabriel corrected him: 'By the western Christians, you should say. Don't forget it is the eastern Christians who are going to pay the price.'

The film was only shown to a few invited audiences in Israel: the general public did not see it. But it was shown widely all over the rest of the world, usually in churches.

CHAPTER SEVENTEEN

In Conclusion

THERE was an unfortunate connection in my own family with a religious organisation: my mother was addicted for as long as I could remember to what was known first as the Oxford Group and then (having lost credibility) as Moral Re-Armament. This undermined her relationship with my father and seriously weakened the links with my sister Juliet and me, and even her beauty and intelligence were diminished because this suspect organisation held her in thrall. When she died in 1975 Juliet and I inherited what furniture and effects remained to her, but no money at all.

Besides working hard for his family as a schoolmaster, my father had pursued many unpaid interests, and I found when I was in Oxfordshire after his death that what he had done for amateur drama and conservation in Abingdon was very much remembered. There were portraits of him in Radley College library and the foyer of the Abingdon theatre.

We despaired of our children's ever getting a decent education in the Palestinian universities since the Israeli authorities so often closed them; and so Simon, Mark and Belinda went respectively to London, Oxford and Birmingham universities. I spent much time in England while they had the last two or three years of schooling and three or four years of university there. After a certain amount of travelling they all came to work for the Guiding Star.

231

Abu Jabra was bed-ridden for some years after he broke a hip which never mended. Um-Jabra looked after him with Azizeh's help; for it was considered 'shame' to put a member of the family in an old people's home. He did not often speak but when he did it could be very much to the point. One day when Gabriel and an Assyrian cousin were drinking coffee in his room, Gabriel told him his contemporary Abu Girias, the 'headman of Isfis', one of my two adopted fathers, had had a son. This was quite untrue because his wife, though a spirited woman, was said to be in her nineties. Abu Jabra roused himself from his customary silence: 'Beshouf?' he said. 'Can he see well enough?'

He died in 1984 on the Christmas Eve of the Syrian Orthodox Church and was buried in Bethlehem on Christmas Day, January 7th.

Um-Jabra 'retired' after this, ending her many gruelling years of domestic work, and starting a new life as an old lady and symbol for her six children and seventeen grandchildren. She died in April 1990 much mourned by the whole family. Azizeh did the housework and cooking, and in time with a maid or maids she managed the whole house, while I concentrated on the office and entertaining whoever had to be entertained.

Of Gabriel's other brothers and sisters: Khalil left the office and the downstairs flat and started a laundry called 'Snow-White' in Bethlehem; Victoria devoted her all to her original family and Guiding Star, Amman, working day and night to make it successful; Widad continued to live and work in Bagdad, occasionally visiting us here; and Mousa had a travel agency in Houston, Texas and lived there with his wife (who came from Bethlehem) and four daughters and a son.

The troubles in Lebanon made us very sad. Um-Jabra's elder sister and her Armenian husband died, while the other sister went to Mexico with her whole family. A very nice Palestinian refugee woman from Sidon, who stayed with me in Oxford, was nearly bombed to extinction by the Israelis, but she succeeded in educating her eleven brothers and sisters, so that the burden of responsibility was finally lifted from her.

Gabriel always talked about retiring but he found it difficult to let go the reins. Though it was really his heart's desire that his sons should run the office, he grumbled when they were in control. His palm revealed a significant thing about him: his life-line was much the most pronounced line in his hand: his fate and fortune lines were practically non-existent. I believed this meant his career was his life and his life was his career. I took it philosophically, therefore, when on our summer visits to Oxford he phoned the Jerusalem office every day, Amman very often and Houston several times a week. The radio in his hand, tuned to the Middle Eastern news, perhaps represented another aspect of his work: to follow the Palestinian problem to its final end. He often fell asleep with the radio still relaying its sad tale of misunderstanding and prevarication.

However he did enjoy our times on Hinksey Hill near Oxford. He was a fanatical shopper when abroad, he loved entertaining and being entertained, he enjoyed walking particularly by the River Isis in the evenings, and he liked to watch the occasional programme about the Middle East on television. He liked to make improvements in the house, and when he did such work or oversaw others doing it, he always asked us:

'Why does one take the donkey to the wedding?'

And we duly gave the answer: 'To carry the wood and water'.

When he forgot the key of the house, had to ring the doorbell and was asked, 'Who is it?' he would always say 'Ahmar', 'The Donkey.'

He made a good speech at Belinda's wedding in Oxford in the summer of 1989. The reception was in a large marquee, and he recalled the party my parents gave when we came over to England after our marriage:

'The speech was given by a don of Delia's and he wanted to know whether she would be living in a tent. Now at last she is in her tent. And he also asked what means of transportation she would have, and I said she would have a camel with wheels.

'You know, when they told me the wedding reception would be in a tent, I thought they meant a circus tent - as we say *khaime caracous* a clowns' tent, but I see there are no clowns here; and I think except that it is not made from goathair it is more like a bedouin tent. When my son Mark was in the Wadi Rum recently, he was invited to a tent as big as this for a bedouin wedding. I should like to make you welcome as the sheikh welcomed him, by saying, "*Ahlan wassahlan*", "Walk in: this is your home".'

Summers in Oxford were just interludes: the main thrust of our lives was still in Jerusalem, the centre of the world. The office was busier than ever with people from all walks of life and all parts of the world. Christian pilgrims began to come from the Far East and Australia, and Moslem pilgrims from countries other than the Arab countries. American pilgrimages and church tours were still a focal point of our efforts, the stress now being more on Catholic and Episcopalian clients; many priests and pastors came back year after year.

Our old friend Ata the taxi-driver ended his life a sad man. One day an exorbitant tax demand reached him: he could never hope to pay the sum required: it bore no relation to his income. It was as if the Israelis, ignoring the maxim, 'No taxation without representation', felt they were entirely outside the law and could extort money as they wished.

When Ata received the tax demand, he gasped, his eyes rolled up and he fell backwards. He had had a stroke. We went to see him afterwards, and he was no longer rotund but a pathetic, shrivelled figure, sitting on a stool and scarcely able to speak. He was only recognisable by his woolly hat. Gabriel guiltily pressed a few hundred dollars into his hand and we drove away in silence. He died not long afterwards.

There were three or four taxi-drivers who worked for us after Ata's time, and one of them gave us a good deal of aggravation but also much amusement. His voice was the loudest I ever heard and he always talked at the top of it. He was called Mahmoud (his surname means 'clown'), and when I first knew him he was a hard drinker, hashish-pusher and gambler. But in 1978 he got religion (Islam) and completely gave up alcohol, drugs and gambling. He prayed five times a day and attended the mosque regularly. He told me once:

'I swear I prayed for you and you husband when I was at the mosque. I think you believe in God, Mrs. Khano.'

'Of course I do,' I said. 'I'm a good Arab'.

I always thought it must require a great deal of effort in the Arab world not to believe in God. He is so built into everyday thought and conversation. And it is difficult to counter the sound of the muezzin soaring untrammelled to the skies every five hours or so.

'God bless you', said Mahmoud in his thunderous voice.

Mark one day played a trick on this pillar of Islam in the best traditions of his father Gabriel:

It so happened that Mahmoud did not hit it off with our accountant Samer Sliheet. (Samer was only a young man but the name Sliheet was quite famous among the Christians of Palestine, because the family had the right and honour to receive the Holy Fire when it was first passed out of the Sepulchre on Holy Saturday. This honour was handed down from father to son.) Mark decided, when Samer went to America for a month, that Mahmoud should meet him at the airport on his return.

He told Mahmoud that there was a very important client arriving and he should go to the airport with a certain George who was to be our new transfer man. George was actually Samer's cousin and not a transfer man at all. Mark gave them a cardboard sign saying 'Mr. El-Sheet' in a slightly dubious adaptation of the Sliheet name, and Mahmoud was delighted to have this important mission.

When the plane arrived and the passengers started coming out to where Mahmoud and George were waiting, George pleaded stomach cramps and disappeared into another part of the airport. Mahmoud clutched the sign enthusiastically and waited for the V.I.P Mr. El-Sheet. Noone showed up; the Israelis came out, the tourists came out, after a gap the Palestinians came out and still no sign of Mr. El-Sheet. Finally came Samer and, seeing Mahmoud and his sign, he raised his arms and did an Arabic dance to mark his arrival on Terra Sancta. At that moment George came back and Mahmoud did not linger: he rushed to the phone to tell Mark he now knew his V.I.P. His voice could almost be heard in Jerusalem without a telephone as he boomed:

'The Jews came out, the foreigners came out, even the Arabs came out and there was no V.I.P. What is more even the Gazans came out! And finally who was it? Samer! May God forgive you!'

What struck him most was not that he had been duped but that an alleged V.I.P. should come out after the poor unfortunate, downtrodden people of Gaza.

In fact the Israelis always searched and questioned Palestinians when they arrived at the airport, and Samer had a portable 'phone he had bought in America, and it aroused deep suspicion and had to be dismantled. That was why he was last out.

Among the regular visitors to the office was Issa (the name means Jesus) who took the garbage away, and Jacob the shoe-shine man. Issa came almost every day in different headgear, but his favourite item was a purple and red headscarf which he wore with matching sunglasses (cracked). Before emptying the baskets in this finery, he would tell us his latest dream in a low voice full of awe and reverence. There was always a smile on his dumpling face and he knew he had a captive audience. The dreams were often about Jesus and Mary, for Issa was a Christian; once I was the subject and he entrusted me with his money; sometimes he dreamt about bombing and the low voice was fearful but still reverent.

The shoe-shine was also confident of a friendly reception and he smiled as he headed for someone's footgear; it was hard to resist his persuasive easing off of one's shoes. On cold, wet days he sat in the office and shone the shoes with a mesmerising syncopated movement. His pride as he brought back the shoes was a delight to see. If Issa did not come he would empty the rubbish and also wipe the linoleum over and hoover the carpet.

Munir, a Moslem from Bethany, came to us at the age of fourteen in 1967 and he progressed far in this time: he learned English, taught himself to type and use the telex, learned passable Hebrew and got to know all aspects of the business.

For a short time we had working for us an Assyrian of eighteen called Saliba which means 'the crucified one'. He was as keen as mustard. Mark employed him one Sunday when Bethany was under curfew and Munir was not able to come to the office. In the afternoon Munir was able to slip out, and when he went to see if there was any mail in the post office box, he saw a strange youth putting the key in the box.

'Hey, what do you think you are doing?'

'I'm looking to see if there is any mail,' said Saliba.

'Where did you get that key?'

'I work for Guiding Star,' said Saliba.

'No, you don't.' Munir was ready to fight him.

'Yes I do,' said Saliba.

And so on until Munir was convinced. A little later Saliba started on the guiding course.

We often took important guests to a very basic little restaurant in Bethlehem. *Shishlik* (pieces of lamb) and *shish kebab* were chopped and prepared on a bench in full view of the guests, and the meat was cooked on a hooded grill. The *hommos* was the best in the country, and Gabriel always leapt up and toasted the pitta bread on the grill. An old man called Abu Itzhak (the father of Isaac) used to do the chopping and cooking - and the *hommos* - until he retired, and he taught the proprietor Zu-Zu (Georgie) all his secrets. Now Zu-Zu wields the huge knife with a skilled rocking motion to chop the meat and tomatoes.

Gabriel often told our guests about the important part Abu Itzhak played in our lives in the summer of 1960 before we married:

'I knew Abu Itzhak from the 1940s. I followed him from one restaurant to another, and he was the reason I first came here.

'Before we married Delia was with us in Bethlehem, and one day she decided she wasn't going to go through with it. She packed and asked me to take her to the British Consulate so that she could make a total break.

'We took a taxi to the Damascus Gate (for the Consulate was in the present Schmidt School); and as it was before eight and the Consulate was not yet open, I asked her if she would join me in a last plate of *hommos*.

'She agreed and we went into the little café where Abu Itzhak was at the time. To this day I don't know if it was the *hommos* or his benign presence hovering near us, but after we finished the plate, she said, "Never mind. I'll stay." '

We usually sent our clients to a big souvenir shop in Bethlehem run by Assyrians called George and Ephram; for Bethlehem was the home of the olive-wood craft instituted by the Franciscans.

George and Ephram did not concern themselves with politics: even when there was unrest in Bethlehem, they concentrated every fibre of their energy on their business. Ephram said, 'We are people of bread and salt. Our parents and their like suffered so much in the persecution in Turkey, we do not involve ourselves in any troubles.'

In the early days the family was terribly poor: the father was a builder and the eldest son helped him, but they did not have very much work. They lived near the well on the southern slope of Bethlehem in a very small house; as the family grew they were very cramped for lack of space.

One day in the late 1950s the father had a bright idea: 'Let's knock down the lavatory and that will give us a little more room'. When his wife protested that they needed a lavatory, he told her, 'We can go out in the fields as many others do'. And without more ado the son started to knock down the wall.

They were surprised when he struck the wall that there was a second wall and a space between the two, but they did not know why till he neared the ground. Two big pots were standing there and the glint of the contents was unmistakeable in spite of the dust and rubble. It was the glint of hundreds and hundreds of gold sovereigns.

The family hid the find at first and spent the money gradually and prudently; but eventually it transformed their lives and they told people what had happened. But there is sadness in the story: the eldest son became ill. The people said that a *djinni* or demon was released with the gold and it struck him. He was taken to a mental home where he has been ever since.

Victor Handal, the former Bethlehem goalkeeper who made the runaway match all those years ago with Vera, died in May 1990 of liver cancer at the age of sixty, leaving Vera to battle with breast cancer. Although the Handal family was formerly one of the richest in Bethlehem, Victor was reduced to penury by the *Intifada* (the Palestinian uprising) which started in December 1987. He spent the little he had left from economic strictures on two operations for Vera, since there was no medical insurance in the West Bank.

Only a month after Victor's death Vera gave up the unequal struggle against grief, poverty and cancer and died too.

There were three different dates for Christmas in Bethlehem: December 25th, January 7th for the eastern Orthodox, and January 19th for the Armenians. Usually my Anglican traditions predominated and we kept December 25th with presents, turkey, plum pudding, mince pies, crackers and funny hats, but we also had a special meal on January 7th: the heads and legs of the sheep.

Sometimes we celebrated Christmas in our house in Jericho, where the weather was warm and balmy, and bougainvillea and mimosa bloomed; oranges, grapefruit and pomelo hung on the trees, and we barbecued lamb and chicken.

We preferred not to attend the Christmas services in Bethlehem itself as long as the Israeli occupation lasted, since the little town we knew and loved so well was besieged by troops on that day, and the churches which had once been packed with Christian Arabs now held only tourists; for Arabs from outside the land could only come if they had a close relative in the West Bank or Jerusalem - and sometimes not even then.

One visit, however, was always part of our celebrations: on the evening of December 24th, dodging the Israeli checkpoints, we went with an American evangelical group to the Latin (or Catholic) Shepherds' Fields just east of Bethlehem, in fact the area that we looked across at from our Bethlehem house when we were first married. In a big cave there, its roof blackened by shepherds' fires of years past, the leader of the group held a simple service.

Elias, the Bethlehemite who always guided this tour leader, was once a Ta'amreh shepherd, and as he led his flock to the bus, he called them in the traditional way, 'Grr! grr!' They followed in a daze. Looking up at the velvet sky pricked by brilliant stars and at pinetrees moving to a gentle west wind, we felt in spite of everything it was good to be in the Holy Land at Christmas.

Bread and salt might be enough for George and Ephram: many Palestinians longed for something more; and in the years after the *Intifada* began hundreds of them died to gain blessings which are only recognised if you do not have them: namely political rights, civil rights, human rights; franchise, representation, power to control you destiny as individuals and as a people; freedom of expression, freedom of assembly, freedom of movement, freedom of religion; your language, education, culture and future safeguarded; your history preserved. Thousands of young men and many children were detained at the Israelis' pleasure and languished in vast prison camps. Thousands of homes were blown up. If people asked how the Israelis could do this after their sufferings at Nazi hands, the Israelis levelled the charge of anti-Semitism. To this Archbishop Tutu had the classic reply: 'If you call me an anti-Semite - well, tough luck!'

The fact that the land was holy to Christians, Moslems and Jews added another dimension.

Gabriel had a radical explanation of the cause of the Arab-Israeli dispute which pleased the tourists.

'The person to be blamed,' he said, 'is Abraham: if he had stayed with one wife, this problem would never have arisen. But when he already had Sarah he took Hegar, and the sons of these unions were Ishmael, the father of the Arabs, and Isaac, the father of Israel. Both sons were blessed and their nations became great. Believe me, the problem started from Abraham.'

Other people did not go back that far.

The English archaeologist Crystal Bennett, who was our friend for many years, was once engaged to a prominent English Zionist and used to work for the Zionist cause. When she first visited Israel in 1950, she was met by Teddy Kollek and Yigal Yaedin. On the way from the airport she saw new *kibbutzim* without much emotion, and then she saw an attractive village. 'What's that?' she asked. 'It looks as if it belongs somehow; it fits into the fold of the hills.' The answer was: 'Oh! that's just a dirty Arab village. We're going to destroy it soon with many others.' Crystal gasped: 'How could you after what happened to you?'

Though she kept some of her Jewish friends all her life, she and the Zionist never married; and she lived and worked with the Arabs almost till her death.

The three hundred and fifty Palestinian villages were destroyed about the time that Khatoun was in the bus that caught fire. Magdala, home of Mary Magdalen, was one of them; another was Motza-Colonia which some scholars favour as the true Emmaus. Some villages like Ein Karem and Migdal - once a great weaving centre - were colonised; a few like Lifta were left deserted. As the psalmist said, 'They despised the pleasant land.' History, beauty and sentiment were swept away together, so that it was no longer a simple matter for the one and a half million villagers to return to their land. The majority of the inhabitants were outside the country and though Palestine has never officially ceased to exist, it was effectively nullified by the influx of Jews.

The problem always haunted me in all its different aspects, wherever I happened to be, and one day in the National Gallery in London I came upon a fascinating picture. It suddenly illuminated for me a moment when history lurched wildly in a certain direction - though whether left or right I could not really say. It was a seventeenth century painting by Honthorst of Caiaphas and Jesus talking on the night of the betrayal and arrest in Gethsemane; Caiaphas was sitting at a table and looking seriously, without antipathy, at the younger man standing opposite him. The features of the two men were caught in the light of an oil lamp and they were isolated from the encircling darkness: nothing distracted from the interaction of their personalities and the urgency of the time. The priest seemed to be a wise man, even kindly, certainly not the villain of Oberammergau, his age and long experience, not his rank, giving him authority; an Establishment (that is pro-Roman) figure only so far as it helped his people and their faith to survive; and I had the feeling that the two Jews were on the same side.

Earlier, when Jesus said the words, 'Render unto Caesar that which is Caesar's and unto God that which is God's,' he was holding in his hand a *denarius* with the head of the Emperor Tiberius on one side and the seated figure of Peace on the other. For the peace of the world was Roman at that time - *pax Romana* - and the coin was two-sided.

In the fevered atmosphere of those last Passover days, Caiaphas realised that if the priests accepted Jesus they could only expect Roman

anger and the obliteration of their Temple and nation. One man had
to die for the Jewish people. As they talked together in the lamplight,
Caiaphas and Jesus both knew that Jesus' death was the only way
out. It must have been a conversation more than an interrogation.
When Caiaphas asked Jesus if he was the Messiah, Jesus said, 'I am,
and you will see me sitting beside the all-powerful one and arriving
from the clouds.' Caiaphas tore his clothes at that; and while this
may or may not be the thing to do when a blasphemy is committed,
it is undoubtedly a sign of great grief.

It fell to him as High Priest to make the sacrifice that would end all
sacrifices, and I believe he knew whom he was sacrificing. The religious
and political scenario gave the meeting of these two great figures and
the ensuing crucifixion the inevitability of a Greek tragedy, and there
was no villain.

One day when we were younger - it must have been in 1977, ten
years before the uprising of the Palestinians - we went to spend the
day in Galilee, taking the three children and their cousins. We left
very early and going by the road through the Jordan Valley, arrived at
the YMCA on the west side of Lake Tiberias in time to swim before
lunch. The place was called Peniel, 'the face of God', and it is just
south of the site of Magdala, which in New Testament times had a
fishing fleet of two hundred and thirty ships.

After lunch the children left us to go to the pool in the neighbouring
Russian compound while Gabriel and I talked to the proprietress of
the YMCA. Later we too went to the compound, and passing the
little church, walked under tall eucalyptus trees which every now and
then shed some bark or leaves and came to a pool. The stone in the
Galilee area is very dark and the pool was almost black in the shadow
of the trees and the encircling wall. But the water was in fact clear to
the black stones in its depths, and some dark fish were swimming in
it. There was a metal Russian cross standing out of the middle of the
pool, and the fish seemed to reproduce the pattern in the arrangement
of their fins. I believe they were catfish which the Jews considered
'unclean' because they have no scales. Water from the pool emerged
from an outlet and ran headlong down to the Lake.

We saw some sudden flashes of an exotic peacock blue amongst the trees, but we could not tell if they belonged to kingfishers or bee-eaters. A pair of pied kingfishers flew chattering out over the lake and suddenly plunged down to the water to catch a fish. Some gulls winged slowly past. The other side of the Lake was only dimly seen in the haze of noon.

We walked past fallen trees and signs of fishermen's fires on the shore of the Lake to the pool where the children had been swimming. It was shut off from the Lake by a wall and high railing, and its limpid olive-green water was very different from the opaque waters of the Lake. The black stones on the floor of the pool were set off by some greenish-yellow ones, and though two eucalyptus trees dappled the surface with their shade, the whole effect was much lighter and happier than that of the stern pool of the catfish. Hiding in the tree-roots were crabs, some golden and some purple and white, but there were no catfish here: only many small fish little bigger than minnows that nibbled one's feet.

The children were fishing in the lake, and as we came up they pulled in their line with a fish about three inches long struggling on the end of it.

'This is the sixth,' they said proudly. 'We put five into the pool,' and they released this one into the clear water to join the others they had caught and the many tiny fish that were there before.

The sight of the slippery, gasping creature reminded me that the fish was a sexual symbol, male and female.

Later in the afternoon the Russian nun who looked after the compound came shuffling down to the pool. She was a sad-looking woman, perhaps in her thirties, but celibacy and loneliness had set her face in lines of defensive gloom. She spoke to us in Russian, and Gabriel, who had never found language a barrier, said 'Christianos' and pushed back his sleeve to show the cross he had tattooed on his forearm. The nun smiled and pointing to herself said, 'Valentina'.

The Madame of the YMCA had told us the spring-water of the pool was a good cure for rheumatism, and Simon dived down to find the main spring in the centre. When he came up, he was holding a chain with something dangling from it. Valentina screamed faintly, and it transpired it was a cross belonging to her which she had lost one day when she was clearing the pool of leaves and pieces of bark. It had settled over the spring. Taking it, she kissed it and clutched it to her breast, repeating her thanks over and over in Russian.

A little later as the shadows lengthened and a breeze got up, we said goodbye to Valentina and Galilee and returned to Jerusalem.

This now seems like a prophetic parable of what happened in the 1990s, when Christianity returned to Russia after lying hidden so long.

As the Berlin Wall unexpectedly came down, so Peace reared its head quite suddenly for the Middle East with the first Oslo Accord, and this has been carried further at the time of writing.

For the Palestinians - especially the West Bankers - peace is still limited: everywhere they are circumscribed and restricted and the refugees are not able to return to their homes; for the Israeli government controls immigration, residential status, travel, movement between cities; the army is very much in evidence; the settlements are in place, the settlers armed and menacing; freedom of religion is not assured; Moslems and Christians are afraid of being squeezed out of Jerusalem because as non-Jews they are not wanted; Gazans and West Bankers are often locked in their towns. Much of the Israeli populace is hostile even to this *soupçon* of peace: the bill in the Knesset for the Peace Process being passed only because of the votes of Israeli Arabs, as the President of Israel did not hesitate to point out.

For us Khanos the only real difference to our lives is an improvement in the Bridge crossing from Jordan: the Israelis no longer make it a nightmare, but leaving from Tel Aviv airport has yet to improve.

The enemies of peace on both sides continue their dark crimes.

It fell to me, as a fairly objective Englishwoman, to know the Palestinians in some of their darkest hours: when they were almost universally equated with terrorists because of the actions of a tiny minority; when they were also tainted with the opprobrium traditionally loaded on 'the Arab'; and when no sympathy whatever was accorded them that they had lost their country, their houses and their land and that furthermore they had to live under an alien power that had a right-wing ideology veering to racism.

For my part I found them excitable, impulsive, gregarious, loquacious, family-minded, fond of children and money-conscious - but lavish spenders and expansive in every way.

On the other hand they could be masters of muddle, and this often necessitated a complete about-turn in one's plans. Luckily this did not often extend to the services of the Guiding Star.

Foreigners like myself, in dealing with Palestinians, do well to be prepared to take what comes and to play things by ear. In my own life I often found that 'what came' was much better than what was first projected, and that 'playing by ear' made one more in tune with the music of the spheres than following the original score.

I learned that, in our case anyway, worry was a waste of time: I became ill with anxiety about our future after we started the agency and was afraid our children would not have enough to eat; but it was not too long before we made the dizzying climb from rags to riches and could provide, not only for our immediate family but also for some of the extended family, a life of comfort and plenty. Furthermore we could travel, keep a foothold in my home country, and enjoy friendships and contacts in many other countries too.

THE END